MW00789977

Endowed by Our Creator

Endowed by Our Creator

How Christians Can Preserve God's Gift of Freedom through Political Activity

Keith W. Johnson

www.lifesentencepublishing.com

Like us on Facebook

Endowed by our Creator – Keith W. Johnson

PRINTED IN THE UNITED STATES OF AMERICA

First edition published 2013

LIFE SENTENCE Publishing books are available at discounted prices for ministries and other outreach. Find out more by contacting info@lifesentencepubishing.com

LIFE SENTENCE Publishing and its logo are trademarks of

LIFE SENTENCE Publishing, LLC
P.O. BOX 652
Abbotsford, WI 54405

ISBN: 978-1-62245-042-8

This book is available from www.lifesentencepublishing.com, www.amazon.com, Barnes & Noble, and your local Christian Bookstore

Cover Designer: Amber Burger

Editor: Donna Sundblad

Share this book on Facebook

Contents

Preface

We hold these truths to be self-evident, that all men are created equal, that they are endowed by their Creator with certain unalienable Rights, that among these are Life, Liberty and the pursuit of Happiness. – Declaration of Independence

The Constitution lays out the structure and rules by which the United States government conducts its affairs. However, it is in the "Declaration of Independence", adopted in 1776, where the underlying philosophy of the new nation was expressed. "Endowed by their Creator" is arguably the most important phrase in that document. It affirms that the rights of men and women come from God – not from government. Properly identifying the source of rights has important ramifications both for defining what those rights are and how best to preserve them. The fact that they are gifts from God also places a high value on protecting them and ensuring they are not infringed. Minimally, a believer who recognizes human rights as coming from God should be first among those who realize the importance of maintaining them.

I do think believers should have a role in preserving that gift of rights. I will make a case for why and how Christ-followers should be involved in such an effort. While I cover many topics in this book, the two primary areas of focus are:

1. Why Christians should be involved in politics, and,
2. How Christians should approach political philosophies and issues.

Our involvement in politics will help preserve God's gift of freedom; our philosophy of government points to how we can do that.

I use the terms "believer" and "Christ-follower" interchangeably with "Christian" to describe those who have admitted their sin to God, accepted His Son's sacrifice on the cross as a payment for those sins, and live in a personal relationship with Jesus Christ.

It is to those with this understanding (referred to frequently as evangelicals) that I am directing this book. I address issues and philosophies of government from the perspective of an evangelical. However, I believe those of any religious persuasion will find many ideas worthy of consideration in the book. Certainly, there are others who do not classify themselves as such who, nevertheless, view the world much the same way as do Christians. There are, for instance, those who have not received Christ's forgiveness personally, but who understand human nature is corrupted.

I direct the book to evangelical Christians for several reasons. The first is that I myself see the political world through such a prism. Second, our theological perspective has much to say on political philosophies and issues. Third, evangelical Christians are a key to turning our nation back to freedom and greatness. Fourth, evangelical believers on the right have erred in several important ways, both in the positions they have adopted and the way they have presented themselves. Fifth, I am concerned about the influence the political left has gained within the evangelical community. Finally, since it is Christ-followers who ought to see the world and its inhabitants most realistically, we should be best able to apply effective and proper principles to politics. We, therefore, bear the most responsibility toward preserving the gift of freedom God has given to us all.

I am speaking also primarily to Americans. Even though the United States has fallen so far from its high point of being a beacon of freedom to the world, we retain much more liberty than most countries. There is still among us enough of a residual understanding of the principles that secured our freedom and made us a great nation that those ideas can be restored and implemented in our political system. If we do that, we can again be an example to the world of how a polity should be organized and maintained.

Although this book is directed to evangelical Christians, I hope many others will also read it, especially liberty-minded people, including those who may be non-Christians or atheists. An open-minded libertarian should come to realize that he has little to fear from the proper application of Christian principles to politics because they provide a strong undergirding for ideas on freedom.

Mark Twain said, "Only kings, presidents, editors, and people with tapeworms have the right to use the editorial 'we'." I have no aspirations of royalty or the presidency, am not serving here as an editor and – as of the writing of this book – do not have a tapeworm (that I am aware of). So, I am probably violating Twain's dictum, although when he referred to the "editorial we," he was primarily talking about a person using "we" to speak for those other than himself. The use of "we" is appropriate here since I am writing as an evangelical Christian. My intent is only to use it in a way that implies I am speaking for all Christians in situations where I am stating a truth generally accepted by believers. But when I use the word "we" (or "us"), I intend it to mean "we Christians" unless the context clearly indicates another use.

Others have written books about such topics that:

1. Present a survey of others' ideas
2. Attempt to prove the superiority of their positions, and
3. Use statistics and quotations to support their views

My approach is somewhat different in that I am presenting the way I believe people of faith should think about political philosophies and issues based on the implications of a Christian worldview. I also recommend other reading that provides more detailed elaboration of the issues I have discussed.

My intent here is not merely to rehash what others have written. Some of the points will be those already made by others. It is necessary in some cases to present the ideas of others to provide a more comprehensive view of a particular topic or issue. But many of my key thoughts are ones I have not heard or read. All said, while I consider myself well-read in both Christian and political literature, I have barely scratched the surface of what is available. As Solomon said in Ecclesiastes 12:12:

"The writing of many books is endless." He also said that "There is nothing new under the sun" (Ecclesiastes 1:9). So, to claim a particular idea is original with me merely because I have not encountered it in another's work would be very presumptuous indeed. I make no such claim. I will also mention ideas I have heard from others but which, to my knowledge, have really not been widely discussed in political circles.

Throughout the book, I also make various individual points on topics I have chosen not to emphasize. This is usually done when I wish to bring out a thought that I do not see as having been part of the discussion of that particular issue.

In discussing any given issue, I make no claims to have dealt with it definitively. Many areas in this book could have been expanded considerably, but I have chosen to maintain a tight focus on the issues covered. Books could be (and have been) written on many of the subjects I am addressing. I have left out many arguments for particular positions well-covered by others. I cite them or present their ideas to elucidate a complete position or to build a bridge to points I wish to make. My intent is to present a Christian perspective on issues – not deal with them exhaustively. My hope in writing this book is that the ideas presented will bring the reader closer to the views that I, as the author, intend to promote.

At times, I use a story, parable, or portion of Scripture as the basis for an analogy to make a point. I can already hear the voices of those who will read those ideas and accuse me of misapplying or abusing the biblical text. Thus, I have tried to make it very apparent when using Scripture for analogies that I am not trying to read anything into the text. Comparisons to make points are often drawn from all areas of life and literature, so certainly the Bible can also be used in this manner. In fact, I believe it is a particularly rich source for analogies.

I realize there can be a fine line between using Scripture for an illustration and interpreting it. So, I will not claim I never engage in biblical interpretation anywhere. I do, in some cases, assume a certain interpretation that has been made by others. In such situations, I am following what I believe to be generally accepted as orthodox theology.

This book is largely prescriptive, presenting ideals I believe should be followed. Christians, of all people, recognize we live in an imperfect world. On this present earth, we will never fully live up to any ideals. Even if I, or any other writer, were able to capture precisely how political life should be organized in perfect correspondence with God's Word and His will (and I certainly don't make that claim for myself!), the reality is that it would never be perfectly implemented. If it were, it would never be completely lived out according to the plan by fallen men and women. However, this should not prevent God's people from attempting to apply His Word to our corporate lives, nor to present ideals, even when we know they can't be completely fulfilled.

In selecting issue areas to address, I have chosen those that:

1. Are of major public concern at the time of the writing of the book
2. Relate to a particularly grave threat to freedom
3. Involve ideas in which a Christian perspective is very pertinent
4. Are issues where I believe many conservative Christians have erred, or
5. Involve points and perspectives I have not heard discussed.

Some of my ideas may at first sound somewhat extreme. I suggest that is because of where we have arrived as a society in contemporary America. These are thoughts that would have been considered mainstream in our country's past. However, we have departed so far from our nation's original principles that even some who generally believe in our nation as it was conceived have been conditioned to think of certain ideas as outside the pale. I believe if you will look beneath the cultural crust which has built up over our national thinking, you will see these ideas as very reasonable, even logical.

Those who dialogue with one another across the wide divide that separates the political left and right on most issues are often talking past their opponents rather than speaking to them. This happens because they frequently use terms that mean something quite different to them from what they mean to those with an opposite political perspective. This is true of people on both sides of the political aisle. A good example is the use of the word "rights." I attempt to make certain the reader knows what I mean when I use one of these loaded words.

No matter what your perspective may be on either Christianity or politics, I ask that you consider my thoughts and not use disagreement on a certain issue as an excuse not to be open to other ideas I present.

Because this book is about Christianity and politics – particularly the believer's role in preserving freedom – much of the discussion is, of necessity, about governmental affairs. As such, a reader could get the impression that I believe political action is the most important activity for a Christians. That is definitely not the case. A believer's first priority should be carrying out the Great Commission by furthering God's kingdom by bringing others into a relationship with Jesus Christ. While political activity relates to and can contribute to that effort, it should never supersede it.

Acknowledgments

Thanks to all who contributed to this book.

My sister and brother-in-law, Marge and Dr. Daryl Rahfeldt, did full edits of the complete manuscript. Marge made many suggestions for improved wording. Daryl contributed considerable theological input.

Mark Griffin and Sarah Desombre edited portions of the text and gave me advice that I applied throughout the whole book.

Stephen White and Greg Beam made helpful suggestions. Norann Dillon helped with proofreading.

Jeremiah Zeiset at LIFE SENTENCE has been a pleasure to work with. Amber Burger created a wonderful cover for the book. Donna Sundblad did a great job of editing. And Laura Paulson's proofreading helped find many errors and inconsistencies. Any mistakes are my responsibility. I apologize if I have forgotten anyone.

I also wish to thank all who contributed to the effort with their encouraging words.

And most of all, thanks to God who gives us all the ability to communicate with our fellow humans.

Dedication

To the memory of my parents, Seymore and Ruth Johnson, who provided a Christian environment with the right amount of discipline for my formative years, encouraged me to read, and were concerned enough that they made a concerted effort to inform themselves and others regarding the threats to our country's future.

Prologue

It was the best of times, it was the worst of times.
– Charles Dickens, *A Tale of Two Cities*

Knowledge comes, but wisdom lingers, and I linger on the shore,
And the individual withers, and the world is more and more. –
Alfred Lord Tennyson, *Locksley Hall*

A Simpler Time?

I rarely look at a Thomas Kincaide painting without imagining myself in the scene – longing to go back to what he called "A Simpler Time." When I less frequently view a Currier and Ives print depicting an even earlier era, I also often find myself wishing I were there. Even a Norman Rockwell picture from a more recent time may evoke a desire to return to a more innocent and blissful life. When I think about my years growing up in rural North Dakota, I find myself asking why our society, or at least I personally, couldn't return to such an idyllic lifestyle.

Even one as logical and analytical as I – one who falls off the northeast corner of the INTF block on the Meyer-Briggs personality inventory grid – can let his emotions wax nostalgic about the perceived halcyon days of the past. I also realize that if I were to be thrust back in time to any of these previous eras, I would likely experience a rude awakening as I encountered a life devoid of many of the conveniences of today's life that we all take for granted. I know we humans have a tendency to remember the good things from the past and filter out negative ones. Images and memories of my early years are from a time in my life when I didn't have the responsibilities of adulthood.

Yet, there are times when it seems like it would be worth it to give up some modern advantages to live without the rampant immorality, vulgar entertainment, pedestrian literature, lack of responsibility, ungodliness, omnipresent government, etc., of America in the twenty-first century. I want to pray: "Lord, couldn't you please transport me back to a time when songs had melodies, poems had rhyme and meter, most families had two parents, and government largely left us alone?" Nevertheless, I believe God has placed me in a time where He wants me, and that He has a purpose for me here.

From a values standpoint, I really do feel like I was born in the wrong century. I haven't determined exactly which century I would best fit into, but it would likely be sometime before the twentieth. It seems as though many Christians would have feelings similar to this. I believe the values we should cherish just don't fit in that century, much less the twenty-first. However, many believers seem too comfortable in contemporary times. Maybe that is at least part of the reason so few of them make any effort to impact society – they just like things as they are too much.

It's not that I don't appreciate the wonders of our modern society. I'm not a technophobe. I love what can be done with computers and the Internet. I eventually get most of the electronic gadgets, although often not until long after most others have them. It is great that jets give us such wonderful access to so many places and that we can communicate so easily across the globe.

It seems that if we would hold to the values of the past, we would, along with modern technological innovations, have the best of both worlds. Unfortunately, we have taken great tools that can be used for much good and made them ends in themselves. Many have become enthralled, if not obsessed, with the technology itself, and/or have used it merely to amuse themselves. However, it is in the areas of religion, morality, and politics that our current era particularly demonstrates a degradation of values.

The good news for us believers is that no matter how out of place we feel in this age, we know this world is not our home and that we are heading for a far better place where we will live forever. If we think *sub specie aeternitatis,* we can live above the unpleasant circumstances and environment in which we find ourselves. However, we should not be so comfortable in our time that we don't care about the state of the world we occupy. Too many Christians have used their eternal security as an excuse to shirk their earthly responsibilities.

A Small-town, Rural Perspective

Some of the positive things I recall from my youth had to do, not only with the time, but also with the location – small-town North Dakota. Also responsible for my good life were my parents, who exemplified those folks in Thomas Gray's country churchyard of whom he said:

> "Far from the madding crowd's ignoble strife, their sober wishes never learned to stray; along the cool sequestered vale of life, they kept the noiseless tenor of their way."[1]

They typified many from our little corner of the world – which is not the end of the earth, but it can be seen from there!

I get quite annoyed when I hear people badmouth small towns. I suspect many who do so have never visited a rural area, much less lived in one. One of the complaints is that residents are cliquish and not accepting of new people. I never found my hometown of Crosby to be that way.

One of the other raps small towns often get is that everyone knows your business. That is true. But if a person is living an honorable and upright life, why would he care about that? There is also a positive aspect to this. They also know your business when you have problems and are there to lend a helping hand. When my father smashed his leg between a tractor and a plow, many neighboring farmers harvested his crop. This type of helpfulness still happens today in Divide County, North Dakota, as I'm sure it does in countless rural communities across America.

What such things are really about is community. Hilary Clinton wrote a book entitled *It Takes a Village.* She was writing to justify government involvement in the development of children. It isn't neces-

1 Thomas Gray, *Elegy Written in a Country Churchyard* (Poem)

sary to have a whole village or town involved in rearing a child, but a community can help in a way that has nothing to do with government.

As a person grows up, there are temptations to do things one shouldn't. In a small community, the eyes of everyone are on you. Most people know whose kid you are, and some are likely to report one of your infractions to your parents. The anonymity that might protect you from disclosure just doesn't exist in such a community. Many who have watched you grow up would be disappointed if you went bad. It isn't just your parents you are trying to please. This acts as a check on wrongdoing. It's not that none of the youth in these communities ever steps out of line. Some don't care what anyone thinks. This seems like an ideal point for a personal example of a time when I strayed from the straight and narrow, but my memory seems to have failed me!

I have heard that the sense of community I experienced in a small town existed in some neighborhoods even in quite large cities, and I believe that is true.

Another advantage to small town life is that such communities are microcosms of our country and, really, of the whole world. In them, one tends to see various classes and subgroups of people up close and personal. Often those who live in a city or suburban environment are isolated from those with values other than their own. Although a greater variety of people live in a metropolitan area, one doesn't often observe how they live their lives on a daily basis. In smaller communities, a person often sees people operating in all aspects of their lives – business, family, community, church, etc. So, growing up in such a setting can give one a better picture of life and enable a more accurate assessment of human nature and what policies will actually work in society.

Those who have grown up in middle-class households (our family was probably closer to lower middle-class) also tend to have a more realistic view of life – particularly on economic issues. For instance, they often realize there is a limited supply of money which must be budgeted, both by families and by government. As such, they are much more likely to be political conservatives. By contrast, many from wealthy and upper-middle-class families got pretty much what they wanted from their parents, and believe government, likewise, can tap an unlimited supply of funds to meet every need (and wish) of its citizenry.

Not everyone who decries this loss of community is a conservative. Some on the left also wish to return to this type of living. They attribute the loss of community to the fact that everything has gotten so much larger. It is certainly true that chain stores, big-box retailers, shopping centers, etc., have reduced the number of independent and mom and pop stores. Typically, people who live in small towns or the country now do much more of their shopping in the larger towns and cities rather than smaller, neighboring towns where they used to trade. Farms have gotten larger, so fewer people live in the country.

In my home county today, only a handful of occupied farmsteads exist in each township as is true in many places in the country. Many of the stores selling basic products like groceries, hardware, and drugstore products have disappeared. I would love to see someone living on every other section of land throughout rural America, and towns where vibrant main streets are filled with buildings that house thriving businesses again. But I know that is not likely to happen. The development of larger scale equipment allows one person to farm much more land, and crop prices have not kept pace with the increases for other items. As a result, a farm family needs to be able to market larger crops to earn an adequate income.

Some on the left who also bemoan such changes believe we can pass legislation that will cause a return to the lifestyles of several decades ago. But we can't go back again. They equate community with government. Not only are they not equivalent, government often works against community. One of the things great about small, local areas is the willingness of neighbors to help those with needs. When the government sets up programs for social welfare, people tend to adopt an attitude that they do not need to assist others since they are being taken care of by the state.

Many look back to the time I grew up as an ideal time as depicted on TV by Ozzie and Harriet Nelson, on the popular *Leave it to Beaver*, and *The Andy Griffith Show*. World War II had been over for a few years, there was relative prosperity, and industry was producing an increasing number of modern appliances and conveniences that made life easier.

The specter of the Soviet Union and the threat of nuclear war caused some concern, but generally it was a time of optimism with a sense of well-being. But were things actually as serene as they seemed? Few would then have imagined that, in a few years, many of our cities would be in flames, campuses would be the scene of massive student unrest, a drug and illicit sex culture would emerge, or that families would start unraveling.

A Family Awakens

It was when we were still in the age of blissful living that a former communist came to speak in our town. Based on his inside knowledge, he talked about the serious problems we faced and that all was not as placid as it appeared on the surface. My parents and a dozen or so others who heard that message started meeting at the Farmers' Room in the county courthouse to discuss the situation and take action to help stop the slide into collectivism. They affiliated with a similar group in a neighboring town and also started studying the Constitution.

My parents, who were already fairly conservative, became activists, which really went against their grain since they were not, by nature, joiners or promoters. They believed that, as Americans, they had an obligation to try to work to reverse the disastrous direction in which our country was headed.

I had an interest in history from a young age. I remember my dad taking me to the county library when I was probably in the second grade, showing me around, and encouraging me to use the services. I recall shortly after that time seeing a new book prominently displayed about our nation's founding that had a picture of the Liberty Bell on its cover. It was recommended for a level several grades above mine, but I asked the librarian if it would be okay for me to check it out. She really didn't say I couldn't, but greatly discouraged me from doing so. Although I wasn't really convinced, I let her talk me out of taking the book.

I don't know if my parents actually pushed my interest in history or just generally encouraged me to read. I developed that interest early

– particularly as it related to our country's founding era. I read every biography of a famous American I could find. We had in our home a battered set of encyclopedias from the late 1800s that had been in my father's family for decades. Using them, I created outlines of the Revolutionary War and the founding of the United States. When I showed them to other kids, they couldn't understand why I would want to do such a thing; to them it just looked like additional school work.

When my parents became politically active, they started listening to conservative radio broadcasts, buying books, and getting various periodicals. Because of my interest in history, I ate up this information. This started what has become a lifelong interest in politics.

About this time, we also changed churches. My parents had become increasingly concerned about the liberal drift in the larger mainline Lutheran denomination with which our church was affiliated. When a congregation affiliated with a smaller, more conservative Lutheran group was started in Crosby, our family began attending it.

My parents believed that what was going on in the church and political world were related. Their assessment was confirmed by some of the sources from which we were getting input. I shared that belief, although I had not yet made a personal commitment to become a Christian.

During this period an incredible smear began in the media of conservative and anti-communist groups and individuals. Communists had murdered millions, were in control of the Soviet Union, China, all of Eastern Europe, had established themselves at our doorstep in Cuba, occupied other countries, and were involved in subversion all over the globe. Yet, it was those who opposed them who were being attacked in the press! Something was seriously wrong in our country! I think that realization convinced me, my family, and others that the forces of collectivism had gained considerable power and influence in America and that we would have to expend some effort to save our country. All I have read and experienced since that time has confirmed that opinion in spades.

The Slide Began Years Ago

Many today have been energized politically due to the bold attempts by the Obama administration to grab power for the federal government at an unprecedented rate. We should be thankful that they have. Some of them believe the real threat started with the election of Obama. Others think it began with Clinton, or possibly back as far as the Carter days. Certainly some have recognized seeds of the problems were sown in the turbulent, late 1960s and early 1970s. As our family studied about the condition of our nation, we soon realized the problem was not of recent origin – that, in fact, we had been moving leftward for some time. Two of the most helpful books I read during this period were *Keynes at Harvard*[2] and *The Great Deceit*.[3]

They were both published by the Veritas Foundation, founded by a group of Harvard alumni who were concerned about the leftward movement of that school. It included Archibald Roosevelt, the grandson of Teddy. "Veritas," which means truth, is Harvard's motto. These studies really look at the change in teaching at several premier American universities in addition to Harvard.

Keynes at Harvard is more oriented toward economics – particularly the ideas of John Maynard Keynes who advocated government spending to stimulate the economy. Our country has been following Keynesian economics for decades. The recent bailout, stimulus mania (2008-2009) could aptly be called Keynesian economics on steroids.

The Great Deceit is probably the one political book that has been the most helpful to me, and one I have referred to often. My copy is battered and dog-eared. Fortunately, I read it shortly before starting college. It prepared me so I wasn't influenced by collectivist ideas and helped me understand why I was getting everything from a leftward slant. My dad ordered multiple copies. He had us give them to our history and social study teachers. It is probably the one book I would most highly recommend.

---

2 Veritas Foundation Staff, *The Great Deceit* (West Sayville, NY Veritas Foundation; 1964)

3 Veritas Foundation Staff, *Keynes at Harvard* (New York, NY Veritas Foundation; 1960)

It deals with how the teaching of various disciplines has changed in key schools – focusing on ideas imported from German and British socialism. It also tells about the racist and anti-Semitic attitudes of key people on the left, and goes into the origin of leftist organizations like the ACLU and forerunner groups that spawned Students for a Democratic Society (SDS). This book really packs a lot into its 300+ pages.

The Great Deceit documented the formation and growth of the Intercollegiate Socialist Society. It later changed its name to the League for Industrial Democracy (LID) due to the negative connotations of the term socialist. By 1915, its founder Harry Laidler was able to say:

> "Ten years have wrought marked changes. Over three score of colleges now contain I.S.S. chapters; hundreds of lectures on this subject are given every season before thousands of collegians; scores of courses in socialism are contained in college curricula, while publishers vie with one another to obtain for their lists standard books in socialism."[4]

> "I am continually coming across professors in colleges, ministers, journalists, social workers, and collegians of various professions, formerly members of undergraduate Chapters, who are now doing splendid work in bringing the Socialist or radical point of view before the great unreached public – working sometimes most quietly, but effectively, nevertheless."[5]

With socialism having that much influence at such an early time, it certainly wasn't hard to see how our society was so suffused with collectivist thinking by the 1960s.

Several key events that happened early in the twentieth century had a profound impact on future political developments. The first was the ratification in 1913 of the 16th Amendment authorizing a direct income tax. Its role in moving us toward larger government became particularly evident in more recent times. There has been a healthy movement in the states to reassert those rights that were never given to the central

4 Harry Laidler, "Ten Years of I.S.S. Progress," "Intercollegiate Socialist" (December-January 1915-1916): p 19.

5 Ibid, p 21.

government in the Constitution, but were merely usurped by it. The fact that individual states retained those rights was reinforced by the Tenth Amendment. This could (and should) lead to states nullifying federal laws which are gross violations of constitutional restrictions. Such nullifications are made more difficult because individuals pay income taxes directly to the federal government. This means states can't cut off funding to Washington. So, although they may elect not to enforce some illegitimate program, their citizens will still be funding it for those states that knuckle under to the federal government.

The second event in 1913 was the passage of the Federal Reserve Act. It, along with later action that removed precious metal backing from our currency, gave the government the power to expand the money supply. The income tax made funds available to spend for an ever-increasing list of new programs, but the ability to increase the money supply meant Congress didn't even have to appropriate tax monies to cover all the legislation they passed, contributing to a further growth in government. It is very unlikely that the federal government would have expanded to such a great extent if lawmakers would have been required to go to the taxpayers for all the necessary funds.

So, two great enablers of the welfare state were both birthed in 1913. But one more major change made in that year was the passage of the 17th Amendment that mandated the direct election by citizens of US Senators. Originally, they had been chosen by the respective state legislatures. This was intended to be a balance to the House of Representatives, which was elected by individuals. The idea was that the House would represent the people and the Senate, the states. This was also consistent with the federal system the founders intended where the central government had only the powers given them by the individual states. The direct election of senators was a step in trying to reconfigure the government as a national rather than a federal entity.

Events also happened before the onset of the twentieth century that started the undermining of the system set up by our founders. None of this should be surprising since there are always forces working against freedom. Trite as it may sound, it is also true that "eternal vigilance is the price of liberty."

Another major occurrence that moved us much further toward collectivism was the New Deal. Whether one agrees with the means taken to ostensibly alleviate The Great Depression, most do recognize it was a great expansion of power at the federal level. Many, though, believe it was something we weathered and that we got back on track after World War II. That was only partially true. Much legislation was passed during that period which remains in place and continues to contribute to the current size of government. One of the most notable was the Social Security system which has made so many dependent on government.

Philosophical movements from the earlier part of the twentieth century also existed that didn't manifest themselves in government policy until somewhat later. The average person doesn't have a lot of interest in philosophy. He tends to believe it deals with abstract, ethereal ideas that don't relate to real life. But the ideas philosophers promulgate impact disciples who become teachers at colleges and universities. They, in turn, influence those who teach at the primary and secondary school levels and others, like writers, who impact the thinking of many in society. As these ideas filter through academia and out into the culture, the basic philosophies get applied to various disciplines and become beliefs prevalent in succeeding generations.

Most people likely have not heard of Michel Foucault, Jacques Derrida, or other promoters of postmodern thinking. Yet, without knowing of such people, many have accepted the premises that flowed from their ideas. Chief among those is the idea that there is no absolute truth – an idea that is widespread in our society.

Another philosophic idea that has impacted us greatly is humanism. "The Humanist Manifesto" was signed by a number of academics in 1933, and two additional iterations have appeared since then. It has impacted the study of many different subjects. For instance, John Dewey, a signer, was one of the leaders in a movement known as "progressive education."

A key development shortly after the time of our family's awakening was the Great Society. It greatly expanded the federal government's involvement in social amelioration and grew the welfare state. A particularly important part of its legacy was the implementation of Medicare, which vastly increased government involvement in medicine.

We are currently in a mess with a debt in the trillions and the government taking over more of our lives. This didn't happen overnight. Some have seen this coming and recognized that what we are experiencing was an inevitable outcome of the policies we followed. Even with the biased media which has withheld information from the American public, many more should have realized what the result of those policies would be. Certainly, there were some who did and made no effort to inform others or try to stop the onslaught.

The situation in our country can be likened to that of individuals who suffered at the hands of surgeons back when the bleeding of patients was thought to contribute to their healing. When they were bled for the original problem, they became weaker. It was decided they hadn't given enough blood, and more was taken. This process was continued until the patient was so weak she often died. But the doctor never questioned whether bleeding was the correct remedy or considered the possibility that it might actually be harming the patient.

In a similar manner, statist politicians and theorists believe money and more government are the solutions for social and economic ills. So, they bleed the productive segment of our society for the funds to finance their subsidies and stimulus programs. When the problems do not improve or even worsen, they assert that not enough money or adequate social control has been directed to the situation. More funds are extracted from the economy and thrown at the situation. This continues with the advocates of this procedure seemingly never catching on to the fact that it is their supposed solution exacerbating the problem, or that they may actually have caused it. In some cases, I believe, they are so enthralled with the process of passing out government funds, they don't even consider the possibility that it isn't the right solution. Some politicians either know the funds aren't helping or don't care because they are more interested in using them to buy votes and/or in growing government. There are also those so committed to statist philosophies of government that they won't abandon them under any circumstances. With all the bleeding that has been going on in recent decades, one wonders how much lifeblood is left in the United States. This process has been greatly accelerated by the various rounds of stimulus spending begun in 2008.

I believe Christians particularly should have recognized what was happening. Many did have at least an idea of what was taking place. Of those, some made efforts to alter the course of our nation – others did nothing. Knowing of the fallen nature of men, many more believers should have seen the folly of concentrating power in the hands of government – particularly at the national level. Recognizing the tendency of men and women to take advantage of opportunities to avoid personal responsibility, they should have realized a large welfare system would result in greater dependency, and should have seen that accumulating increasing amounts of debt was an unsustainable and disastrous course that could only end in financial shipwreck.

Those who understand the nature of men and women should have been able to discern what was happening. The ones who did see what was going on, but did nothing, should at the very least have warned their fellow Americans. These things have gone on over a period of decades and we should never have let it get this far out of hand. It is possible many of the problems we face today would not exist or at least not be nearly as severe if even just a majority of the Christians in the country had opposed the trends in some way.

But this presupposes Christians should be involved in politics. Some believe such effort by believers is not appropriate. In Chapters 1 and 2, I will make the case that it is not only proper, but it is incumbent on us to be so engaged. In subsequent chapters, I'll describe how Christians can apply their beliefs to political philosophies and issues, and I will also evaluate current and past efforts of believers in such endeavors.

Chapter 1

God's Purposes for Life on Earth

Yet, I doubt not thro' the ages one increasing purpose runs and the thoughts of men are widen'd with the process of the suns. – Alfred Lord Tennyson, *Locksley Hall*

I have lived, Sir, a long time; and the longer I live, the more convincing proofs I see of this truth, that God governs in the affairs of men. – Benjamin Franklin

To assess the role Christians should play in politics, it is helpful to look at the purposes God has for human life on earth. Christians know this life will not last forever, and those who believe in Him look toward a future time quite different from those who don't. Since God, until now, has chosen to continue this earthly existence, we know He has things He wishes to accomplish before terminating it. While His people remain here, God has roles for us to help further His objectives.

In this chapter, I will cover some of God's purposes and how believers have, and should, participate politically in achieving His ends. This will include a short look at the colonial period in America as well as the time of our country's founding. The next chapter will address more specifically how Christians' involvement in politics relates to facilitating the Great Commission, carrying out commands from Scripture, and providing salt and light for society.

A Review of End-Times Beliefs

Christians differ in their views of what the chain of events will be in the end times. I will make a number of points in this chapter and other places in the book based on my beliefs regarding eschatology. Before I launch into a discussion of God's working in history, I will offer a quick review of the various end-time views and what I believe, to provide a foundational understanding of why I make certain assertions. Of course, if you don't agree with my eschatological beliefs, you may also not agree with the ideas upon which I have based them.

The Bible describes a one-thousand year period of rule by Jesus Christ known as the millennium. Believers who hold to a postmillennial view assert that He will return to earth after a thousand years of ruling from heaven. Others do not believe in a literal millennium (amillenialists). Some from both of these camps believe it is the duty of Christians to take dominion and establish the rule of Christ on earth. Believers who advocate this view follow what is called dominion theology.

What I believe is the correct view is called premillennialism. Those who hold this view believe Jesus will return to earth and then reign for a thousand years. This period will be preceded by a terrible seven-year period called the tribulation. Some in this group think He will return prior to the tribulation to remove Christians from earth in an event called the rapture (a pre-trib view), others believe He will perform this rescue around the middle of the tribulation (mid-trib), and still others believe this will happen at the end of the tribulation (post-trib). I believe in the pre-trib scenario, although I think a case can be made for a rapture at the middle of the tribulation.

Many, if not most, premillennialist advocates, see events in recent decades pointing to the likelihood of the end times being close at hand based on biblical prophecy. I see evidence of that possibility. Since I am neither an amillennialist nor a postmillennialist, I do not think we as believers should be taking over the world for Christ. So, when I talk about applying Christian principles to government, I am not advocating an effort to build the kingdom of God on earth. However, I believe that if Christian worldview ideas were followed to a large degree in the political realm, we would likely see a great transformation of our society.

Christian Participation in God-Ordained Government

God Moves in History

Most Christians believe, as Tennyson said in the quote at the beginning of the chapter, that an increasing purpose runs throughout the ages, and God guides the course of history to bring about His desired ends. Many believe the ultimate denouement of His workings will be a millennial kingdom ruled by Jesus Christ which, in time, will be succeeded by the new heaven and earth where His followers will dwell with Him forever.

This does not mean things on earth have increasingly improved in a deterministic way as implied by Tennyson, and as believed by some historians and philosophers. Civilizations have risen and fallen; nations and governments have come and gone. For several centuries, it appeared to many that Western Civilization would result in the pinnacle of life on Planet Earth; however, perceptive believers recognize the West has actually been in a period of decline for some time.

In spite of the ebbs and flows of civilizations over the years, most Christians believe God is accomplishing His purposes through history. In this way, we could say history is deterministic – it is ultimately determined by God, and it is moving toward an end: His end. That doesn't mean all that has and will take place necessarily relates to God's larger objectives. We do not always know how God uses certain events to further His desired outcomes, although we may recognize, after the fact, how they have contributed to furthering His kingdom and, thus, appear to have been engineered by Him.

Whatever God's wishes may be for man-centered earthly governments, they are not of ultimate importance since all human institutions will eventually pass away. His desires for them are subordinate to His eternal purposes. However, various human authorities are tools who have been, are, and will be, used by Him to further the establishment of the heavenly kingdom that will replace all temporal rulers.

God's Direct Rule on Earth

In Genesis 1:26, 28, God commands men to rule over the earth. Since it was issued right after creating the first man and woman, it appears this instruction is intended for all humans and their descendants. It is not completely clear how much of that job is to fall to governments, but presumably they should at least be involved in maintaining the political environment that would facilitate the task. Of course, it was given while God was still directly in control of what happened here on earth and before separate nations existed. The command appears to be intended to give the humans He created authority over the earth. It is not likely that He would want to exclude those who are believers from having a role in that rule.

In the times succeeding the giving of this mandate, God ruled the nation of Israel directly. This went beyond the definition of a theocracy where a government is ruled using God's principles. Since God Himself was in control, it could almost be considered a super-theocracy.

When God chose Moses to lead Israel out of Egypt He initiated a more formal type of government. In Exodus 18, at the suggestion of his father-in-law, Jethro, Moses established leaders and judges over groups of ten, fifty, a hundred and a thousand. The Ten Commandments issued through Moses were rules directly from God about how individuals were to live their personal lives. The many additional laws specified in Exodus and the other historical books draw on these commandments and, in effect, flesh them out. Specific punishments laid out for many of these laws indicate they were to be enforced by Israel's government.

Since God created the rules, human legislators were not needed. Men were called upon to administer the laws, although not too much is said about how that was done, or how those wielding executive power were picked – except for main leaders like Moses whom God personally chose. In cases of major disobediences like the incident of the golden calf and Korah's rebellion (Numbers 16), God directly acted as a judge and meted out punishment through leaders such as Moses. Presumably, in cases of individual violations of the laws, a system of justice to judge and punish lawbreakers existed.

In a later period, God used judges to rule over Israel. One assumes the rules He laid down in Moses' time remained in effect. It is likely those judges had some type of judicial and penal system that used Israelites in its administration. God dealt directly through the judges on matters affecting the whole nation. We have the biblical reference to chiefs of the various tribes in Judges, but we are told little about their rule over civil society. The book of Judges primarily discusses the role of the appointed judges as head of the military.

Kings and Prophets

After the period of the judges, God established a system where kings were the rulers. This was not His choice , but the result of the Israelites' request for a king. God warned them of how such rulers would abuse their power. From this, we know the vesting of authority in one person was not His ideal. Much later in history, when some adopted the doctrine of the divine right of kings, they were not following God's Word.

It didn't take long for God to be proven right about kings. The very first, Saul, was disobedient to the point where God intervened to replace him with David. God's warnings were borne out by the actions of other kings of Judah and Israel – only a few of whom were obedient to Him. Some also oppressed their subjects as God had indicated they would. Rehoboam, for example, against the advice of his elders, put a heavy burden on the people which resulted in a rebellion that divided Israel (I Kings 12), and Ahab, with the aid of his wife Jezebel, caused the death of Naboth in order to acquire his vineyard (I Kings 21).

Even the best of Israel and Judah's kings, David, who was described as a man after God's own heart, abused his power by having sex with Bathsheba, the wife of one of his military men. He then set up a situation where that military man, Uriah, would be killed in battle, effectively murdering him.

If kings wouldn't follow God when He was dealing with them personally and through His prophets, we certainly cannot expect them to rule in accordance with His laws now that He is no longer speaking to them as directly.

Many of God's warnings about kings equally hold true for oligarchies where a small group of people rule or, actually, for any system where a central government has unchecked authority to do as it wishes. Throughout history, we have seen countless examples of how kings and oligarchs have abused their power, oppressed their subjects, and ruled in a way not pleasing to God. We certainly can see what He meant when He warned the Israelites about kings.

During this period God used prophets to communicate His desires to Israel's leaders. Most often the kings did not listen to them or heed their warnings. Again, it can be assumed that laws given earlier by God were still in force. In looking at Old Testament times as a whole, we can say that God, as legislator, established all the laws for Israel, and that both He and its leaders participated in the executive and judicial functions of government.

God's rule over Judah and Israel was a very special case since they were His chosen people. God did not assert as direct a control over other nations in Old Testament times. He did, however, use them in various ways, such as punishing both Israel and Judah – which were also used, in turn, to punish those nations for their evil and idolatrous ways.

Will Nations Continue?

God really established separate nations when He scattered the people at the Tower of Babel by causing them to speak different languages. Most nations in this time were ruled monolithically, but we have no evidence God approved this. In fact, when the people of Israel asked for a king to rule over them, their reason was so they would be like the other nations, and He clearly warned them this would not be a good idea.

It seems separate nations are God's intention as long as this present earth remains. Not much is said about their role in the millennial rule. However, at the end of the thousand years when Satan is released from the pit, he will deceive the nations from the four corners of the earth and gather them for war against the saints (Revelation 20: 8, 9). Those nations are said to include Gog and Magog which are mentioned in Scripture references to times before the millennium. This indicates not only the existence of nations during Christ's reign, but also shows that at least some of them may be continuations of those that exist prior to the establishment of His rule.

Government in New Testament Times

God's Word indicates that He expected separate nations to exist in New Testament times. The term "Gentiles" used so frequently actually means "nations" in Greek. Roman hegemony over much of the Middle East and Europe at the time probably disguised the fact that many nations and cultures existed. When Paul took the gospel to the Gentiles, he was going to places that, although ruled by Rome, still thought of themselves as separate countries. That was certainly true of Judea itself.

By New Testament times, the situation had changed dramatically. While the Jews were still involved with the ceremonial and moral law, they had only a limited role in the civil law. Rather, those rules were primarily set and administered by the occupying Roman authorities. Nothing in the New Testament indicates God would re-institute a direct rule over the Jews or any other country, until the time of the millennium when Jesus would reign over the whole earth.

Of the types of law God established in the Old Testament, the sacrificial law is no longer needed after Christ's death. And men and women are responsible to God for keeping of the moral laws. What remains to be enforced by human governments is the civil law.

Some suggest that the New Testament does not counsel Christians to be involved in politics and that examples of believers participating in such affairs are nonexistent, and because of this we should not be involved either. However, at that time, Israel was under the iron-fisted rule of Rome with little opportunity for individuals to affect the law. That fact should not preclude such involvement by believers where it is possible. Nor does it mean Christians shouldn't be a part of the establishment of a new government system for a nation, as they were at the founding of the United States.

The rationale some Christians use for saying believers shouldn't be involved in politics is very similar to that employed by believers to justify slavery. In both cases, the justification is provided by citing societal situations that were in play in the biblical ages as being normative for all periods of time. In the case of slavery, it has been said by some Christians that since it was practiced during the time when scripture was being written, and was not specifically condemned, that God, therefore, condones it, and it should be acceptable in all societies. Yet, most believers recognize this type of thinking as fallacious and applaud the efforts of Christians like William Wilberforce in ending the practice. It is instructive to note that to be in the position where he was able to further this change, Wilberforce had to be involved in politics as a member of the English Parliament.

Just as the cultural and political climate in New Testament times included slavery, it also did not provide opportunities for believers to participate in politics. Since such activity was not specifically prescribed in the Bible, some say it is prohibited in any era – regardless of whether conditions in a later cultural period allow for it. This is similar to how some have tried to justify slavery, because it was prevalent when the Bible was written. But history has shown that Christians involved in politics have furthered God's kingdom – most notably through the establishment of the United States and the influence American Christians have had throughout the world.

It is apparent that what is written in the New Testament about government (as in Paul's discussion in Romans 13) is intended to apply to civil rule over nations and their subordinate political jurisdictions. It seems to assume believers will live under a variety of different polities. It does not state or imply that Christians should try to re-establish the type of theocratic government we see in the Old Testament. In fact, unless God starts speaking again to believers directly or through prophets, it wouldn't be possible to operate in the manner practiced in Old Testament times.

God's Use of Human Authorities

Today, Christians who assert believers should not be involved in politics at all frequently say such efforts are unnecessary or futile because God raises up government and its leaders. That is true. It says in Daniel 2:21, *It is He who changes the times and the epochs; He removes kings and establishes kings.* But God does not send angels down to earth to establish governments or take positions in existing jurisdictions. He uses flesh and blood humans in these efforts – just as He does in other things He wishes to accomplish.

Some Christians think that because God will achieve His purposes, believers can sit back and watch as He works, and that they need not participate at all in what He is doing – at least in anything beyond evangelism. It is true God will achieve His goals with or without the cooperation of Christians, but it does not follow that we should not be involved in working toward those goals. It would certainly seem that some of the people God raises up to govern would be His believers.

God also raises up people to positions in His church. That does not mean Christians should not seek His will, and, when finding it, should not either take on such leadership positions themselves or prepare others for them. The church is God's primary vehicle for carrying out His command to go into all the world and make disciples. However, just as God ordained the church, He also ordained government. Both institutions serve His purposes. If Christians are not involved in governments, they will be totally controlled by unbelievers. Does it make sense to say that He has or will in the future raise up only non-Christians as governmental authorities?

Christians should be receptive to God's will and respond to His leading. When believers are in tune with God and involved in the political process, it is more likely the outcome will be what He desires. Of course, God will accomplish His ultimate purposes, and He does use unbelievers, although we don't really know how He gets them to do His bidding. However, would he not also use His people who are sensitive to His wishes? May He not even prefer to use us?

Looking at history, we can see certain nations have worked to thwart God's purposes. Some have tried to prevent the propagation of the gospel within their borders. Others have conquered nations previously open to the salvation story, and within nations, leaders and groups have worked to suppress the spread of God's kingdom. But some countries have allowed God's message to be disseminated freely – most notably in the United States.

God's chief purpose for earthly life is to propagate the gospel and bring as many people as possible into His kingdom. Arguably, the establishment of the United States has contributed as much to that goal as any development in history. Does it not seem that those involved in creating and maintaining our nation were doing God's work by enabling the spread of the gospel?

It is God's intent to use government to further His larger purposes. It is also certainly true that believers are expected to advance God's objectives. If government is one tool He uses to achieve these objectives, it should go without saying that some Christians would be involved in political affairs. To assert otherwise would be to say that God would use government to promote His purposes solely with those who do not believe in Him.

It is stated in scripture that believers will rule with Christ during the millennium. We do not know the details of how that rule will be carried out. We do know this will not be a time of perfection since many will rebel against God at the end of the thousand years. So, some type of political structure and laws will be needed to try to restrain unregenerate men and women who are part of the earth's population. We do not know how much of the political structure that exists at the time of Christ's return will be carried over into the millennium. We do know Jesus will be the head ruler, but if nations with governments are still in place (either as constituted at the beginning of the period or as reorganized by Christ), believers will likely serve in them. It is possible that our role will be based on our experiences on earth before the millennium. If so, our life now could be partially a preparation for our rule with Christ. In that case, involvement with politics now is an important activity for at least some Christians.

A small number of Christians have promoted the view that Christians should establish a theocracy where all the non-ceremonial laws of the Old Testament would be implemented and that Christ will not return until this is substantially accomplished. This movement is known as Christian reconstructionism. However, I see nothing in the New Testament that suggests the purpose of government should be to impose God's complete moral law on all people through human law. We are not even told for certain that Jesus Christ will establish such a government or governments when He returns to rule the earth for 1,000 years in the millennium.

One belief that is quite prevalent among believers is that since God ordains all government, we should, therefore, make no effort to oppose evil regimes or rulers, that such action is actually thwarting His will.

While God allows such people as Hitler, Stalin et al. to gain and maintain power for a time, and He will sometimes use these leaders and their governments to accomplish certain aspects of His ends, this does not necessarily mean He desires that type of tyranny to be in place. We, as believers, should always oppose evil wherever we find it.

God's Purpose for Civil Government

Although God's ultimate objective is to bring as many people as possible to be with Him in eternity, in conjunction with that goal, He works to bring history to a culmination that will lead to the millennial rule. He also has a vision for how government can aid life on earth in the meantime.

The passage of scripture that talks most directly about this is Romans 13:1-7. In these verses, God tells us through Paul what those purposes are and what our responsibilities are to be to those who govern. He tells us that all authority is actually established by Him to be *a minister of God for you for good* (Romans 13:4). In doing so, it punishes evil.

Surely He would want his children to assume roles in an institution He has prescribed. If we don't, control of governments will be completely in the hands of those who have not experienced God's redemptive power, do not understand His laws, and have not subordinated their wills to Him. Such governments will likely not do good, but rather oppress their citizens. History is replete with examples of tyrannical governments void of Christian influence. In the Romans passage, rulers are also said to be servants of God. Who better to perform that function than Christians who, if being obedient to Him, are already His servants?

We get further ideas of why government is ordained by God in I Timothy 2:1-2, where we are asked to pray for kings and those in authority, *so that we may lead a tranquil and quiet life in all godliness and dignity.* This indicates that government must punish evil men and women because they disrupt order in society and, in so doing, prevent us from having an environment where we can live such lives. For Christians, this is a society where we are free to be obedient to God, and if governments are to restrain those who would prevent us from living a tranquil quiet life, it should go without saying that they themselves should not take actions that disrupt our ability to lead such lives.

Christians' Roles in Government

Governments that carry out their mandate properly are not very prevalent in the world's history. Rather, the tendency for government leaders has been to grasp power and restrict freedom. A Christian who understands the nature of the world and human beings will have a better idea of how to construct a government with a greater likelihood of maximizing liberty. If believers actually serve in government leadership posts, they are not as likely to abuse power and squelch freedom. Christians, who should have as a priority being obedient to God, have a vested interest in maintaining a political environment where they have the freedom to do so.

A government based on God's principles and a proper notion of man will be more likely to best carry out the appropriate functions of government. It is possible there could be such a government without believers participating in any way – where no Christian has a position in it, nor has given any input into its formation. But is that likely? A government could exist that is good because those in authority, although not necessarily believers, are not power-hungry and sincerely seek to do the right things. However, unless the form of that government discourages the obtaining of power, the reins of that government in the future will likely pass into the hands of those who will use their positions for personal gain or power.

The best chances for a government that allows the unbridled growth of God's kingdom will occur with involvement from believers. That would include counsel and input in the process of actually founding a government as well as advice in ensuring its continued adherence to founding principles. Christians should have the discernment to recognize when government moves away from sound ideas and practices. In order to do so, they must keep themselves informed about what is going on in political affairs. I believe Christians have an obligation to do that and also to inform others about threats they see to the polity under which they live.

If Christians engage in commentary on issues and influence people politically, but none of them are willing to actually get involved in the political process, it would likely be perceived as adopting a superior attitude. It communicates an attitude of "let us tell you how it should be done," while also saying, "we're not going to get our hands dirty doing any of the actual work." Such an attitude is similar to what James related about a believer encountering a needy person: *If a brother or sister is without clothing and in need of daily food, and one of you says to them, Go in peace, be warmed and be filled, and yet you do not give them what is necessary for their body, what use is that?* (James 2:15, 16). This does not mean that all Christians must actually be actively involved in politics. But if we, as a body, comment on political issues, we should also acknowledge that some of our number should be willing to participate.

If God does, indeed, ordain nations and uses them to further His ends, it doesn't seem like He would want all of His children sitting on the sidelines and not taking part – like spectators at a dramatic performance. This is particularly true when He has given them gifts through the Holy Spirit that could aid in what He is trying to accomplish. Does it also not make sense to use those who are attuned to His will?

The United States has been used mightily by God throughout our history. Christians put forth much effort in the setting up of the nation. God has used even those who disobey Him to achieve His purposes. So, it is possible that everything done by Christians to the end of freeing us from Britain and setting up a new nation was displeasing to Him. However, what cannot be denied is the considerable (even monumental) amount of involvement on the part of believers in the forming of our country. Is it likely God was unhappy with all those believers who contributed in some way to the establishment of America? It resulted in a nation that produced unprecedented freedom to worship God, and which has sent missionaries all over the world to preach the gospel of Jesus Christ. Doesn't it seem more likely that believers were obedient to God by participating in His raising up a government like none other in history – one that has facilitated mightily the promulgation of the Word?

Political Involvement that Fits God's Timing

We cannot know for certain what God is working to accomplish in a given time in history, or how He intends for Christians to contribute to his plans for that era. However, it is possible that whether and how He wants believers to participate in the political arena depends on His objectives for that period. In New Testament times, it may be that God did not wish for His people to be involved in politics not only because of the difficulty in doing so under Roman rule, but also because His most important objective at that time was to firmly establish His church and have it provide a witness to the various parts of the world.

In later centuries in Europe, it may be that God wanted believers to be active in governments to develop Western Civilization as a prelude to causing the gospel to spread throughout the world. In our colonial and founding eras, He may have wished to create a nation which would be used as a base for sending missionaries to all points on the earth. Today His interest may include having Christians oppose the coming world system described in Revelation.

Responsibility for God's Gift of Freedom

When believers find themselves in a political situation that fosters considerable freedom to grow the kingdom of God, it seems He would want them to expend effort to maintain that ability. That is the position in which believers in America found themselves after our government had been firmly established. Christians did a reasonably good job of contributing to the preservation of our liberty for a while, but over the passage of time, believers have paid less attention to political affairs – particularly in recent decades when the insights of believers were needed as our freedoms were slipping away.

Whatever has gone on in the past, when we reach a place where freedom is severely threatened, as it is now, Christians should not just sit idly by until it is gone completely, since we know that the loss of liberty will also greatly curtail our efforts at furthering the kingdom. Believers should have seen this situation coming years ago and worked to prevent it from getting this bad. It is irresponsible to see a danger and allow it to become so serious, without making efforts to stop it. It may be said many believers did nothing since they did not recognize the threat, but my contention is that if they were really paying attention to what was going on in the world and truly looking at those events through the lens of Scripture, they would have seen the approaching perils. If, as the Declaration of Independence states, and I assert throughout this book, freedom is a gift from God, then we believers have a responsibility to care for it. Such care surely includes the establishment and maintenance of governments that protect this freedom and which do not infringe on it.

I feel particularly bad when I break or lose an item I received as a gift. I am especially bothered if the loss was due to carelessness on my part. It shows a lack of regard, not only for the item, but for the person who gave it to me.

A couple of years after college, my mother gave me a set of silverware that our family used for years, but which she no longer needed. In one of my many moves at the time, I placed all the utensils in that set in a bag, intending to take them to the car just before leaving. Somehow, I forgot them and didn't realize it until much later. This incident troubled me for years and still does somewhat, even though my mother has been gone for more than six years. I doubt if it would have bothered me if it had been something I had purchased myself, but it just seemed like I had slighted her by not caring for the silverware properly.

I may be more sensitive than necessary about such things or at least more so than the average person. However, I think many people feel a particular responsibility for taking care of something given to them. Certainly, we should feel that type of responsibility to an even greater degree for the gifts God has given us – particularly when the gift is such an important one as freedom. To have a lackadaisical attitude toward it demonstrates ungratefulness to, and a lack of regard for, the God who gave it to us.

Politics in the End Times

Some say that since the return of Christ is so imminent, we should do nothing to try to salvage society or its governments; rather, we should put all our efforts into saving souls. One cannot argue with the priority of evangelism. However, it is not an either/or choice. We should be active in politics for a number of reasons – even if facing the impending end of the world as we know it. First, we do not know God's exact timeline. The signs have been such that it seems to me (and I'm sure, others) that the rapture should have already happened, but it hasn't. It appears God may be moving at a slower pace than many of us expect. What if the Lord delays His coming for another fifty or a hundred years (or more)? At the speed events are happening in the world, being able to hold off efforts to control Christians for that number of years could mean a big difference in our ability to proselytize in the time remaining.

Second, we as individual Christians and as the church are to be Christ's witnesses on earth. That is equally true whether the world goes on for thousands of years or it ends next week. The likelihood of Christ's return should not change that. If we are to be involved in political affairs, then it should not matter how long we have to do it. This does not mean we should not have an increased sense of urgency about evangelism as we see the time grow seemingly short.

As the end does approach, conditions in the world will likely worsen considerably. Non-believers will be looking for answers. Christians should not be surprised to see problems escalating. But if our attitude is that we are not going to help address these problems because "we're out of here, you guys are going to have to stay and clean up the mess," it is not going to attract anyone to Christ. Many who see this cavalier attitude may, as a result, never be open to the gospel message. So, we need to involve ourselves in trying to straighten out a world which we believe may not last long. It is possible the opportunity for the church to be a corporate witness in the world will never be greater than near the end.

Third, we are to oppose evil in the world. As the end approaches, we should expect more strong signs of a developing evil world government which will be working against God. Moves toward establishing that government should be actively resisted by Christians.

Historical Perspective on Christian Involvement in Politics

Political Environment of the Old Testament

In the discussion of "Christian Participation in God-Ordained Government" above, we looked at how God governed Judah and Israel in Old

Testament times. I will now discuss the roles of some of God's people in other governments during that time.

Joseph ultimately became the *de facto* ruler of Egypt. Daniel was in the governments of Babylonia and the Medo-Persian Empire at a high level. Both of these men were very strong witnesses based on how they did their jobs and how they remained true to God.

Esther is another example. Although she lacked any real authority, her influence saved the Jewish people in Persia. Mordecai, her uncle, was an advisor to the king, Ahasuerus.

Joseph was plucked from prison and placed in the government of Pharaoh. He didn't apply for the job, and it doesn't appear he really had a choice in whether he wanted the position he received. Daniel was in Babylonia as a member of the Jewish captive people. It is questionable whether he had any choice about serving in the positions he held. Mordecai was in Ahasuerus' government of Persia as part of the Jewish captive people, and his service likely was also not voluntary. So, we probably shouldn't use any of these Old Testament people as examples in answering the question as to whether a believer should choose to be involved in governmental affairs.

In looking at the New Testament, we don't really see examples of believers involved in politics. Given that all the areas where Christians lived at that time were part of the very authoritarian Roman Empire, one would not expect any of them to have had opportunities for such activity.

The American Experience

It is instructive to look at the beginning of the colonies in the New World – particularly the one settled by the Pilgrims at Plymouth. If they would have followed the counsel that Christians should not be involved in politics, they would have made no effort to establish a government. They also could have said they didn't need to do so, since God would raise one up and provide it with leadership.

That does raise the question of where God was to get the people to run His government. We never know for certain which individuals are true believers in Christ, since we cannot see inside the hearts of others.

But from what we do know, it is likely that most of the Pilgrims were born-again believers. If they had been thinking like some Christians today, they would have considered those who came forward to organize a government as disobedient believers. If such a view is right, then from God's perspective it would have been best if those setting up the government were actually unbelievers, since then none of the Christians would have been disobedient.

It is possible that among the Pilgrims, as in most Christian bodies, some were not true believers – that tares lived among the wheat. If the true believers thought political involvement to be wrong and, therefore, obediently declined to be involved in the running of the colony, God would have had only a few colonists (the phony Christians) to work with to raise up a government. The Mayflower did have a crew that may have included those who were not believers. It might have been possible to put together a government from the crew and non-believing Pilgrims, but that would have resulted in an essentially Christian colony being ruled by unbelievers.

It is also possible that if the Pilgrims had not established authority over the colony, God could have raised up the Indians as their government by having them conquer the Pilgrims and rule over them.

Maybe they could have placed advertisements in European newspapers such as:

Wanted: Men and women to establish and run the government of Plymouth Colony in America

Qualification: Must not be a believer in Jesus Christ

The problem is that even the effort to seek governors for their colony would be involvement with politics, which they weren't supposed to do, remember?

The only option they had, if they wanted to be obedient to God, was to do nothing. This is close to what was initially done at the Jamestown colony in Virginia, and the results were disastrous. Although it had a government of sorts, with little organization or Christian influence, it suffered from disease, starvation, theft, fire, Indian attacks, and much loss of life.

I have been intentionally facetious in presenting these various options for Plymouth Colony based on the assumption that God does not want His people to be politically active. My objective was to show a contrast between those alternatives and what was actually done. Doesn't it make more sense to believe that the Pilgrims recognized the need for order in their colony, and in acting to meet that need, those who became their leaders were the people God raised up to establish the governmental authority He prescribes for civil society? The Pilgrims actually began their effort to create a government before they even left the ship by drafting and signing the Mayflower Compact. It became one of the precursors for the government eventually founded for the United States.

To be consistent, opponents of Christian political involvement would have to believe the Pilgrims were disobedient in setting up a government for their colony. But, realistically, if they were to have a government as called for in God's Word, it would have had to be established by believers. It is likely that even the most ardent opponents of political activity by Christians would acknowledge that, in this highly exceptional case, it was okay for believers to be involved, because no government previously existed, and primarily only Christians were available to create one. But, again, if they were to be consistent, they would have to question continuing involvement when a government was well-established. At what point would they feel comfortable turning it over to unbelievers?

Is the United States a Christian Nation?

What Does it Mean to Be a Christian Nation?

Whether the United States is a Christian nation is a question addressed frequently in recent years by both believers and non-believers. However, rarely do those answering that question define what they mean by "A Christian Nation." Most often, they just launch into a discussion of why we either have or have not been a Christian nation.

What are some of the possible definitions of a Christian nation? Does it mean a majority of people in the nation are true believers in Jesus Christ? The problem with that definition is that one cannot see inside another's heart. Orthodox Christianity says that a Christian is one who has received the gift of salvation. It is particularly difficult to look back more than two centuries to determine who was and who was not truly a believer.

Is a Christian nation one where a majority of residents profess to be Christians? What if 95 percent of the people claimed to be Christians but only a small minority lived their lives according to the principles of the Bible? It doesn't seem like we would be justified on that basis to designate the country as Christian.

Is a nation Christian if its culture reflects Christian principles and acknowledges the God of the Bible in its public institutions? Under that definition, we might say the United States was a Christian nation at the time of our founding, but it has experienced a marked change in recent decades. Due to recent Supreme Court rulings, the Ten Commandments are no longer in many classrooms. In many schools, Christmas programs or concerts are called holiday or winter concerts. Many Bible verses remain in public buildings, because they are chiseled in stone, but they mostly serve as a reminder of when the Christian religion was dominant in the United States. We could, legitimately, have been called a culturally Christian country in the past, but little evidence warrants that classification today.

The questions I have been asking deal primarily with the culture and the beliefs of the people of America at the time of the founding. People who ask whether the United States is a Christian nation are most often addressing whether our government was established as Christian. A better question would be: "Was the United States founded as a Christian nation?" However, even that question has different answers depending on what one means by "founded." Some would say it would only be founded as a Christian nation if its basic law was intended to carry out the mandates of the Bible. Such a government would involve passing laws against activities prohibited in Scripture. This would truly be a theocracy. If that is what is meant, I believe few of any political or theological stripe would say we were founded as a Christian nation. I think few believers would want our nation to operate in that manner.

Before returning to the question of whether we were founded as a Christian nation, let's examine some of the issues discussed by those dealing with the question.

Reasons Some Say the United States is Not a Christian Nation

Many who deny we were established as a Christian nation say important founders were deists – not orthodox Christians. Some cite the fact that God is not mentioned in the Constitution. Others suggest many of the presuppositions underlying the government our founders set up were based on ideas from the Enlightenment. Others believe many of the founders were elitists. These points are made by those who are quite conservative, including Christians. Is there any validity to such claims? Let's look at them individually.

1. Certainly, there were founders whose religious views could be categorized as being deist – a belief that God created the world, but then let it operate without His direction. Those include some well-known names associated with our nation's founding – like Jefferson and Franklin. However, of the other men who contributed their thinking to the formation of our governmental system, some were Christians, though they may not be known as well as some of those identified as deists. Nevertheless, they had a profound impact on the form of our government. These included: Samuel Adams, Patrick Henry, John Jay, Roger Sherman, and Charles Cotesworth Pinckney.

Several signers of the Constitution had been students of John Witherspoon at the College of New Jersey (now Princeton) and were deeply influenced by him. Witherspoon was a Presbyterian pastor and a very orthodox Christian. His pupils included James Madison whose influence at the Constitutional Convention earned him the appellation of "Father of the Constitution." Witherspoon himself was a member of Congress and the New Jersey Senate, and was a signer of the Declaration of Independence.

Franklin, in urging that daily prayer be instituted at the Constitutional Convention said:

> "I have lived, Sir, a long time, and the longer I live, the more convincing proofs I see of this truth – that God governs in

> the affairs of men. And if a sparrow cannot fall to the ground without his notice, is it probable that an empire can rise without his aid? We have been assured, Sir, in the sacred writings, that 'except the Lord build the House they labour in vain that build it.' I firmly believe this; and I also believe that without his concurring aid we shall succeed in this political building no better than the Builders of Babel."[6]

He certainly doesn't sound like a deist who believes God leaves men to their own devices and doesn't intervene in their world.

2. God actually is mentioned in the Constitution. It is indicated as being signed "in the year of our Lord." Some defenders of the idea that we were founded as a Christian nation cite that as partial proof, but I believe that is stretching a point. At the time of the writing of the Constitution, such a designation was in general use.

However, the lack of any substantive mention of God in the Constitution does not indicate we were not founded as a Christian nation – nor should it be considered surprising. A constitution is basically a technical document which lays out the nuts and bolts of how an organization conducts its affairs.

It is really in the Declaration of Independence where the philosophic underpinnings of our system were laid down, and that document very specifically declares our rights come from God. This statement has far-reaching ramifications that are dealt with throughout this book.

It is interesting that many of the state constitutions did have specific references to God. They also had requirements that office-holders be Christians. In fact, at the time the Constitution was being debated, several states had established religions. If one looks at the America of 1787, as not the federal government, but rather the sum of the various states, then a better case could be made for saying we were a Christian nation – even that we were founded as one. There is some justification for such a view. People tended to look at themselves more as Virginians, Pennsylvanians, etc. than as Americans. They saw the national government they had created as very limited – rather than one that

6 Benjamin Franklin, Motion in the Constitutional Convention, June 28, 1787

would command greater loyalty than their state. It may be the desire to leave the question of religion to the individual states is one reason for the lack of any mention of God in the Constitution.

3. Was the United States based on principles of the Enlightenment rather than Christianity? There certainly was some of that thinking among founders. However, many assume all the ideas of the Enlightenment were in direct conflict with Christian beliefs – that a strict dichotomy exists between Christianity and those ideas. But in reading about the Enlightenment it is difficult even to come up with a hard-and-fast definition for what the term means. Many who write on the topic view it quite differently.

Isaac Newton and John Locke (who are considered Christians) are two names associated with the Enlightenment. Locke had a particularly large amount of influence on the ideas of several founders. Born into a Puritan family, Locke did move away from their religious views. His ideas on religion (as well as many of his other thoughts) are somewhat complicated. However, he did not reject Christianity.

Montesquieu is another person who has been identified with the Enlightenment. He was a Frenchman who advocated the separation of powers in government in his major work *The Spirit of the Laws.* He was very influential in colonial America, being one of the most frequently quoted thinkers prior to the Revolution. Separation of powers is an idea many founders – particularly Christians – recognize as necessary due to the tendency of fallen men and women to increase their power through government. This is one example which illustrates how ideas that influenced our founding from an Enlightenment thinker were actually very compatible with Christian thinking.

In general, one could say that the Enlightenment was a movement toward more use of the mind to evaluate ideas, rather than merely accepting the authority of the state and church, which had dominated European society for some time. There is nothing implicitly anti-Christian about using the mental facilities which God gave us, and we should not, as believers, uncritically accept the pronouncements from human institutions – be they church, state, or other. Of course, when we elevate our minds to the point that we accept ideas in conflict with God's Word, we are going too far.

Merely because some philosophic concepts were arrived at by developing ideas that came out of the Enlightenment does not, in and of itself, make those concepts anti-Christian. We need to hold up all thinking against God's Word to see if it is consistent with it.

The Enlightenment liberated thinking from human institutions. This led to more people thinking for themselves. One would expect some would use this freedom to oppose God but others to develop ideas consistent with a Christian worldview.

4. Some assert that many founders were elitists looking out for the interests of the well-situated and not that concerned about the common man. Some who have called them elitists have done so because they come to the discussion with a social-leveling or Marxist perspective. They believe the function of a government is to equalize the economic statuses of society's members, and they assert that the structure laid out by the Constitution militates against government assuming such a role. That is true, but that doesn't make the founders elitists. They merely believed that an open-ended constitution that permitted government to do whatever those who gain control of it wish is detrimental to freedom. They were actually protecting the interests of the common man that tend to get overrun by the power of big government.

If one believes government should provide for people, then one could look at the system set up by our fathers as protecting the interests of the powerful and mighty and those who set it up as elitists. However, as asserted throughout this book, that is not what government should be doing.

If our founders were primarily elitists who had their own interests in mind, why would they have set up a form of government where the power was so dispersed? Why wouldn't they have concentrated power in a way they could more easily use to maintain control? Since they were highly respected and had the confidence of so many people, they may have gotten away with establishing such a system. But they, in effect, gave away their power, rather than arrogating it onto themselves. Also, many of the signers of the Declaration of Independence paid a heavy price for opposing England. They suffered losses of members of their families, possessions, and their health. Elitists don't normally make such sacrifices for the good of others.

A More Relevant Question

This raises a more important question that needs to be asked about our country. Are the basic documents upon which our national and state governments were founded based on biblical principles? Do they reflect a Christian understanding of the nature of man and the world? Are they consistent with a Christian worldview?

One of the main ideas incorporated into our government was the concept of limited, specified functions. Another was the recognition of the need for the separation of powers among the various branches of government. These ideas sprung from the Christian conception of man – the belief that humans have a fallen nature. Because they are flawed, men tend to gain and maintain power in their own self-interest. Recognizing this, the founders created a government with limited, specified functions – one where attempts to gain power would be difficult, and where power would be divided.

Even Thomas Jefferson, who was not an orthodox Christian, recognized this when he said, "In matters of power let no more be heard of the confidence in man but bind them down from mischief by the chains of the constitution." Although he may have been a deist, he recognized that men were fallible – which accorded with the Christian view of human nature prevalent at the time.

It is because of this view of human nature that the founders recognized the necessity of limiting government and not concentrating its power. Although not all those who shaped the form of our government believed in the presence of a sin nature in man, the pervasiveness of such a view at that time certainly caused a majority of them to see the need for placing restrictions on governmental power.

The question regarding Christianity and our founding has been phrased wrongly. Rather than asking whether we are a Christian nation or whether we were founded as one, we should ask if we were founded on Christian principles – particularly with a Christian understanding of the nature of men and women. If the question is asked that way, the answer is definitely in the affirmative.

Perhaps the best indication that political involvement is proper for the Christian is the testimony of American history. Christians played predominant roles in establishing this country on biblical principles, and we have been blessed as no other nation in history. If God had been displeased with the efforts of those early American Christians, would He have allowed us to prosper as we have? Would He have blessed us as He has?

In reality, the proper way to look at this situation is that human government is an essential part of life on earth – just like many other institutions and occupations. We, as believers, are "in this world, but not of it." It is unrealistic to think Christians will not have a part in all legitimate activities that take place here on earth – including those that involve politics.

CHAPTER 2

Christians' Involvement in Affairs on Earth

Go therefore and make disciples of all nations, baptizing them in the name of the Father and the Son and the Holy Spirit. (Matthew 28:19)

You are the salt of the earth; but if the salt has become tasteless, how can it be made salty again? (Matthew 5:13)

Let your light shine before men in such a way that they may see your good works, and glorify your Father who is in heaven. (Matthew 5:16)

Enabling the Great Commission

Working for a Political Environment Conducive to Evangelism

Some counsel Christians not to become involved in politics since the time and resources we have available are quite limited. They contend that everything we do should be focused on spreading the gospel. This should, of course, constitute our primary work. However, in those countries where believers do not enjoy religious freedom, a great deal of exertion is required just to avoid being detected by government authorities. Worship and Bible study often take place in secret. Believers cannot legally witness in public. Effort that could be used to evangelize must be expended to evade the government.

If we Americans lose our freedom, we could find ourselves in a similar situation. Working at this juncture to preserve our liberty may be preventing a situation where our time and effort can only be used much less effectively in the future. Americans would likely not be in a position where our liberty is as threatened as it is if we had paid more attention to the gradual loss of freedom that has taken place and expended more labor toward preserving it. That is true of both Christians and unbelievers. However, we who understand the fallen nature of man and the consequent propensity of those in authority to assume more power should have had more discernment and recognized the threat to our liberty. Certainly, some have been sounding the clarion call of warning for many decades, but too few paid attention or did anything to stop the slide.

Serving Christian Ministries through Political Activity

Many Christians involved with foreign missions or in a domestic ministry help in a support role. They provide services like accounting or computer functions for a given ministry. They do this to allow others to focus on the primary purpose of the organization. What they do is not less important; it is often vital to the continued operation of the ministry. They are using gifts God has given them to serve. Many believe they have been called to assist in this way. Although they are not directly evangelizing in their ministry role, it does not mean they should not personally be proselytizing whenever an opportunity arises (as should all Christians).

Christians who are involved with politics could also be seen as filling a support role for Christian ministry. Their efforts help maintain an environment where Christianity can thrive with the least interference from government. Such a person is supporting Christian activity in general – rather than a specific ministry. Why would it not be proper for some to work to maintain the liberty that provides an environment conducive for evangelism?

Protecting the Wall

The role of such people is not unlike that of those guarding the workers who rebuilt the wall around Jerusalem (Nehemiah 4). The objective was erecting the wall. Yet, Nehemiah assigned just as many men to protect the laborers as he did for the actual construction. Were their jobs any less critical to the overall goal of building the wall? No. Without their efforts, it is possible it would never have been built, or that it would have been torn down by the Jews' enemies. The actions of believers today who provide protection for the building of God's kingdom through political activities are no less important to that task.

In addition, Nehemiah's wall-builders did their work with one hand and held a weapon in the other, and at least some of those who did construction during the day were asked to act as guards at night. If we were to follow that pattern, some whose primary focus is with Christian ministries would also spend time and effort to help maintain conditions in society so God's work can proceed with minimum impediments.

Preventing a Hostile Environment for Christians

The quality and quantity of government establishes the social environment in which Christians carry out the commands we have from God. Throughout the centuries, Christians have had to do that in very hostile surroundings. Many governments have persecuted them, discriminated against them, and forbade activities such as worship and proselytizing. In other cases, authorities have turned a blind eye and allowed persecution of Christians by others.

We must be obedient to God's directives no matter the circumstances in which we find ourselves. Many faithful believers have done so to the point of martyrdom. We need to be prepared to do whatever is necessary to follow God's will and to be witnesses regardless of the political climate in which we may find ourselves. This raises the question: isn't it legitimate to work to prevent such a situation and to establish and maintain a political environment conducive to furthering God's kingdom?

We, in the United States, have been immensely blessed in that we have been able to practice our faith with little interference from government. This is largely because we have had a limited government severely restrained by the Constitution. Christians have had a major role in creating and maintaining the resulting freedom. Have not these efforts been a substantial aid in furthering God's kingdom and carrying out the Great Commission? For those who placed a large percentage of time into those efforts, could it not be considered a ministry?

Politics as a Calling

When we think of a calling from God, we properly think first of roles needed in the body like pastor, missionary, and evangelist. However, not all Christians are asked by God to serve in these capacities. Many believe He calls people to stations in society where they also serve Him as well as their fellow humans. This surely would include positions where a person could use their influence to nurture a political climate hospitable to the spreading of the gospel.

Believers who are not called to be evangelists are still expected to win people to Christ. Likewise, those who are not called to participate in the political arena should still do their part by being somewhat knowledgeable on issues, influencing others, voting intelligently, and performing other civic duties of a good citizen.

If believers spend all their available time on evangelism, then we are relying on unbelievers to maintain the political situation that allows us to do that in an unfettered way. This results in several problems. First, those who aren't Christians will not have the understanding of human nature essential to keeping a nation free. Second, they will not have the proper concern for ensuring believers have the liberty required to carry out the Great Commission. By relying on others to maintain the environment we require, we become, in effect, parasites on the body politic – asking others to maintain conditions under which our work will thrive. The Amish and other such groups are able to live separated lives in America only because they are protected by the rule of law that surrounds their communities, but they contribute little to maintaining that shielding environment.

The Threat of Lost Freedom

Americans are rapidly losing the freedoms we have enjoyed. This situation could eventually devolve to the point where our right to present the gospel is severely restricted or actually outlawed. Faithful Christians would then be compelled to either take political action to attempt to restore the right to evangelize, or practice civil disobedience to spread the message of Christ. Is it not better to expend effort to maintain the freedom we have now, rather than have to work to restore it in the future, under adverse conditions?

If such a situation should occur, the spreading of the gospel would continue as it always has. In some cases, the church has actually grown rapidly under conditions where it has been greatly persecuted. Some might think it would be better to allow our freedom of religion to be lost, since believers might then become more serious in their commitment to Christ. To purposely let that happen would constitute irresponsible and almost contemptuous treatment of the gift of freedom God has given us.

Some of those saying we shouldn't be involved in politics due to the priority of winning souls for the kingdom, nevertheless seem to find time for all sorts of activities that do not directly (or even indirectly) relate to building God's kingdom. This includes excessive time for personal pleasure. God does expect we will enjoy the wonderful things He has given us, but should people whose priorities seem to be things other than winning souls criticize those who are involved in political activity? Is time spent protecting our right to evangelize not as important as time used to amuse ourselves?

Christian leaders who say believers should only be involved in activities directly related to evangelism seem to assume the ability to continue to do that freely will go on indefinitely. If we lose our freedom, the course they advise may not be easily followed. At the present time, it is a simple decision to opt for an evangelism-only lifestyle. However, doing so under an oppressive, anti-Christian regime would be much more involved and difficult. At least some of us should work to ensure an easier path will still be available in the future for those primarily engaged in proselytizing. And we shouldn't wait. We should anticipate the growing threats to liberty and take steps to stop them before the tasks become much more difficult. Many signs and trends today point to the likelihood of losing our freedom to evangelize unless something is done to prevent that loss.

In spite of our freedom to do so, many, if not most, Christians in the United States do not use the time they have very wisely or devote much of it to carrying out the Great Commission. Believers in other countries put us to shame, since they have much less time available and yet effectively use what they do have for kingdom activity. The fact that many American Christians are poor time stewards when it comes to serving God does not change the fact that having the freedom available for building His kingdom is a good thing. Such an ability is worthy of being preserved.

Increasing the Financial Resources Available for God's Work

When a person has to use almost all his resources to keep him and his family alive, little time or funds remain to contribute to God's work. The great surplus available to American believers, beyond that used for personal needs, has been used mightily to fund missionary work throughout the world. Many have not given what they could from their great bounty, but that does not alter the fact that our economic system has created great prosperity and provided large amounts of funds to aid the spread of the gospel throughout the world. Our forefathers had the foresight to set up a system that provided the incentives and freedom that led to a prosperous economy. Therefore, many have an abundance of time and resources available for God's work, and many believers toiled mightily and sacrificed to establish and maintain the system from which Christians still benefit today. They did this by being involved in politics.

In this way, believers who are politically active are really supporting the Great Commission by working to obtain and preserve an economic system that produces abundance for contributing to Christian ministries.

Is It too Late for Politics to Help Us?

From prophecies in the Bible, abundant signs seem to indicate we are approaching the end times. One of the most visible is the movement toward a world government system. Some Christians see the culmination of that movement as being so imminent and inexorable that any activity against it is pointless and futile. They believe whatever limited time we do have remaining should be devoted to proselytizing. The signs do seem to be the birth pangs mentioned in the Bible. However, we do not know how long they will be experienced before the end actually comes.

Although we may rejoice because such signs point to Christ's return when we will be rescued from the trials of this world, we should not be happy about events signaling this development. Those times will see the raising up of powers and people opposed to God and His plans. They will do many evil things in pursuit of their ends, and we believers should not in any way be abetting their efforts.

In fact, as God's representatives on earth, we should recognize and oppose them. Just to say they are inevitable and do nothing to stop them is not an appropriate response from God's people.

Is Revival the Complete Answer?

Some Christians say that being involved in politics is futile because our country has moved so far away from God. They believe that only a revival will restore our nation and that God will not bless us while we are so disobedient to His laws. They may well be right. Believers should always hope and pray for revival, but doing so should not preclude working for political renewal.

Some believers assume a revival would automatically result in a reformation of government. However, even if a spiritual revival occurred, we have no guarantee a political regeneration will necessarily follow. It may be that not enough believers would recognize that need and take the actions that would result in such a restoration.

Even if a return to a limited, constitutional government occurred, could it be maintained without the adequate understanding that comes with a Christian worldview? A revival will bring many new believers. A large number of them will likely not be schooled in Christian beliefs, and will initially not be discipled. It is also true that most will probably know little, if anything, about a Christian worldview.

A revival is definitely desirable, but that does not remove the need for political involvement from believers. It is not likely a revival would result in a majority of those in the United States being saved. That could happen, since with God anything is possible, but even if a revival resulted in seventy-five percent of the country being true believers, it would not automatically transform our political system. It would mean a substantial portion of the people would be receptive to learning the principles required to re-establish our republic on a firmer basis. This would not happen, unless enough believers actually worked to apply these principles to our polity, any more than our nation would have been founded without the efforts of believers – no matter how high a percentage of colonists were Christians. God works through people – particularly those who are faithful in applying His Word. Many believers seem to think of revival as a magic potion that would automatically make all things right.

If a revival should occur but a majority of those saved through it continue to live sinful, destructive lifestyles, would we expect society to be reformed? Most believers would not. It is not likely God would choose to allow us to return to our roots and experience the concomitant blessings while such a large percentage of our populace is living so far from Him and His principles. Nor should we expect that a revival where most of the converts don't understand how God's laws apply to government would result in a restoration of our founding principles. Believers should be developing political philosophies consistent with God's laws now so, if a revival happens, believers will be available to teach them to new believers and actually implement them into our body politic when the new spiritual climate makes this feasible.

This is really analogous to what should be happening on an ongoing basis in our churches and in the community of Christian ministries. The better God's people understand His Word and the more discipleship programs are put in place, the better the church will be prepared for a revival if it comes.

Here's an interesting possible scenario. What if the greatest Christian revival in history occurs in America, and when it's over, we find that ninety percent of the country's residents are now believers? Would those who assert that Christians not be involved in politics suggest that we turn over our country, states, cities, counties, school boards, etc., to the ten percent who remain non-believers? Should all those who had been in government and had been converted then resign their positions?

The most important reasons Christians should desire a revival is the harvest of souls for God's kingdom and the spiritual and moral renewal of our society. This would be a cause of great rejoicing. But, contrary to what many Christians maintain, a revival would not automatically result in a political restoration.

Supporting Christian Life on Earth

While the Great Commission is the primary command for believers, God gives us other directives in Scripture that have a bearing on whether, and to what degree, Christians should be involved with politics. We are to: 1) Bring up our children in the fear and admonition of the Lord, 2) Work to provide for our own and our families' needs, 3) Help the poor and needy, and 4) Be stewards of that with which God has entrusted us.

Raising Christian Offspring

We are told in the Bible to raise our children to fear the Lord. This involves their training – much of which should be done within the family. However, in the United States and most other countries, a system of formal education has been established. Much teaching is done in public, private, or parochial schools. Also, a growing number of students are being taught by their parents with many Christians opting for home schooling. Other believers have chosen private or parochial schools – particularly those with an evangelical emphasis. However, those choices are not economically feasible for some. Others live where such schools are not available. Some do not home school for a variety of reasons. Possibly neither parent believes they are competent to teach, or both parents work outside the home. The result is that students from Christian homes attend public schools. Their parents should certainly be concerned about what is being taught to their children.

Increasingly, mandates from states and the federal government dictate what is taught in public schools and how it is taught. Christian parents with kids in those schools need to be aware of such mandates. They also should know about pending legislation that will impact the schools. Even if policies for schools were not being dictated from higher levels, they would be at least partially determined by the local school board. For this reason, it is important to have people serving there who will support the right things in education, since a humanistic, anti-Christian agenda is currently being promoted in many public schools.

Christians who don't have children in public schools should also be concerned about education. If students from believing families are learning things that will undermine their faith or contradict what they learn at home, it will impact the mission of the church. What is taught in schools will help determine the direction of society – something all believers should be concerned about. In this respect, all Christians have a definite stake in education.

In order to have an influence, one must do such things as review curriculum and teaching methods, go to school board meetings to express concerns, track legislation in the education field, and contact representatives regarding laws being considered. It may require working to get good people elected to the local board. Who would be better suited to serve on a school board than an informed Christian who would stand up for the interests of believing parents and children and for values that will positively impact future generations? All these things are political activities. For Christians – particularly parents – to participate in this way is aiding the ability to raise up responsible Christian children.

There hasn't been excessive direct interference yet by the federal government in private, parochial, or home schooling. States vary in the amount of mandates placed on those schooling options. However, if Christians are not vigilant, there undoubtedly will be greater efforts to control such schools. One reason there has not been more restrictions on home schools is that teaching parents are well-organized and have prevented more controls by being politically aware and active.

Proverbs 22:6 says, *Train up a child in the way he should go. Even when he is old he will not depart from it.* Increasingly, government is interfering with parents' ability to do this; not only by mandating what their children are taught, but also by intervening more in families. The signs suggest this trend will continue. If not reversed, we can expect parents will eventually be told how they can discipline their offspring, what they can feed them, and what they can teach them. It will take a political effort to prevent this from happening. Christian parents will need to be involved if they wish to continue to be obedient to God in the upbringing of their children.

Providing for Ourselves and Our Families

Men are told to provide for their families, and in today's society many women participate in that responsibility. This is done primarily by working. Meeting the needs of our offspring should not only involve caring for them while they are still in our homes. It should not be only to help them when needed throughout our lives or leave them a substantial inheritance. Providing for our families should also include doing what we can to ensure they have a political environment that will allow them to provide for themselves and their families when we are gone. We currently have a profligate government that has run up unimaginable and unsustainable debts. This will be paid for by future generations through increased taxes and by destruction of purchasing power through inflation, which will effectively reduce the value of any inheritance left to them.

Liberties are also being taken away by government which will impair our children's ability to provide for themselves and their families, to evangelize, and to be obedient to God. What good will it do to take care of our children while we live, but then make no provision for them in the future – leaving them with a political system that will ultimately make them slaves and/or indigents? That is not even considering the situation in which it will leave their progeny for generations to come if the Lord tarries. Surely, the mandate to provide for our families should extend to leaving them with a political and cultural legacy as well as a financial and spiritual one.

We are commanded to work as the method to provide for ourselves and our families. There is no question that what happens politically has an impact on our ability to obey these commands. In many countries throughout history and in our current world, people have to spend most of their waking hours working just to scratch out a subsistent living. Contrast this with the United States where most of the populace has plentiful spare time. The difference is due primarily to government policies. People who use most of their time earning a living have little left to fulfill God's commands to evangelize and make disciples.

This also has an impact on the raising of children. The amount of time required to feed and clothe families has a direct bearing on how much remains for parents to instruct children in God's Word and ensure they are brought up with positive values. The time saved by a reduced number of working hours can be used for our church, Christian ministries, and our families. The political environment is a major determinant of the amount of time required to meet our families' needs.

Our economic system is now being severely threatened. Does it not make sense for believers to work to prevent its destruction or impairment? If it is seriously harmed, it will reduce our earning potential and many will have fewer resources to provide for their families. Many parents would also have to devote more time and energy to working and have less of those resources available for their spouses and children.

A believer can engage in a wide range of jobs to fulfill his or her obligation to provide for himself. Many elective positions are full-time jobs that are quite essential to the functioning of society. So, it should certainly be appropriate for Christians to hold them. The main difference between them and other jobs is that voters, rather than managers, make decisions on hiring. For such jobs, a campaign and election replace the typical application and interview process used for private sector jobs. If it is proper for Christians to hold these positions, it must be proper to seek them by running for the office. It must then also be acceptable for believers to participate in the process of helping others obtain these jobs. These are political activities.

Assisting Those with Needs

The Bible tells us many times to help the poor. The percentage of needy people has been considerably lower in this country than in most others. That is largely a result of our free market economy. This is, I believe, the system most consistent with the Christian view of the world. Having the right type of economy is a great boon to the poorest in society. Doesn't helping them include working to establish and preserve a system that dramatically reduces the number of indigent people and creates the most opportunities for them to provide for themselves and rise out of their lowly economic status? And of course, efforts to strengthen and restore our economic system enable us to prosper more – and, thus, to have many more resources to help others.

Since countries with more Christian influence are more likely to set up such systems, our evangelistic efforts throughout the world are indirectly also helping the poor. But even if a country is predominantly Christian, that is no guarantee of its being prosperous. The dots must be connected between a Christian worldview and economic freedom – and believers are best equipped to do that.

Regardless of the economic climate of a country a certain part of the population will include needy people for various reasons. Christians should be in the forefront of those assisting them. Since a free market creates more wealth, a nation with such a system will have more surplus resources available to contribute to the needy. This is another reason for Christians to promote economic liberty. Actually, working for a free economy (which is a political activity), both in America and in other parts of the globe, might be the best thing a believer could do to carry out God's mandate to help the poor.

Being Stewards of God's Gifts

The way we take care of our finances is a great responsibility. It affects some of the other commands God has given us such as helping others, providing for our families, bringing up our children, etc.

We, as believers, should always advocate that government itself be a good steward of the income it receives. The way it gathers and uses monies definitely impacts our ability to be stewards since every dollar it takes from us is one less dollar over which we are able to exercise stewardship. That, in itself, should be a reason for the Christian to advocate limited government and low taxes.

Christians differ about whether tithing is still required under New Testament teaching, but whatever one believes, it is instructive to see what the Old Testament requirement was. When added together, the varying mandatory offerings amount to about 23.3 (rather than ten) percent of a person's income. Old Testament Israel was a theocracy, and these payments amounted to a tax. They went to finance both the spiritual and secular functions of the nation. One would think that the total percentage of our income we pay for taxes to all levels of government should not exceed the percentage God asked for both the governmental and spiritual functions of Israel. What we give to the church is over and above our taxes. Yet, the amount required by just government today often actually exceeds the percent God asked for both spiritual and secular purposes. Our priorities as a society are seriously out of line if we are mandating more revenue for our government than God asked Israel to give for His work.

A person who serves as a steward is given a great deal of control over what they have been asked to manage. This is certainly true of governments. While we should expect them to be good stewards of the tax monies we give them, the amount should only be enough to cover legitimate functions of the state. Beyond that, we should not transfer our stewardship responsibilities to any level of government since doing so is giving them control of those funds and enlarging their domain – reducing our choices of how to use the money we have earned in the way we believe God is directing us.

An essential part of stewardship is not to waste resources. Government has been wasteful by subsidizing efforts and enterprises that otherwise would not receive adequate funding in the free market. By doing so, they have diverted money from endeavors where it would have been spent in ways that the marketplace deemed more useful. In this way, government has been a poor steward by squandering economic resources on less beneficial purposes – reducing the amount available to those who would be better stewards. This happens, for example, when government takes money from productive enterprises to give subsidies to inefficient forms of mass energy generation such as solar and wind power.

Recently, discussion about Christians' stewardship responsibility for natural resources has increased – an issue that has come to be called "creation care." That topic will be dealt with separately in Chapter 15.

Stewardship of God's Gift of Free Will

There is an important area of stewardship which has bearing on the appropriateness of Christian political activity. We believe men and women are created in the image of God. This involves free will as we make rational decisions and act on them. Believers know humans are flawed and often make choices that violate God's laws and/or are displeasing to Him. This is a misuse of the gift of volition God has given us. The fact that the capability is not always used properly, however, does not diminish its importance. For without the ability to choose, neither could we voluntarily submit ourselves to God and His will.

God gives each of us a set of natural talents. We are also given gifts by the Holy Spirit. But more important than either natural or spiritual gifts is the endowment of our minds and the ability to choose, for this allows us to use and develop the other gifts He has given us. Of course, no gift is as important as His giving of His Son, Jesus Christ, to pay the price for our sins with His death. I believe second only to that sacrifice, is the gift of our minds and the ability to use them to make decisions, without which we would be unable to accept the gift of salvation and to effectively use God's other gifts.

We use this gift of volition naturally; it is intrinsic to our humanity. It is what defines us as humans possessing the image of God – separating us from other life forms. However, other parties can intervene and prevent us from exercising our choices. When individuals or groups injure us physically, limiting our ability to perform some actions, or rob of us our belongings or wealth, they prevent us from having the wherewithal to pursue certain choices. In some cases, they may prevent us from making any further choices by taking our lives.

Therefore, one of the most legitimate functions of government is to restrict those who would infringe upon the exercise of our wills. It is important to have laws to defend our freedom to use that ability. Unfortunately, governments, rather than protect its use, can, and often have, interfered with it by preventing us from making a whole host of choices.

As individuals, we can be good stewards of this cognitive ability God has given us by making wise choices. As believers, this means obeying God's Word and attempting to learn His will and to follow it.

Through psychological techniques like brainwashing, our ability to use our mental abilities can be seriously impaired or virtually destroyed. Currently, in this country, most people are still able to make free, rational choices. However, we are often fed inaccurate or deceptive information, causing us to make wrong decisions based on inadequate knowledge. Certainly, part of the stewardship of our rationality is to try to prevent such assaults against it and make an effort to get good information.

Unless we retain the ability to act on choices, our volitional capability is very hollow. In addition to stewardship relating to our personal use of time and financial resources, stewardship also involves preserving the rational ability of everyone in society by preventing forces that interfere with its exercise. This is done by creating human laws which restrain and punish private parties who seek to prevent individuals from acting on their choices. Just as importantly, it involves restricting government so it does not infringe on our right to act on our decisions. Such actions are really part of preserving our mental abilities and, therefore, involve being stewards of the volitional capability God has given us. As such, it seems appropriate that Christians should be involved in politics to promote stewardship of this important gift of God.

Believers who recognize humans are endowed with an image of God that includes the ability to make free choices should be the most concerned with preserving that right. We as individuals tarnish that image when we make decisions to dishonor Him. The capabilities we have as part of the image of God are diminished when a person's ability to use her mind is restricted by criminals or arbitrary decrees of government. Such violations of God's image in us really bring those being transgressed closer to the level of animals that act out of instinct and cannot make or execute rational choices. Fortunately, to this point, attempts to control people's thoughts have been limited. Even though governments may prevent people from acting on their decisions, they are not yet able to prevent them from thinking right. However, we face major efforts to get people to think like collectivists through the increasingly centralized control of our education system.

It is not surprising that materialists who deny man has a spirit or mind independent from the physical brain usually value freedom of thought and action so little. They are much more likely to support government policies that treat people like animals by herding them around. We cannot rely on them to restore our free society. That is only likely to happen if Christians lead the way, because we understand the marvelous gift of liberty God has given us is worth preserving.

There are non-theists who believe in individual liberty. Some are working hard to preserve that right. We should acknowledge and express appreciation for those efforts. However, such individuals should recognize they have no philosophic basis for their belief in liberty. They are materialists, and such a position leaves no room for a mind independent of physical life. This means thinking and corresponding actions by humans are just random occurrences. It leaves no rationale for saying we have any more natural rights than an animal since, in this view, we are little more than masses of matter with no true volitional ability.

God has not only created us in His image, He has given each of us an individual, unique personality. The more of our freedom we keep, the more we are able to be the distinctive people God intended us to be. Government mandates tend to reduce the individuality of its subjects. They promote the conforming of citizens into patterns of thinking and acting deemed to be correct by the rulers. The bureaucratic mentality tends to see people as numbers and statistics. Those who would control society realize it is easier to do if people act and think alike. By promulgating laws that reduce our choices, they rob us of the ability to be true to who we are as persons designed by God.

Care for the use of our freedom will also aid in other areas of stewardship. It increases our ability to unrestrictedly use our talents and gifts as God pleases. It restricts others from stealing resources we might otherwise use for God's glory. And it reduces the amount government takes in taxes – leaving us more to use in God's works.

We have a situation in the United States today where the government is not only not allowing us to exercise stewardship over the volitional gift given us by God, but it is positively working to harm, if not destroy, that gift. If it is right to exercise stewardship by protecting plants and animals, is it not much more important to preserve the marvelous gift of human freedom given us by God?

Stewardship involves making choices. It is only possible to the extent we maintain our ability to freely make decisions. All stewardship is dependent on preserving that capability. Since government is a great – if not the greatest – threat to that ability, Christians should be involved in politics to protect the continued use of our freedom to exercise stewardship in obedience to God.

Being Salt and Light in Society

In addition to the specific commands from God, more general ones also exist. For example, Christians are commanded by Jesus to let our lights shine before men and to be salt for the world. If we are salt and light personally, as a church, and in various ministries, the collective effort will certainly impact the world and be a witness to its inhabitants. But does being salt and light also include political activity?

Salt Throughout Society

Frequently, biblical commentators cite the use of salt for a preservative as the basis of comparison for what Jesus said about being salty. Based on His reference in Matthew 5:13 about salt becoming tasteless, it seems more likely its property as a seasoning is the analogy He intended. If that is true, we can say Christians in society stimulate it in a manner similar to the way salt brings out the flavor of food.

When persons use any seasoning, they sprinkle it over the whole serving of food – not just on one corner of the portion – so the flavor of the complete helping is enhanced. Similarly believers should be sprinkled throughout society by occupying various stations in life. In a given community, you would find them in different neighborhoods, and in various social strata and occupations. You might encounter one checking out your purchases at a grocery store, fixing your teeth, or helping you prepare your will. Why should they be in all those places but not in legislative halls, city council chambers, or on school boards? If we find no Christians in these places, are we truly being salt?

We are to be positive influences and witnesses wherever we are. The potential for doing that in a significant way is actually greater in a public office of some type than in many other pursuits. As a legislator, for example, a believer has the opportunity to originate and/or help pass laws that impact the whole society. Also, people in public positions have a higher profile, allowing a greater number of people the opportunity to observe their behavior.

The Amish generally live admirable lives as far as their personal character is concerned. They also live in what is usually a close Christian community where they assist those in need. In one sense, they are good witnesses, since most people are aware of how they live. But they are not truly being salt in the larger society, since the communities they live in pretty much isolate them from others. They do not interact much with those outside their world – so few get to see and experience first-hand the testimony of their Christian living.

If one believes being salt refers to Christians being a preservative in society, the same thinking holds. For a preservative to be effective, it, too, must be dispersed throughout that which it is intended to keep fresh.

Christian Light Needed in the Political World

Can Christians be a source of light through political activity? Surely what God's Word says about the nature of the world He created has some bearing on how governments ought to be organized and operated. Those who study His Word will find insights that can be applied to political issues. If such insights could improve the way nations or other political entities are governed, we have a responsibility to share them. To fail to do so would be akin to knowing a cure for a disease and withholding that information. When we give such input on issues, it is the equivalent of shining God's light on them.

Should we go beyond comments and get into the trenches to implement policies that reflect the Christian perspective? And should we work for candidates who support those policies? To say we shouldn't is like saying Christians can speak out about feeding the poor, but shouldn't be personally involved in the actual work. This would not demonstrate the servant attitude the Bible commands.

Some suggest Christians shouldn't be in politics, because it is so dirty. But will politics be dirtier with Christians involved or without their influence? Has it possibly become fouled partially because good people (notably believers) have stayed away from political activity? Due to the fallen nature of humans, all life is dirty – and messy. Isn't it in the darkest places where it is most important to let God's light shine? We don't need a flashlight on a bright, sunny day. If politics are dirty, that is all the more reason for us to bring God's light to bear on it. In response to those who criticized him for eating with tax collectors and sinners, Jesus said in Matthew 9:12, *It is not those who are healthy who need a physician, but those who are sick.* I believe one could appropriately say our political environment is suffering from a type of sickness, and it is doubtful much healing will take place without the involvement of Christians bringing the word of God to bear on our problems in this arena.

The whole world is dark since it is influenced so much by Satan. To stay away completely from that which is tainted by evil we would have to head for the hills or migrate to islands where only Christians live. We might *let our little lights shine* in such situations, but the only people seeing it would be other believers. It certainly wouldn't be living in a *city set on hill* (Matthew 5:14), nor what Jesus meant when He told us to let our light shine. It sounds a whole lot more like hiding it under a bushel.

The effective operation of society requires some political activity from its members. To teach that Christians should not be involved in politics is, in effect, to counsel us to be poor citizens. That is certainly not being a good witness. Nor is it being salt and light. Some make much of the fact that Jesus did not encourage people to work for changes within their government. However, unless one was a Roman citizen, political involvement was not really an option in His time.

Political Influence by Churches and Pastors

Beyond the issue of individual Christian involvement in politics is the question of whether churches or pastors should participate. Churches can legally discuss political issues without losing their tax exempt status if they don't mention candidates. A pastor should be able to freely do the same – even from the pulpit. And it is proper for him to participate in politics outside the church as a private citizen.

The question arises of what should appropriately be discussed and advocated officially by church bodies. Evangelicals assume it is proper for churches to discuss positions on things like pro-life, gay rights, etc. – the so-called moral issues – but they also tend to assume other issues are off limits. However, Christian perspectives on almost all political issues and positions follow logically from our worldview. Why shouldn't pastors preach on such topics? Doing so would definitely become controversial in some congregations. Many might even protest such proclamations from the pulpit.

But if pastors had preached in this way in the past, believers likely would not be as politically divided as they are today. Most would recognize the clear connection between Christian beliefs and the concepts of limited government, upon which our nation was founded. The result would be less controversy about such a practice. Had this generally been practiced continually from the time of our founding, our nation may well not be in the dire straits in which we find ourselves today.

This type of involvement by preachers was more prevalent in our early years. Pastor Thomas Hooker was a founder of both Hartford and the colony of Connecticut and is believed by many to be the inspiration for its first constitution: "The Fundamental Orders of Connecticut." There is actually a book called *Political Sermons of the Founding Era*. If this type of preaching had continued, we may well live in a very different America today. This is not to say political preaching couldn't be overdone. It should never overshadow the teaching of the key tenets of the Christian faith or be emphasized above the growing of God's kingdom, but that does not mean it should not be done at all.

If pastors were preaching on some of the larger political issues, it should not be necessary to mention candidates. Most congregants would be able to connect the dots to determine for whom they should vote. Nevertheless, it is wrong to require churches to refrain from mentioning candidates to retain their tax exemptions. Laws mandating that should be reversed to take away all restrictions.

While those rules remain, any church which believes it is God's will to endorse candidates, should. A failure to do so is to let our actions, as Christians, be determined by man rather than God. If being obedient results in the removal of tax exemption and a consequent financial loss, we know God will be able to meet the needs of the church in other ways.

Contributing to a Better Society

Our society is faced with many troublesome problems. People are looking for answers. Christians believe God created the world and is ultimately in control of all that happens. Many expect those who believe this will have at least some insights into the world's problems, and rightfully so. We, as believers, know what is ultimately most important to each person is where they will spend eternity and that all other concerns pale in comparison. We need to communicate that to others.

If we properly apply our views of humanity and the world to politics, we will also have answers for the more secular issues of life. Not that those answers will provide complete solutions since we live on an imperfect earth, but our perspectives could have major, positive impacts on society. To provide such guidance in the addressing of human problems is truly bringing God's light to the world. Of course, God's light will not always be accepted in a dark world – particularly in an age that is becoming increasingly materialistic. This should not stop us from allowing it to shine through us. To fail to respond to the sorry state of the world, or to say or imply that all we care about is the hereafter, will not attract anyone to Christ.

The Church as Salt and Light

Jesus' commands to be salt and light most often seem to be given to individual believers. However, as Christians join together in various endeavors, they, as a group, can also provide salt for society and cast light on various situations in the world. This is particularly true in our age when, through advanced technology and enhanced communication capability, people are much more aware of activities of various groups within society. When they are composed of Christians, these groups provide a public witness, just as the words and actions of individual believers are testimonies.

This has been the case with those who have been involved in conservative politics. Perception of that activity has been both positive and negative, but I think most would agree it has been more on the negative side. This is due primarily to the way Christian conservatives have been portrayed by a media hostile to both Christianity and the conservative philosophy. However, the Christian Right has itself contributed to such opinions.

Negative images, like those of some politically active believers, have caused many to be less receptive to the gospel. Fortunately, individual Christians can dispel and overcome negative views of believers by the testimony of their personal lives lived out in a positive way among acquaintances, neighbors, etc. A public witness by Christian ministries is also helping people and has been more positive.

Some might suggest the negative images Christians have presented by being in politics are a reason to stay out of that arena, but such thinking overlooks the potential for a very positive witness by believers involved in political affairs. Fairly or unfairly, many believe the goal of Christians on the right is to impose their morality on others. This is not primarily what the Christian Right is trying to do. However, some actions and words by leaders have contributed to such a perception. These are discussed in Chapter 17. If, rather, we would use our influence to promote the maintenance of freedom for all, we would be looked upon more as salt and providing light for society. We would still be opposed by the media which doesn't like liberty very much, but if our focus was on freedom, it would be more difficult to portray us as moral enforcers.

Christians as Objects of Hate

In addition to saying believers should be salt and light, Jesus said we would be hated and suffer persecution (John 15:19, 20). We tend to think of being salt and light as those things we do to provide a positive witness – like helping others. We should be doing such things, but we also need to be preaching and teaching against sin and bringing people to salvation. That is also being salt and light. It is doubtful whether many Christians have been persecuted or hated for feeding hungry mouths. Even evangelizing doesn't arouse much opposition if it is not done too publicly. But when believers work politically to do things like save unborn lives, limit marriage to one man and one woman, or try to stop the indoctrination of children in public schools, they begin to raise the ire of secularists and liberal Christians. Such Christians are primarily the ones who become the objects of the hate Jesus says all believers should expect.

It is true that some of the anger directed at believers in the political arena is a result of the distortion by the media and opponents. When some Christians try to impose their morals on society (see Chapter 5), it results in antagonism. However, even making allowances for these facts, there is much unwarranted hatred against those believers who engage in politics – much of it expressed by those who decry the supposed hatred conservatives practice. We don't experience much in this country that really rises to the level of persecution yet, but that will likely come as things get worse.

I wonder whether the real reason many Christians decline to be involved in politics is that, in doing so, they can avoid much of the conflict and controversy attendant to being a believer. They know if they only engage in the "nice" part of being a Christian, people will like them rather than hate them. And if they can convince other believers it is wrong for us to be in the political sphere, it helps assuage any guilt they may have for staying out of the fray. But if they are suffering none of the hatred Jesus said we will experience, they should ask themselves if they are truly living the lives expected of faithful believers and whether staying out of politics is just an excuse for avoiding animosity. We have different callings as Christians and not all should be in politics, so this is a case of wearing the shoe if it fits.

Forcing Us Into the World's Mold

The world, the flesh, and the Devil are described in Scripture as three of our enemies. They often work together to draw us into sin or divert us from fully following God. For example, Satan will tempt our flesh with the attractions in the world. We are not helpless against such temptations because, with God's help, they can be resisted. We ultimately choose when we do wrong. We cannot legitimately use the plea of Flip Wilson's character Geraldine that "the Devil made me do it."

However, the world attempts to force us into its mold through legislation. An example is when the state tries to impose humanistic values on our children through public education. Another is the attempt to force Christian colleges and companies like Hobby Lobby to offer health care plans that cover abortion pills. Those organizations can choose to not follow that mandate, but that involves civil disobedience and could conceivably result in them shutting their doors. Government is able to impose such requirements on believers because we have allowed its scope to expand so greatly. As the state continues to grow, we can expect it to become more oppressive and impose additional rules that conflict with Christian values.

Knowing that Satan wants believers to do his bidding rather than God's, it would be surprising if he did not use his influence to get government to compel people to do his wishes. It seems likely he has had a hand in things like the attempts by Communist governments to stamp out Christianity, and in the forced abortion that takes place in China. However, he could also be behind some of the more subtle efforts to use government to force people into ungodly activities since he is a master of deceit. Whether Satan is involved, it certainly seems legitimate for Christians to work politically against efforts by authorities to pressure us into acting according to the principles of the world.

What Would Jesus Do?

Some say Jesus didn't get involved in politics when He was on earth. Others argue that if Jesus came back, they don't believe He would be a political activist. Jesus Christ came to earth for some very specific purposes. First and foremost, it was to provide a sacrifice for our sins by dying for us. He was also a teacher of God's principles. Jesus didn't get married, nor did He have a job in the earthly sense. At least in His years of ministry, He did not appear to have a permanent home. If we were only to do things He did, no obedient Christian would marry or be employed, and we may not have a house of our own.

Our role on earth is different from Christ's. The fact He wasn't involved in politics does not mean we should not be. As to what Jesus would do if He returned to earth, we don't need to speculate about that since He will be coming back. When He does, He will rule over the earth for 1,000 years. That certainly sounds like involvement in governmental affairs to me!

Chapter 3

Thinking Politically as a Christian

In this chapter, I will discuss how I believe Christians should approach the way they think about political ideas. It is important to look at such ideas through the framework of a Christian worldview. I cover how our view of the world relates to politics philosophically. In later chapters, I will address how our worldview applies to specific issues.

This chapter discusses a Christian mindset regarding the following questions:

1. Are conservatives really anti-government?
2. What should a Christian's attitude be about the use of power?
3. Is an intellectual approach to politics appropriate for Christians?

I also talk about whether it is proper to bring Christian values into the public sphere and discuss what issues I believe should be most important to believers.

Applying a Christian Worldview to Political Affairs

Christians' views on life should be shaped by what they believe about the nature of God, man, and the world. These core beliefs are reflected in day-to-day life and are described as a Christian worldview. Discussions of worldviews by believers have drawn increased attention in recent years.

Much has been said about how few of those who call themselves born-again believers actually have a Christian worldview. In a recent George Barna survey, only 19 percent of people classifying themselves as such had an outlook on life that conformed to a biblical worldview. [7]As dire as this sounds, the situation may actually be worse. Of those who do have such a worldview, how many actually apply it properly to the various aspects of individual and corporate life. To have a worldview and not live by it is akin to traveling to a remote, difficult-to-find location but never referring to the map in your possession.

A Christian Worldview Is the Starting Place for Political Beliefs

Our worldview should have a bearing, not only on how we look at the world, but also on how we live our lives. And pertinent to our discussion, it should influence how we view political philosophies and issues. Just as we should follow a Christian worldview in our personal lives, we should seek to employ it in our political thinking. Some believers, who have a view of God, man, and the world consistent with orthodox Christianity, and may even live their lives in accordance with these values, do not base their political ideas on them.

My intention is not to discuss all aspects of a Christian worldview, but to look at some key components with direct pertinence to political views. I will first review what those are and then go back and discuss how each should affect our political beliefs. Implications of the various aspects of our worldview for political policy will sometimes overlap.

1. We believe men and women are created in the image of God. This includes having a free will. We can make decisions about the course of our lives. This view is in contrast to those of materialists who believe men are descended from animals. Many materialists admit their view of the world is not consistent with a belief that humans have free wills. If they were honest, all those believing that only matter exists would have to agree such a world cannot accommodate free will.

2. Our worldview assumes God has laid down laws He expects men to follow. We are responsible to Him for our words, actions, and

7 http://www.barna.org/transformation-articles/252-barna-survey-examines-changes-in-worldview-among-christians-over-the-past-13-years

even our thoughts. God will punish those who disobey His laws. He has provided forgiveness through Jesus Christ for those who receive it, but those who become believers by doing so are still expected to follow God's rules. We who believe do have the Holy Spirit to aid us, so obedience should be easier if we live in His power.

3. The Christian view with immense implications in relation to our political beliefs is the fact that men and women are fallen. They are prone by nature to sin against God and their fellow humans. As such, they are self-centered and tend to look at their own interests first when making decisions and determining courses of action.

4. Christians believe God built fixed, immutable rules into the world He designed. These include laws that govern the physical part of the world (such as gravity), and the nature and character of humans.

5. We also believe we live in an imperfect world. Not only are we humans flawed, the physical world itself has been impaired. As a result, life most often is a struggle. Bad things happen – even to those who are followers of God. We believe the ultimate source of all the problems in the world is sin. That does not mean a person who is suffering is necessarily doing so because of their own errors. Sometimes people who are innocent in a given situation may experience difficulties because of the sin of others. Due to our marred creation we should not expect to see perfection on this side of heaven.

6. Christians also realize life on this earth is not the end of our existence. We will live on – either in a new heaven and earth or in a hell where we will be punished.

7. Believers know it is important to do what is right, in accord with God's commands, rather than what we think will provide the correct result. The means are often more important than the ends. We do know, however, that using the proper means (ones of which God approves) is the better course. And although doing what is right may not always seem in the short-term to be beneficial, it will ultimately result in the ends He desires.

We who believe such things should look at the world differently from others. Our expectations for this life will not be the same as those without a Christian worldview. We should have different ideas about what type of political systems will actually work on this earth. We should not, however, use that as the sole criteria in advocating policies. More important than judging issues pragmatically is evaluating whether they accord with God's will and whether they allow individuals the freedom to be obedient to Him.

Men and Women are Created in the Image of God

Having God's image, we are moral agents who can choose to do right or wrong. It is because of our free will that we can say our rights come from God – not from government. This is acknowledged in the Declaration of Independence where it says "men…are endowed by their Creator with certain unalienable Rights." This is very important because if we believe rights are given to us by government, then they can also be taken away by government.

Because God has given men free will, we should work for a government system that maximizes freedom – one that gives each individual the greatest opportunity to be obedient to God, to whom he or she is responsible. Being created in the image of God and having souls, our lives are precious and governments should protect them. As important as caring for our physical bodies is, preserving the volitional ability God has given us is even more critical. This freedom to choose should be protected from those who would take it away – particularly from government, which has been the greatest threat to freedom.

Humans are Responsible to God

Because humans are responsible to God, governments need not attempt to enforce all of God's commandments. God has set up the physical laws of the universe such that disobedience to them often carries its own punishment. If a person abuses his own body (the temple of the Holy Spirit) with drugs, alcohol, a poor diet, recklessness etc., he often suffers the physical consequences. Even if he is able to escape any severe repercussions in this life, God will punish him in eternity if he doesn't repent. So, it isn't necessary to mete out punishment for all infractions of God's rules in this life. Laws should primarily be enacted to protect people from another's actions – not for those things done primarily to oneself and/or against God.

Believers are also responsible to God. We are expected to seek and do His will. A political entity should maximize freedom which results in minimum impediments to obeying God.

Men and Women Have a Fallen Nature

The one aspect of the Christian worldview with the greatest bearing on our political views is the belief in the fallen nature of man. Its ramifications for politics reaches to many policy areas.

One defining difference between how Christians and non-theists see the world is how they view the nature of man. Christians believe humans are deeply flawed; non-theists often believe they are perfectible. This difference has perhaps the greatest impact on why these two groups look at political issues from such different perspectives. Much of what we believe is based on our recognition of the fallen nature of man. Humanists' views of government are largely predicated on the idea that man is basically good or capable of great improvement. They often blame social conditions on lack of education and/or institutions. One does wonder how such basically good people as they claim we humans are have managed to create all these awful institutions!

Although unbelievers – particularly non-theists – may consider such ideas simplistic or reductionist, Christians know sin is the ultimate source of all that is bad. Because we know all men and women sin, we are not surprised by the amount of sorrow, tragedy, etc. in life or that many social problems seem difficult to solve. We also know proposed solutions not dealing with the root problem of sin are likely to fail.

Ironically, humanists or materialists have a major disconnect between a couple of their key tenets. On the one hand, they believe all is matter. Therefore, there is no mind independent of the body. All that occurs is the result of physical events. Since there is no God or overall designer, all events must be the result of random happenings.

Yet those who believe this also believe in the perfectibility of man. This is to be achieved by proper education and training, and a highly-regulated society, which will usher in an ideal (or at least much better) society. But if all is random, how can anyone control what happens? And how can educating a person cause them to act in any way other than what would randomly occur?

It gets worse. How can the humanists who claim men are naturally good, and yet believe what happens is beyond control, even know whether any randomly occurring event is beneficial or not – since it just happens? We are all at the mercy of haphazardly occurring events. How can people be taught to do right if no one knows what that is? Materialism and a perfectible society are mutually incompatible.

Much of politics is the proposing of solutions to social problems. However, to solve any problem, it is first necessary to properly diagnose its cause. It is not surprising that those who believe man is flawed would have very different ideas on what causes the world's problems than those who believe man is basically good. And those with different ideas on the source of problems will also differ considerably on how to address them.

Christians should recognize that fallen people are prone to take advantage of government programs and use them to escape responsibilities to themselves and their families. We should, therefore, be very dubious of programs that aid and provide welfare for people – knowing and understanding the tendency for flawed people not to extend effort when they have an opportunity to have something handed to them. We should not be surprised at seeing the government social welfare system in this country breed dependency and irresponsible behavior.

Those with our beliefs should be very realistic regarding the prospects of peace in our world. We should not naively believe a country laying down its arms will bring peace. Nor should we trust that nations signing disarmament agreements will necessarily honor them.

Believing in the tendency of humans to do wrong, a Christian will often advocate strong forms of punishment for lawbreakers. They believe such punishment is necessary to provide a deterrent to those whose natural bent is to do wrong.

Christians generally do not believe that merely educating people will result in a better world. It is first necessary to transform individuals to change society. We believe true change comes only when a person receives Jesus Christ as their Savior and allows God to work in their lives through the Holy Spirit. Non-believers often think if social conditions are first changed and/or people are properly educated, that humanity will be improved. They have inverted the necessary sequence of events.

We also should not believe another nation can simply import the US system of governance and necessarily experience the freedom and prosperity we have. The form of our government cannot be overlain with positive results onto a culture that has no appreciation for the concept of God-given, individual rights.

The World has Fixed, Immutable Rules

Christians believe that because an all-powerful, all-knowing God created the earth, there is an order to it. We also believe in fixed truths about God, man, and the world. Because of the fall and the fact that the earth is now populated with flawed people, the order that God intended has been disturbed. Nevertheless, because the earth is governed by unchangeable principles, it should be possible to develop a consistent philosophy about how men should be governed – particularly if one factors in the fallen nature of man.

Humanists who believe life and ultimately man appeared on the earth as a result of random, undirected processes would have a harder time coming up with a consistent philosophy of government. One wonders how they can even account for the order that obviously exists in the universe.

We also believe God and His laws are immutable – neither He nor His world is evolving. His character and standards for men's behavior remain unchanged. We believe society, therefore, must be governed with consistent, timeless truths. Thus, the rules (such as our Constitution) should not be changed just because society has changed. This is not to say we never need to make modifications due to things like new technology, etc. However, some ideas that relate to the character of the world and the nature of man should be non-negotiables.

We Live in an Imperfect World

Those who believe in the goodness of man will often propose things they believe will be a total solution – for instance, the elimination of poverty. Christians, however, who reject a rosy view of human nature, should be very skeptical of most of these panaceas. We should recognize that few, if any, problems will be completely solved in this life.

As such, Christians should reject utopian systems and ideas. Various books have been written throughout the centuries (such as Sir Thomas More's *Utopia*) that describe perfect societies. Other movements have sought to establish earthly paradises. Two in nineteenth-century America were *New Harmony*, and *Brook Farm*. The motivating ideas are invariably based on the perfectibility of man – which is at odds with a Christian worldview.

Believers should realize that ideas for centralized authority and highly regulated societies will ultimately result in self-focused men and women using their power in a tyrannical manner. Humanists, on the other hand, often are not concerned about powerful governments and the men who control them.

The humanist viewpoint leads to legislation intended to prevent certain happenings. For instance, a defect in a certain product may have caused injury or death to a person (or persons). A law is then proposed to ensure "that this will never happen again." In some cases, it may prevent most recurrences. However, the law may have other unintended consequences – which sometimes can be worse than the original problem (e.g. a design modification to meet the law creates other difficulties). A believer is more likely to realize that, in this imperfect world, humans can't solve every problem no matter how many laws we pass.

In a seeming paradox, it is not highly engineered governments, but rather our own here in the United States (which has provided the least amount of central direction) that has resulted in what is closer than any other to a perfect earthly society. For Christians, though, this should not be seen as a paradox at all. Recognizing that man is flawed, our founders built into the system they set up many checks against the tendency for rulers to arrogate power to themselves. James Madison said it best:

> "If men were angels, no government would be necessary. If angels were to govern men, neither external nor internal controls on government would be necessary. In framing a government which is to be administered by men over men,

> the great difficulty lies in this: you must first enable the government to control the governed; and in the next place oblige it to control itself." – Federalist No. 51

This has resulted in a society where people have been left largely free to introduce and implement many improvements to the way life is lived.

The best policy is to have a system with many checks and balances that will frustrate those who attempt to use government to gain power. It is because our founders recognized the necessity of foiling those who seek power that our American experience produced a society that – while not perfect – is vastly superior to any other. It is primarily those with a Christian worldview who, knowing of the deficient nature of men and women, realize the need for this requirement to restrain the powers of government. Christians recognize that the root of so many of our problems is disobedience of the principles God has built into His creation. Solutions proposed involving government merely attempt to remove symptoms resulting from such disobedience without any attempt to deal with the ultimate problem. As such, those attempts result in futility and often actually exacerbate the situation.

Life on Earth is Not the End of Existence

Another difference in worldviews has a bearing on the addressing of problems. The unbeliever thinks this life is all there is and, although it ends for individuals upon death, the world as a whole will go on indefinitely. They believe if they can find an ultimate solution to a problem, it will continue to benefit mankind forever. However, Christians realize our earthly existence is just a prelude, and that life as we know it will have a limited duration. We tend, therefore, not to be as concerned about wiping out certain societal ills – knowing that they will go away either in Christ's reign on earth or in the new heaven and earth. This does not mean we should have a cavalier attitude toward problems. Nor should we fail to propose policies that will ameliorate them. But we should do so with the realistic recognition that it is not possible to create a perfect society on earth – some problems will not be totally solved this side of eternity.

To those who do not believe in an afterlife, it's important to grab all the gusto they can in this one (*If the dead are not raised, let us eat and drink for tomorrow we die* – I Corinthians 15:32). As such, they want to make things here and now as perfect as possible – to build their paradise on earth. Many of them believe the way to do it is through central planning by a very activist government.

Humanists who believe life is unending are very concerned about the need to preserve natural resources – believing they will have to last forever. Christians, on the other hand, who know life on earth is for a limited time, will not be as concerned about the supply of such things.

Ends do Not Justify Means

Because we do not believe that ends justify means, we should reject policies that take away one person's rights to provide what is believed to be a benefit to another. This principle is violated frequently in today's political environment – particularly in the economic area where redistribution by the government has become *de rigueur.* A large number of people believe it is perfectly acceptable to use the immense power of government to transfer wealth from one person to others. We, as Christians, should recognize this as an attempt to justify what is perceived as a good end with an improper means.

Although the philosophy of utilitarianism, which promotes policies that result in what is believed by some to be the greatest good for the greatest number of people, is rampant in our society, it should not be the rationale used by believers to justify positions on political policies and issues. The perceived good end may well require a means that tramples on the rights of those not included in the "greatest number" who putatively experience the "greater good".

As such, we should reject majority rule as the ultimate value in a polity – although it will inevitably and rightly be used as a method to choose leaders through elections and for voting in legislative halls. In any political system, a mechanism must be in place to prevent majorities from achieving an end by taking away the rights of individuals and minorities. The limited, divided power granted to government in the US Constitution is one such safeguard. In fact, the protection of rights should be the primary, stated objective of any political establishment. Christians should especially recognize how important this is since they know these rights are gifts from God.

The assumptions about these aspects of a Christian worldview will be used throughout this book as they apply to more specific issues.

Are Conservatives Actually Anti-government?

Many who are enamored of centralized power accuse those who oppose excessive legislation of being anti-government or of hating government. Actually, most such conservatives not only are not against government or hate it, but realize that it is absolutely essential for establishing and maintaining order in a society. Many conservatives do assign a very limited role for government – particularly at the national level. We assert that it was such limitations that made us the greatest nation in history.

Our heroes are people like George Washington, Patrick Henry, James Madison and other founding fathers who spent most of their lives serving in government. A quote attributed to Washington by some made one of the most profound statements ever made about government: "Government is not reason; it is not eloquence; it is force! Like fire it is a dangerous servant and a fearful master." Whoever wrote it very concisely stated the conservative's attitude toward government.

Government is a Tool

Government is a tool, and like any tool, it has proper uses and improper ones and can actually become dangerous if used in an abusive manner. Would anyone say that a person hated fire or was anti-fire because they wished to confine it to furnaces, fire pits, forges, etc.? Does not the fireman who uses fire in a furnace to heat his home also spend time containing fires that have gotten out of control? Does the person who opposes someone using a hammer to bludgeon another to death hate hammers? The potential examples of the inappropriate use of various tools are almost endless.

Beyond the outright abuse of tools, it is important to use the most effective one that does not cause collateral negative effects. A person could use a crowbar or a battering ram to open the door to their house, but using the key and the door knob generally works better. And though one could say "at least it gets me in" the result threatens the future use of the correct tools and the security of the home. In a similar manner, proponents of a liberal welfare policy will say "at least people are being fed." However, the conservative would point to the destructive impact on the structure of families and the sense of responsibility, and say that government was inappropriately used for the solution of the problem.

Our nation's founders provided for some very limited, specified uses for government. They saw it as a tool with some very specific purposes. We are now at a point where we turn to government for solutions to all social ills. It has become the tool of first choice for almost any such problem.

As fire must be contained to be useful and not become destructive, so government must be contained so as to not become all-consuming. That which is to contain our national government is the Constitution which severely confines its use. Our founders who held to the Christian view that men have a fallen nature understood that, if the power given to those who would govern were not strictly limited, we could not possibly maintain the free society they envisioned.

We have seen these limitations ignored by legislators, with the complicity of the courts, as our national government has usurped more and more power and taken on so many functions never intended by the founders. The growth of government is completely out of control; like a wildfire, it is threatening the freedoms we hold dear. It is this we conservatives are against – not the idea of government itself.

People may reasonably disagree about the proper role and level of government. But those who believe in more government should be advocating for that position, rather than making *ad hominem* attacks that inaccurately portray those with whom they disagree as hating government.

The Proper Use of Power

Many contemporary men and women are obsessed with power; that is certainly true of Americans. Some talk of empowerment for their class, race, gender, etc. which they usually seek through political means. It can often be questioned whether many have gained the power they sought. Often what happens is the government is empowered while other parties or interests have their power reduced and/or their rights and freedoms infringed.

What Types of Power Are Legitimate?

Should power even be sought? Christians particularly should question the seeking of power. It is legitimate to have personal power sufficient to exercise one's rights and make decisions that affect his life. A national government should have enough power to prevent other countries from invading it – thus protecting the lives and rights of its citizens. Lower levels of government require the power to restrain the actions of those who would deprive others of their rights. Another appropriate power in society is that which parents have over their children.

Power is a tool and when used properly can be a good thing. When misused, it becomes a dangerous weapon in the hands of those who wield it. In the case of such abuse, government's legitimate power grows until it is being used against the very people it is supposed to protect. As Lord Acton said: "Power corrupts. Absolute power corrupts absolutely."

The primary power individuals and groups in a free society should exercise is the power of persuasion. If one has an idea she believes will be a benefit, she should be approaching potential supporters to attempt to convince them of the merits of her idea. Too often she will rather lobby for legislation to force the implementation of her plan or at least to subsidize it. This approach seeks to have government use power in an illegitimate way rather than using her power of persuasion to get others to voluntarily join her effort.

Such a person often justifies her lobbying by saying government action is necessary because people will not voluntarily do what she believes they should. The rationale is that if people don't do what we think they should, we'll just force them to do it – no matter whether their rights are violated or not. This is a prime example of justifying the means by the ends.

For example, they will say things like not enough funds will be contributed to charities to meet the needs of the poor. Therefore, we need government programs to help. But what if all those lobbying for such programs spent their time and effort raising funds for the needs they are calling for government to meet? They might be amazed at how much is contributed. Regardless of whether adequate money is raised to meet all needs voluntarily, taking contributions by government force is an improper use of power.

When people seek empowerment for their group through government, it usually comes at the expense of others. Those who have lost in this transaction then attempt to empower their interests through a political move that either overrides that loss or provides some compensatory benefit. This results in various segments of society constantly trying to one-up each other through the legislative process. The inevitable result is considerable conflict among interest groups playing this game of political leap-frog. It is difficult to achieve harmony in society when so many believe others have gained an advantage over them and they need to have some law or program to balance the scorecard.

Appropriate Use of Power

How should we as Christians view power? Knowing that humans are fallen, we should realize the great potential for its abuse – particularly when it is concentrated in the hands of a few individuals. We should also recognize the wisdom of the dispersal of power incorporated into our original federal system and seek to maintain and restore it.

The power God gave us should be used through our minds to make decisions consistent with His Word and His will. We should rely on the greater power of the Holy Spirit who indwells us to accomplish those things God wishes for our lives. The power of persuasion should be used first and foremost to convince unbelievers of the truths of the gospel message by emulating the apostle Paul who reasoned with the Athenians on Mars Hill. We should also use persuasive power to counsel others to live in accordance with the Bible.

However, we should not seek power for ourselves, the church, or other groups we may be a part of by gaining political advantage over others through legislation. If we find ourselves in a political office, we need to be particularly careful to exercise only those powers proper for that office, not use our position to gain personal privileges, and not abuse our position in any other inappropriate way.

The bottom line is that we must acknowledge all power is ultimately God's power. When humans use the power He has given them the only legitimate uses include the very limited use by government, parental prerogatives, and persuasion.

As believers, we know evil resides in the hearts of all men and women (Jeremiah 17:9). As we look at history, we can see the potential for manifesting this propensity for wickedness increases proportionately as a person gains more power. The more authority those in government have, the greater opportunity they have to exercise the corruption in their souls.

We see this displayed many places in the Bible. One particularly egregious example occurred when Herod, backed by the power of the Roman Empire, had all the male children under two slain when he heard of Jesus' birth. The Magi had told him a king had been born. Believing Jesus would be an earthly ruler, Herod became concerned that this king could displace him in the future. Those with political power can become particularly savage when that power is threatened.

The Danger of Concentrated Power

In more recent times, we have seen the ruthless regimes of Nazis and Communists murder immense numbers of their own fellow citizens. Occasions of "man's inhumanity to man" on Planet Earth have always existed, but even the worst of personal mass murderers number their victims in the dozens. It really takes a position of authority in a government to enable one to kill huge numbers of people. Recognizing the potential danger of concentrated power, our wise founders set up a government with very limited powers and with many checks against its abuse.

As a Christian takes positions on the issues of the day, a key question they should always ask is whether a particular proposal will enhance the power of government. If it does, that in itself should be a very strong reason to question its adoption.

Giving inordinate power to government doesn't always result in its abuse in the short-term; not every person who rises to a position of immense authority uses it in an inappropriate way. One would hope a Christian in such a situation would not. And there are non-believers with the moral strength to resist the temptation to misuse great authority. However, once a particular position has been invested with such authority, it is likely someone who assumes it in the future will use his power in an evil manner. When considering whether to give some new power to government, decision-makers should visualize the worst person imaginable and ask whether they would want him to have such authority. If they would be uncomfortable with such a person having that authority, they should not provide for the enhanced power. No one can possibly know who might, in the future, obtain a position where they could exercise its powers.

As such, anyone who works to give more power to government is enabling the potential for evil actions. Many non-believers seem blinded to such possibilities and advocate increasing roles for government. It is likely they have swallowed the canard that people are basically good – although history contradicts this in a major way. The Christian who knows of the corrupt nature of men and women is, in effect, an accessory to evil when they seek to empower big government.

We are told by those with a statist mentality that we need big government or at least a large solution in a given situation to handle a big problem. The fallacy stems from the assumption that such a problem came about from a very complex set of circumstances. That is often not the case. Frequently one very small misstep can result in a major problem, and very often the offending item is something government itself is doing. What is needed is just having government stop causing the problem, it doesn't require a huge (and often expensive) solution. Frequently, the action government has taken that created the problem was undertaken in an attempt to solve some other crisis. We often suffer from solutions.

Is an Intellectual Approach Proper for a Christian?

There is often a strongly negative reaction to intellectualism. Many conservatives (whether primarily influenced by Christian thought or not) have a distinct dislike for the word and have a negative impression of anyone perceived as an intellectual. They are thought of as impractical people who dream up ideas largely divorced from reality. If they are statists (as they often are), they try to foist their ideas on society. Back in the 1950s, they were often referred to as eggheads.

It is often said that "the Devil is in the details." But in this case, as in many, it could be said that "the Devil is in the definition." One definition of intellectual is: "Guided by the intellect rather than by feelings." Certainly, we should apply our minds and intellects to address political principles and to posit cogent, coherent, philosophies to apply to the issues of the day. God gave us our minds and expects us to use them. Many Christians too often let emotions rather than their intellects drive their political views. The problem comes when we use our minds to deny God and His Word or believe we can decide better than He what is right for our lives.

Many on the left are self-styled intellectuals and wish to be categorized that way. They use the term to look down their noses at those they consider ignorant anti-intellectuals. Many times their proposed solution to societal ills is merely throwing tax money at them – a very unimaginative and decidedly un-intellectual way of addressing problems. Such people are best described as pseudo-intellectuals. This is not to say liberals never use intellectual arguments to make their points.

I believe those conservatives who attempt to develop consistent philosophies of government and apply them to issues are truly intellectuals. This applies also to believers who evaluate political ideas by applying a Christian worldview.

People often dismiss those who discuss things such as philosophy – believing their ideas have no relation to real life. However, the ideas discussed by the philosophers of one generation often become part of a society's common culture in the next generation or so. We may then find those ideas incorporated into the laws of nations.

A low view of intellectuals exists in some Christian quarters. It is often directed at those who exalt human reason and reject God and His truth because they can't be thoroughly explained. It is certainly true that some things God tells us in His Word, at least on the surface, do not seem to square with what is reasonable. It is also true that we must obey biblical directives that may not make sense from a human standpoint. Nevertheless, God gave us our minds and mental capabilities. They are gifts he surely expects us to use. As with all tools, they can be used properly or improperly, and pertinent to our discussion the gifts become very valuable in applying God's principles to political ideas. When we do so, it can be said we are appropriately using an intellectual approach. Those who do that consistently might even be known as intellectuals!

Intellectualism and Academics

Academics are often associated with intellectualism. Some exhibit this attitude by stating or implying one cannot be an intellectual unless they have advanced degrees and/or are in an academic setting. Certainly many who have participated in formal studies in various disciplines have acquired the kind of knowledge that would well prepare them to be intellectuals.

However, being an intellectual is more about having a frame of mind and disposition to approach topics in a logical, analytical way. On that basis, I consider my father, who had only a high school education and dressed on a daily basis in striped overalls, to have been an intellectual – although it is likely he would have bristled at being characterized in this way. It is also true that not everyone who has accumulated a lot of academic information necessarily uses an intellectual approach. Certainly, Christians should eschew the snobbish attitude that one must have academic credentials to be an intellectual.

I certainly do not wish to be mischaracterized as badmouthing people with academic achievements. I much appreciate reading books by scholars who have studied a particular topic in depth as academics often have. Such a person is able greatly to enhance people's understanding of what often is a very specialized area of learning. However, some in this arena have a tendency to be overly concerned about having views that comport with those of their peers. I'm sure many in this category consider themselves to be quite the intellectual because they are in intellectually-oriented disciplines. However, an intellectual should always think deeply about subjects and be willing to consider ideas that go against commonly-held ones, and to be willing to speak out when he finds his research, observations, and/or thought processes have brought him to positions that are not in the mainstream. They should go where the evidence and their beliefs take them even when it means going against majority or even consensus opinion in their field, and even if it means they may be ostracized for expressing their disagreement.

In some discussions, a good share of the so-called authorities actually engage in intellectual incest by only allowing an intercourse of ideas to flow between those who largely agree with consensus beliefs. The blood of new ideas that promotes healthy discourse and a robust debate is not allowed into the forum. They refuse to engage in any discussion that challenges the status quo. Two areas where this is particularly true are in the theory of evolution and in the various positions that surround the belief in man-made global warming.

Conservatives who challenge the establishment views in these areas have been characterized as anti-intellectual or even ignorant by those who do so in an attempt to silence opponents by claiming such issues are settled, refusing to address challenges, and using their positions to deny a forum to any opposing views. Such actions are not those of an intellectual, but rather an intellectual bully. A true intellectual would defend their views with ideas and counter those with opposing thoughts instead of just huddling with their like-minded associates in the safety of their privileged enclaves.

Christians should be more concerned about what is right than about pleasing colleagues or conforming to consensus positions. We should have the courage to go against the grain when such an action is warranted – whether or not we are in an academic setting.

Bringing Christian Values into the Political Sphere

If one assumes it is proper for a believer to be involved in politics, the next question is: Should he bring Christian principles into the arena with him? This can be broken down into two questions: (1) Is it appropriate to apply religious values to political affairs? and (2) Is it legal and/or constitutional to do so?

Christian Views in the Public Arena

The question is really whether persons should bring their religious values into politics. If it is okay for adherents of other faiths to apply their beliefs to political views, it should also be acceptable for Christians. If it is appropriate for atheists to use their values in political matters, it should be equally proper for theists to do so since a belief in no god is as much a religion as beliefs that posit a supreme being.

What we frequently hear is that it is okay for religious people to be involved in politics, but that their religion should be private and not influence their votes – whether that is at the ballot box or in a legislative body.

To address this from a Christian perspective, one needs to review some of our doctrine. We believe an all-powerful God created the world and everything in it – including humans. We assert that He also left instructions in the Bible, and that through reading it and listening to the Holy Spirit, we can determine His will.

Such a God will certainly have some valuable insights on how best to govern in the world He created. Those who read His Word should get a sense of the nature of His world and of the humans with which He populated it. Do you think possibly such people just might believe they have at least an inkling of some principles to follow in making laws for the humans He created? If a person involved in politics has such beliefs, does it make sense to ignore them and not use them in dealing with issues? A believer who makes no attempt to apply those beliefs to political issues would be a fool. This would be akin to knowing the inventor of a very intricate machine and not seeking his advice in operating it.

To ask persons involved in political issues to leave their religious views at the door is to ask the impossible. A person's religion must of necessity color his views of God, the nature of men and women, origin of good and evil, etc. These beliefs are woven into the fabric of their very being. It should be as impossible for obedient Christians to separate their religious beliefs from their philosophies of government as it would be not to apply those beliefs to the way they live their personal lives. That is as true of atheists as it is of the adherents of various organized religions. Those who claim no belief in God also have views on the nature of the world, men and women, etc. These are religious views and have as much bearing on how they approach issues as do those of theists who profess a religious creed. However, one seldom hears anyone asking atheists to leave behind their religious values when entering the political arena.

Quite often people who believe others should not bring their religion into politics really mean they should not be trying to impose their practices on those of other beliefs. This thought holds some legitimacy. This is usually expressed in relation to those who are part of the legislative process in regard to the passing of laws controlling certain behaviors.

Two Ways of Applying Christianity to Politics

Much confusion is caused by the way many conflate two different issues. One is whether Christian views of God, the world, and man should be applied in determining the role and structure of government. Should it be used as a guide for determining whether proposed legislation involves a proper role for government and/or whether it will be effective in addressing a problem, and/or whether it will result in a loss of personal freedom? These applications of our Christian views are entirely appropriate for believers. In fact, it is essential. Basing a political system and/or legislation on a faulty view of the world will almost guarantee it will not be successful. When Christian principles are considered and applied, it creates the possibility for a free and prosperous nation as evidenced by our successful history as a nation.

A separate, quite different, issue is whether Christians involved in politics should try to impose biblical standards of behavior on residents of a particular jurisdiction. This is something we should not generally do. I believe this second action is what most people think of when they hear talk of bringing Christian values into the political realm, and it is also what causes concern. I think most believers who are involved in politics do not generally want to impose Christian rules on all people. However, they are quite concerned about preventing the imposition of non-Christian values on them and their families. Since some believers do have a few behaviors they wish to outlaw, it makes it easier for our opponents to point to them as an example of bringing Christian values into the political sphere. They thus discredit all Christian input to political affairs, including the very legitimate and beneficial effort to influence the creation and maintenance of effective political entities. No one should be against believers using a Christian worldview to guide the structure of government. In fact, they should welcome the application of such principles since in the past it has been a boon to the wellbeing of those nations that have followed them.

Many believe a person should not bring his religion into the public sphere because they see such beliefs as psychological tools to ease the burdens of life – something that will make them feel better, give them confidence, etc. They apply it like a salve to their pains and aren't really interested in whether a particular belief is true. That is immaterial since they believe what matters is whether a religious belief works for them – i.e., makes them feel better or perhaps provides a personal moral code for them. That's why they can keep it private for themselves and believe everyone else should also. It is also why such people are able to say a religious belief can be true for one person and not for another. Truth for them is not an objective fact, but whatever appears to work for them.

But Christianity is built on some very specific, foundational truths about the very nature of the world. It doesn't primarily deal with our feelings, but rather reality. As such, it has implications for all areas of life – certainly including political affairs.

Is it Legal to Mix Religion and Politics?

The constitutional question has become distorted by the use of the phrase "wall of separation between church and state" – which does not appear in the Constitution. The First Amendment states: "Congress shall make no law respecting an establishment of religion, or prohibiting the free exercise thereof; or abridging the freedom of speech, or of the press; or the right of the people peaceably to assemble, and to petition the Government for a redress of grievances."

It is clearly meant to prevent the national government from designating one religion or one denomination of Christianity as the official religion of the country. It does not even imply there needs to be a strict separation of anything spiritual from the affairs of government.

The "Congress shall make no law" portion indicates the restriction is on the national government – as does this language in other amendments in the Bill of Rights. This is further substantiated by the fact that several states did have established religions at the time of the ratification of the Constitution. In fact, an amendment was proposed to prohibit individual states from having established religions, but it failed. Such an amendment would not have been proposed if it were believed the First Amendment already prohibited states from designating an official religion. This does not mean it was, or is, a good idea for a state to have a designated denomination. It just demonstrates that nothing in the Constitution would preclude that possibility.

Some agree with this, but argue as the Supreme Court has done that the Fourteenth Amendment made the states subject to the Bill of Rights. The purpose of that amendment was to ensure that states provided due process for freed slaves. Surely if the drafters of the Fourteenth Amendment would have intended such a major change as applying the Bill of Rights to the states, their language would have stated that explicitly.

The government was intended to have a federal form where the only powers the central government was to have were those ceded to it by the member states of the federation. The effect of imposing the Bill of Rights on states would be to change the central government from a federal to a national government. Such a fundamental change would not have been done without using precise language mandating it.

In actuality, the courts through their misconstruction of the Constitution have effectively turned our government into a national one. We still refer to the monstrosity in Washington as the federal government, but it is totally inaccurate to do so. Indeed, a federal system was established by our founders, and it was largely operated as one for the earlier part of our history. We should return to doing that.

The terminology referring to the separation of church and state is not in the Constitution, so, where did it come from? It was used in a letter from Thomas Jefferson to Baptists in Danbury, Connecticut in answer to a concern raised by them. His response assured them that the new government would not interfere with the practicing of their religion. The whole issue of the separation of church and state is covered well in *The Separation Illusion* by John Whitehead. (See bibliography.)

The only prohibition on religion in the Constitution is against the federal government establishing a specific religion and/or requiring adherence to it. It certainly in no way prevents a believer in any religion from applying principles of their faith to issues – either as an individual or as a participant in government. Of course, it is not legitimate for anyone in government in an executive or judicial position to perform their job in a way contrary to the law. Christian office-holders who find themselves in a position where carrying out their duties according to the law would cause them to disobey God, should resign. That is the honest and honorable thing to do.

To Have or Not Have an Agenda

I mention in various places in this book that at least those behind the scenes on the left often have agendas beyond the stated reasons for their positions on various issues. Most often these agendas relate to their desire to increase the size, power, and scope of government.

Those on the left also accuse conservatives of having agendas. My response is: "I certainly do have an agenda. It is to restore the limited, constitutional government that enabled the United States to become the most free and prosperous in history, and to prevent our government from attaining all-consuming power." For that agenda, I make no apologies. And I know many of my fellow conservatives share this noble motive. Having an agenda is not in itself a bad thing. It is what a given agenda entails that determines whether it is good, bad, or indifferent. In addition, it is important that one's agenda is clearly and openly stated – that it is not hidden or disguised.

Following Christian Values While Serving in a Public Office

Believers should apply Christian values when working with others while in a governmental position. They should always try to get along personally with all those they work with – no matter how much they may disagree with their politics. They should make it clear to others that we do not consider them as enemies.

At first blush, it seems like in a law-making setting a believer should be willing to compromise. Isn't that what reasonable people do when they can't agree? And Christians should certainly be reasonable. Political commentators often talk about the need for legislators with different political philosophies to compromise to get things done. But believers should not compromise their principles. When two opposing groups have almost opposite beliefs about the role of government, it becomes a problem. If one wants to cut a program or a budget and the other wishes to increase it, they are going in two opposite directions, so reaching an agreement without one side compromising their beliefs is practically impossible.

One reason government has grown so large and obtrusive is that conservatives have compromised. Their opposition proposed a substantial growth in government and conservatives have agreed to a lesser increase in its level. However, the movement has been toward a larger role for government; it has just happened at a slower pace. The accumulated effect of this incrementalism is the monster we now have. With government way too large, we now need to reverse this process. If conservatives propose to cut a certain amount, but the other side will only cut a lesser amount, a compromise can be considered, since the effect is movement in the right direction. However, conservatives should never agree to a compromise that grows government – no matter how small that growth may be. That's how we got into this mess.

Christians Should Always Speak the Truth

In arguing for or against a given policy or philosophy both those on the left and the right sometimes stretch the truth (or even lie). They use misleading statistics (or doctor them) and cite historical events in ways that obfuscate what actually happened. They will also exaggerate the impact of various facts. Believers should not do these things. In most cases, it should not be necessary. We should not be relying on such facts to make our cases. Rather, we should primarily be advocating our positions based on what is right – not on what works. It is not wrong to try to prove our views are superior. Certainly, citing facts can be useful in our arguments, but we should make sure they are truly facts. I believe a preponderance of the evidence will support the Christian conservative belief in limited, constitutional government, but he force of the moral precepts we should use to build our cases for or against policies is more powerful than pragmatic reasoning.

Issues That Should Matter Most To Christians

Should Pro-Life Issues be considered the Most Important?

Although life issues include more than abortion, I will use it as a representative of those issues when comparing them to other political concerns. Christians often state directly or imply the so-called moral issues are the most important for believers. Many will particularly say protecting the right to life is of key importance for believers. In fact, most of those Christians, as well as other conservatives, who would be classified as "single-issue", make pro-life the determining factor when voting.

Is protecting life the issue we should be most concerned about? To answer that question we need to look at what the Bible says Christians are to be about in our lives. Certainly a high, if not the highest, priority is evangelism – to spread the gospel. So, preserving the right to propagate the gospel without restriction is an important objective.

We take this for granted in this country. In many countries, believers do not have such rights. Since we have always had this freedom in an unrestricted way in the lifetimes of all who are living today, many are not concerned about the possibility of losing it. However, the right to forthrightly proclaim the Word of God is currently under attack from several directions.

One example is the attempt to pass so-called "hate crime" legislation. Such laws could well outlaw preaching against homosexuality. We only need look at other countries to see examples of similar laws being used to curtail such preaching.

The protecting of human life is very important and should have a high priority. However, the laws that currently allow abortion do not affect Christians directly since they do not mandate anyone terminate pregnancies. But legislation that restricts the gospel would affect the Christian's ability to legally carry out what God has commanded.

It is possible to make the case that preserving our freedom to evangelize should be the most important political objective for believers – with even a higher priority than protecting the right to life. The problem is that legislation regarding pro-life is often very clear-cut in its consequences: it either protects innocent life or makes the taking of it easier. With laws that impact freedom, a particular bill may just be one more step down a slippery slope. The ultimate effects may not be known for years or sometimes even decades. Many times such laws may, in themselves, seem quite innocuous and merely set a precedent for much more obtrusive legislation in the future.

We have been gradually losing our liberty in this country for many decades. Many of the individual laws passed have been just one more straw on the camel's back.

I am strongly pro-life. I have demonstrated at abortion facilities, donated to pro-life organizations and written a rather lengthy poem about an abortion clinic. I certainly am not in any way even remotely implying the pro-life position is not important, or that Christian voters should not make this a key criterion for selecting candidates. I do believe some who have been almost solely focused on that issue need to pay more attention to other very important issues – particularly those involving potential loss of freedom. Some people should be asking themselves if they should be voting for candidates who support a lot of increased government control just because they happen to be right on life issues. Ultimately, if we come to the point in this country where the government has almost complete control, we will also have lost on the abortion issue. Generally, those forces in our society who work for more government are also the ones who identify themselves as pro-choice. If they are in charge, they will certainly permit abortion.

It seems the ability to evangelize may be the most important right to preserve, but the threat to the right to life is more immediate since so many unborn children's lives are being terminated. Believers have exerted a lot of time and resources on the effort to stop abortion, and not nearly as much attention has been paid to stopping the erosion of rights that could lead to severe restrictions on the ability to proclaim God's Word.

What about the Economy?

Many issues classified as economic are very important. If the government controls the economy, they ultimately can determine who will eat, get health care, etc. We all need to eat to live, so they then effectively control all activities. If they wish to stop the preaching of the gospel, they can do so by economic pressure on those who are evangelizing.

This is precisely how communist governments operated. By having almost complete control over national economies, they were able effectively to outlaw the free exercise of religion. Christians did still spread the gospel in those countries – but it was much more difficult. Shouldn't we who still have our freedom work to preserve that freedom? A large part of doing that is maintaining our economic liberty. If we lose that, it would be so much easier for our rulers to impose restrictions on religious liberties.

When we think about economic issues, it should not just be about how much money government is taking from us in taxes. More importantly, we should be concerned about loss of economic freedom since that also leads to the loss of other freedoms – including religious ones. Christians (and other conservatives) should work to preserve economic liberty, not primarily because it promotes prosperity, but because it is right and because it helps safeguard other freedoms.

Another issue area with a similar threat is health care. If the government comes to control medicine to the point they can decide if, where, and when an individual can be treated, they will have achieved complete control over us and can, in cases of life-threatening illnesses, determine whether we live. Nothing prevents them from using that power to dictate to us whatever they wish – including how we practice our faith.

One particular area where the practice of our religion is being threatened is in the use of non-discrimination legislation to force Christian organizations to hire certain people or to prevent individuals or businesses from refusing to provide services that promote immoral lifestyles. Examples include not allowing a hotel to refrain from renting a room for a reception to celebrate a homosexual union or for a printer to decline to print invitations for such an event.

How Should We Classify Issues?

Often one will hear a certain person described as a social conservative and another as a fiscal conservative. A distinction is made which classifies issues as either social or economic. Often, all issues that are not very specifically economic are tossed into the social category. For some people being a fiscal conservative means little more than favoring a balanced budget for governmental bodies. If that qualifies one to be a fiscal conservative, a socialist could be one. And if a social conservative is merely one who opposes abortion and homosexuality, one could be a socialist and claim that label. In fact, one could be both a social and fiscal conservative and be a socialist.

To divide issues into fiscal and social is really to create a false dichotomy. For a conservative, most issues should be freedom issues on which they will be advocating greater personal liberty against those who would give government more power over our lives.

Issues that appear at first glance not to be about freedom, in fact, often are. One example is abortion. The self-styled "pro-choice" movement claims they defend the freedom of women to choose whether they wish to terminate a pregnancy. For a conservative, this issue is really about ensuring the freedom of the newly formed life in the mother's womb.

It is a freedom issue in another way, too. In our federalist system of government, states used to have laws preventing the termination of unborn life. However, the Supreme Court in *Roe vs. Wade* took away the freedom of the people of an individual state to protect such lives through their elected representatives.

In segregating social or moral issues from economic ones, the left makes a direct or implicit assertion that those labeled "social conservatives" care little or nothing about other issues than the moral ones. This criticism is made particularly against Christians.

It is certainly true that many so-called "social conservatives" do place a higher priority on issues that deal with moral activity. One can certainly find some people (Christians and others) who are only concerned about a narrow set of issues, but they are a clear exception. In fact, you will find very few conservatives who don't care about issues beyond those categorized as "moral" (which issues are the "immoral" ones?).

Another problem has arisen with the classification of issues. Some (particularly candidates for office) will say they are pro-business because they favor policies that benefit those who engage in commerce. However, one who supports subsidies or other special considerations for businesses could legitimately say they are pro-business. The huge bailouts of 2008-2009 could be said to be pro-business. These are not things conservatives should promote. We should describe ourselves as pro-freedom – not pro-business. We know freedom in the marketplace is good for business, and that is one reason for advocating limited governmental regulation of trade, but to avoid misconceptions and make our position very clear, we should never describe ourselves as pro-business.

I believe some Christians do contribute to bringing criticisms on themselves. They do so by mentioning primarily moral issues – thus implying other issues aren't that important. The whole question of morality and government is dealt with in Chapter 5. More thoughts that relate to this topic are also presented in Chapter 17 on the religious right.

Believers need to broaden their focus and become more concerned about the rapid growth of government in almost all areas. We also need to adopt an integrated philosophy that is concerned about all threats to freedoms and rights for all people – born and unborn.

Chapter 4

Christians on the Political Spectrum

"Power tends to corrupt, and absolute power corrupts absolutely" – Lord Acton

"In questions of power, let no more be heard of confidence in man, but bind him down from mischief by the chains of the Constitution." – Thomas Jefferson

"God who gave us life gave us liberty. Can the liberties of a nation be secure when we have removed a conviction that these liberties are the gift of God?" – Thomas Jefferson

"What's in a name? That which we call a rose by any other name would smell as sweet"
– William Shakespeare, *Romeo and Juliet*

This chapter will cover two main, related topics:

1. A Christian perspective on the proper role of government, and
2. The labels that should be used to describe political groups and their views.

Christian Perspective on the Proper Role of Government

God created an orderly world. Believers recognizing this, and hopefully having a reasonably good understanding of the nature of that world and the humans with which He populated it, should also be able to define a role for government which conforms to His principles and the reality of fallen men and women. We ought to be able to establish rigorous, consistent criteria for judging what functions are appropriate for government. Some situations do not fit neatly into any philosophy of the role of government. There will be (hopefully limited) exceptions since such definitions have been created by flawed humans and will, thus, never be perfect. On the other hand, those who believe there is no God and that humans are merely randomly occurring masses of protoplasm really have no basis whatsoever to posit any system for the proper role of government.

A major premise of this work is that the most important thing government should do is to protect God's gift of freedom. This is consistent with the Declaration of Independence's assertion that governments are instituted to secure the rights of life, liberty and the pursuit of happiness. Without life, any other right is impossible. Without liberty, countless millions have found life to be exceedingly oppressive and have been stymied in efforts at pursuing their objectives – whether they are happiness or any other endeavors or callings. Thus, any potential activity of government should be evaluated by looking at whether it contributes to or detracts from the practice of individual freedom.

Since the Declaration describes the gifts from God as rights and because the meaning of the term generates so much confusion and differing opinions, I will take a short detour to discuss what I believe rights to be before discussing the role of government.

What are Rights?

It is not possible to address the proper role of government adequately without discussing rights. People have many opinions about what that term means. And, unfortunately, many use it without having thought about the fact others may not share their definition, and without thinking about the implications of the way they view rights.

Many books have and will be written solely to present various ideas about what rights entail. So, it is difficult to do justice to any definition in a few paragraphs. Nevertheless, it is important for me to present a rudimentary explanation of how I view rights since that underlies the ideas I present throughout the book.

Humans have the ability to move their arms and legs and other body members in various ways to perform activities. So do animals. But we also have minds that rationally make decisions on how we use our bodies. And our minds allow us to create physical and mental constructs in a way no animal can.

We use our volition to direct our mental and physical capabilities without the need for any external force. We do this with the inherent abilities God has given us. Exercising these abilities can be construed as natural – it is part of our very nature as humans. Certainly, no government gave us these abilities, nor is any government necessary for us to use them. We have a right to do so related to our volitional control over our minds and bodies. It exists totally independent of, and predates, any human agency such as government. This is how I view natural rights – although it may differ some from how others have used that term. This definition brings into focus a very strong tie between rights and the gift of freedom from God.

As a Christian, I believe the bases of these natural rights are the bodies and minds God gave us. Even if one is not a theist, he could acknowledge our rights derive from our natures as humans and that they are not conferred by government. However, such a person does have a philosophical problem in explaining where our free wills come from. Without a god, there is nothing but material in the world and no real way to account for an independent mind that can be used to exercise volition.

If one can use their natural rights to create physical objects, it follows that they are able to use, trade, or dispose of those items freely. At that point, it can be said they have the right to things, but only those items they have produced. They should also be able voluntarily to join with others to exercise rights cooperatively.

But men and women often use their abilities to restrict the exercise of another's natural rights. This should not be a surprise to Christians who know humans are fallen. At this point, it is appropriate for government to step in and prevent the infringement of those rights.

Unfortunately, a fallacious view about rights has become increasingly asserted. It assumes a person has not only a right to use his or her faculties to create, but that they have a claim on what someone else has created or produced. It also often asserts that rather than a right to do something, there is the right to have certain things beyond what he has created himself. This, of course, means someone else must have first created these things. Since that person used their natural right to create them (or voluntarily cooperated with others to do so), such a view is really advocating that one person has the right to something others used their natural right to produce.

Most do not advocate that a person can just on their own seize items from a party producing them. But some people believe government can do so on the behalf of others, and that those who benefit from this transfer have a right to what they have received. Such rights are not natural since they require the intervention of a third party (read "government"). So, to one such as I who believe in natural rights, taking what is produced by one party and giving it to another (or forcing them to sell it for a price that government – rather than the producer – has determined) can never be considered a right. If one believes such action by government involves rights, then how much can be expropriated from others is limitless, since the right is no longer tied to the use of the voluntary natural ability to create.

Rights must be what we have naturally – not what we are given. If they are not, then some other entity must give them. That entity (usually government) then determines what it will give, and its decisions on what is granted can, and likely will, at times be arbitrary. If we acknowledge that it can give rights, it follows that it can also take them away.

Some people think of rights as being what is right in the sense of what they consider fair. The problem with that way of thinking is that fairness is very subjective, so such a view is built on very shaky ground.

I do believe many, if not most, people try to incorporate a moral code into their personal views of rights. They attempt to determine if an action should be considered a right based on whether it is a proper thing to do. This presents a couple of problems. First, it greatly complicates the definition of rights. Second, since no two people have identical views about what is ethical, using such criteria makes it next to impossible to establish what rights should be for a society. In practice then whatever group manages to gain control of the levers of power will determine rights based on their moral outlook. This may seem good if those defining rights for a society have moral views informed by a Christian worldview. However, I believe the greater likelihood is that the ethical framework will be a humanistic one – particularly in today's philosophical climate.

Rights should be defined independently from moral rules. It is very important to have such rules. As Christians, ours should conform to those God presents in His Word. We should desire that all men and women follow His moral code, and work to accomplish that objective in society. But the roles of rights and moral rules are different. Rights establish our ability to make free choices, which we then use to assert and practice our moral and ethical codes.

Some may protest that the definition of rights I have been speaking of is too closely tied to our abilities as humans to use our minds to choose our actions – that I am saying we have a right to be whatever we wish. But that cannot be allowed in a society. It is necessary to restrict some activities. However, I do believe our capabilities should be the starting point, and from there those things which should not be permitted should be detailed – primarily those things which take away others' rights.

With any other method of defining rights, one is forced to, in effect, make lists of what should be considered a right. It is almost impossible to come up with such a comprehensive list, and the implication is that if something isn't mentioned it is not a right. The default should be that what is not expressly prohibited is allowed. Another problem with itemization methods of defining rights is that it implies the entity defining rights (usually government) – rather than God – is their source.

If one considers rights as the exercise of our God-given natural abilities, many things that are called rights are not rights at all. Voting isn't a right. Marriage isn't. Neither is collective bargaining. For many, rights just seem to cover anything to which they believe they are entitled or any privilege some government body has conferred upon them. Once a given privilege has been granted by government that fact is cited in the future as proof that it is a right. This is a man-centered view of rights rather than a God-centered one.

Most things that are called "civil rights" are not rights either. The term itself is really oxymoronic. Such so-called rights are called "civil rights" since they are put into effect by civil authorities. But if rights are natural, they can't be given by government. A "civil right" like voting is certainly a prerogative that ought to be allowed for most people – with some exceptions like not allowing felons to participate in elections. In a sense, one might consider them "artificial" rights – but not natural rights. However, I believe it is better not to use the term "rights" in such cases since it muddies the water and diminishes the importance of naturally-occurring rights.

I discuss marriage and collective bargaining elsewhere. Voting is really a government-defined process used to assert the public's will for representation or, in some cases, legislation. The voting franchise should be as broad as possible, but that does not make it a right. I discuss voting more thoroughly later in the chapter.

The term "human rights" really contains a redundancy since no one but humans can have rights. If what I have described about rights is a proper view, it certainly vies for the most misused word in the English language.

We often hear about conflicts in society between the rights of various individuals and groups. This is true in some situations and court cases are required to sort out the claims of opposing parties equitably. However, I believe many of the alleged conflicts do not involve rights at all. The disputes arise due to the faulty definition of that term. If we would follow the idea of natural rights and would no longer recognize artificial ones, it would vastly reduce the amount of conflict. For instance, if we would once again acknowledge the right of parties to freely associate and carry on transactions with those they choose, many legal disagreements would disappear.

Having defined what I believe rights are, I will proceed to discuss the role of government. I approach this rather philosophically. I will primarily talk about guidelines for determining whether certain activities should come within the purview of government. It is not a complete discussion of the role of government. I do, throughout the book, address what involvement I believe government should have in specific issue areas.

A Philosophical and Theological Dilemma

As believers approach the task of defining a political philosophy, we are confronted with a problem. Those who know the Word of God have a tendency to be both idealists and realists. On the one hand, we believe God created an ideal world. We know He laid down a perfect law for the people He created. Many of us believe Jesus Christ will personally rule the world for 1,000 years in a society much closer to God's ideal than the one in which we currently live. And we know that ultimately those who accept Jesus Christ as their Savior will live forever in a heaven where God's perfect vision for life is finally realized. We recognize the way things should be – although as flawed humans with limited understanding we see in this life only a small part of what God sees as I Corinthians 13:12 says: *For now we see through a glass, darkly.*

On the other hand, Christians know that humans have been tainted by sin since first disobeying God in the Garden of Eden. The world at present does not operate according to the rules He gave us, so we, as believers, are continually faced with the reality of the way things really are. We must look at the world through God's lens as much as fallen humans can – seeing it as He conceived it, but also discerning the reality of life on earth with its imperfect people and its corrupted nature.

In defining proper principles for a human government, we encounter a dilemma. Do we idealistically follow God's perfect law by incorporating all of His directions from the Bible (including the Ten Commandments) into our human laws? We know that as men we would be woefully incapable of keeping such mandates. The Bible says that none are able to obey His laws. (*For all have sinned and fall short of the glory of God* – Romans 3:23.) Enforcement of such a code would be virtually impossible. This was essentially done in the Israel of Old Testament times. Even with God Himself effectively in direct control, it didn't work out too well, and He had to use other nations to punish Israel and Judah.

Do we rather realistically make allowances for the flawed nature of humans and provide a very permissive set of laws? This would lead to anarchy and make a jungle out of our society. It seems we need to have a system idealistically conceived – which realistically considers the fact that both the governed and the governors have a propensity for error.

Men and Women Must Answer to God

An idea we can start with is that all men and women are answerable to God for what they do or do not do while on earth. God will judge them in eternity based on how well they obeyed Him in this life, so we don't really need to empower government to punish people for infractions against His rules that don't interfere with the rights of other humans. Thankfully, God is merciful and has provided a remedy for our inability to obey Him through the sacrifice of Jesus Christ as a payment for our sins.

Because Christians believe we are responsible to God for our actions, we should advocate a form of government that minimizes the making of decisions for its citizens. Laws that go beyond the scope of protecting rights often require us to conform to what government wants us to do. Whenever this is done, we are forced to disobey either God or government. The more laws a jurisdiction has, the more difficult it is for its believing citizens to be obedient to Him. Christians who are particularly sensitive to the leading of the Holy Spirit will find that government may prevent them from following His direction.

Importance of Political Freedom

Often Christian commentators have written that modern men and women, particularly Americans, are obsessed with exercising their personal freedom; they do not want anyone telling them what to do. That message is particularly directed to believers. The point of most of these observers is that we tend not to want anyone controlling us – including God. They are correct. While God does give us a lot of freedom, He also has expectations of us. There are areas in our lives where He particularly wants us to be obedient to His will. Sometimes that means following a specific call in our lives. Many believers in today's society do have a sense of autonomy that causes them to rebel against what God may want them to do.

The problem with such discussions is that they can be interpreted as indicating that we are too concerned about our political freedom. But that is a separate issue which should not be confused with flaunting our freedom before God. In fact, we should be very concerned about our loss of liberty in the U.S and involved in trying to preserve and restore it. It is this freedom that allows us to be obedient to God. The more of it we lose, the more we are doing what government wants us to do – not what He wishes. We are to be His slaves – not the government's. For a believer, freedom should not be doing what one wants, but rather not being prevented by government from doing what God wants.

Are Humans Too Individualistic?

A similar confusion occurs when Christians are criticized for being too individualistic – a fault with which Americans also are particularly charged. It is said we are too concerned with what affects us personally and not enough about what impacts others or society at large. This is a legitimate claim and many of us are guilty as accused. As believers, we should first be concerned with what God is concerned about, and we should certainly base our actions on how they affect others.

It is also true that we are individually responsible to God and that personal political freedom facilitates that. Our concern about individualism should not extend to allowing government to take away the freedom that helped make the United States a great nation and has allowed Christians to unrestrictedly serve God. We don't want to fall into the trap the liberals have when they assail individualism and say we need more cooperation in society – a need they wish to meet with more government action. They do not seem to understand the difference between cooperation and coercion. It is a noble thing for those with common goals to voluntarily band together to achieve their ends – that is cooperation. This is what Christian ministries do. It is quite another thing when people with agendas enlist the heavy hand of government to force others to carry out their agendas – that is coercion, the very antithesis of cooperation.

Government Should Protect Our Freedom – Not Infringe On It

God gave us minds with which we can exercise free will; we are given freedom by Him. If we truly believe this, our laws should presume the right to use that freedom unless a very convincing reason to restrict it exists. The burden of proof should always be on those seeking to curtail freedom in the same way a prosecuting attorney must prove a person charged with a crime is guilty, but is otherwise presumed innocent. Since we are given our freedom by God and are responsible to Him for how we use it, it should not be restricted unless absolutely necessary. This will mean many in society will use their freedom to engage in activities disapproved of by most Christians, as well as by God.

Many of man's actions are not only disobedience of God, but also violations of our fellow human beings.

Without laws to control this interference from others, it would be virtually impossible to be obedient to God. In fact, without some rules, life of any sort on earth would be difficult, if not impossible. Since people can use their freedom to prevent someone else from exercising theirs, it is legitimate for government to intervene to protect the liberty of the person who is being violated. Essentially, man's law should cover those actions (including spoken words in some situations) directed against other humans, whereas God's law covers all transgressions (including thoughts) against Him. Infractions against another man or woman are, of course, also violations of God's values.

Other nations can infringe on a country and, in so doing, impact the lives of its citizens. So, it is also legitimate for a nation to take actions to counteract such infringements. In fact, the primary function of government should be to prevent anyone from interfering with another's freedom. And it must be recognized that government itself can and does infringe upon our liberty. We currently have a situation where the government that is tasked with preserving our freedom is not only failing to do so, but is actually actively working to take it from us. How outrageous is that? Government really presents a greater threat since it has been given authority that an individual or private entity has not received. That means there must be rules for government itself.

The laws for government must be stricter than those for others since it has a much greater potential for doing harm than individuals or private organizations. Establishing those rules should be the first order of business for creating a government. While in the past they have evolved through precedents and do not appear in one document, most nations today have written constitutions. Those should primarily contain the rules by which the government must abide.

Some Christians will say that because men are flawed, there needs to be severe regulation on activities in society. But the fallen nature of humans is actually an argument against government control since those who do the regulating are also imperfect humans. As previously quoted, James Madison said it well:

> "If men were angels, no government would be necessary. If angels were to govern men, neither external nor internal controls on government would be necessary. In framing a government which is to be administered by men over men, the great difficulty lies in this: you must first enable the government to control the governed; and in the next place oblige it to control itself."

In order to regulate something, you need to give power to someone. With such power comes the opportunity for much mischief. Many in positions of authority have certainly proven themselves to be far from angels.

If a particular activity is not regulated, a person who engages in it wrongly will generally impact only a small number of people. However, those who have regulatory power over some aspect of society have the ability to affect the lives of countless numbers. They do so by inappropriately wielding power, by over-zealous prosecution of the law, or outright corruption. Even when acting lawfully, they often prevent actions that would have benefited society. One of the most negative effects is that they give people a false sense of security that the regulators will prevent some improper action. As a result, people are not as careful as they should be in safeguarding their own interests.

Many regulatory agencies have been given power to control aspects of the marketplace. In actuality, the free market does a better job of policing than any government entity could ever do. Those businesses that engage in unfair or unsafe practices, or peddle shoddy or unsafe products are ultimately punished by reduced profit or financial failure.

Currently, it is government that needs more regulation. At the federal level, we need once again to enforce the strict rules for government that were placed in our Constitution and which have been largely ignored for some time. A government that tells its people what kind of toilets they can use, the type of light bulbs they can have in their homes, and that they must have health insurance has gone off the deep end in exceeding its proper role.

On the surface, it may seem as if providing stringent rules for government is being legalistic – and, in a sense, it is. However, doing so minimizes the rules it can make for individuals and other entities in society. If such strictures are not adopted and closely followed, governments, experience indicates, become very legalistic in the rules they make for their subjects. So, we make legalistic rules for government to prevent it from being legalistic toward us.

We have seen the growth of legalistic government at all levels in this country in recent decades. The Pharisees in the New Testament who added countless rules to the few, simple ones God had given them have nothing on those in our contemporary society who wish to regulate every aspect of our lives. They really can be well-described as "control freaks" – like those individuals who wish to manipulate the lives of their families and friends. They are actually more offensive – and more dangerous – in that they seek to use the law to give an aura of legitimacy to their obsessions. Those with a bureaucratic mindset are also much like the busybodies who constantly put their noses into other people's business.

Licensing by Government

One of the most questionable government practices is many of the situations where they require licensure. Often such requirements are set up at the behest of operators in the field being licensed. It is an advantage to those already practicing a given skill, because it is a hurdle that makes it more difficult for new competitors to set up shop.

One can engage in hardly any commercial activity without a license anymore. Most are unnecessary. A woman by the name of Darlene Ryan does a wonderful job of cutting my hair. I don't go to her because she has a license, but because I appreciate her work. If she would quit cutting my hair as I like it, I would stop going to her. The fact that she had a license wouldn't keep me as her customer.

If I were to find out that the license which hangs on her wall is a forgery, it would not change my evaluation of her as a hair stylist – although her use of deception would alter my opinion of her as a person. My rating of her hair cutting is based on my experience – not on her having received a license.

The whole idea of state licensure is based on the faulty premise that we need to seek permission from government before taking a given action. This is directly opposed to the idea that rights are inherent – that they are endowed by our Creator. It implies they come from government and can only be exercised when the state says it is okay.

When this happens the whole relationship between a government and its subjects becomes a gigantic game of *Captain, May I?* As in that game, where a player cannot move forward until the person designated as the captain tells them to take a specified number of steps (baby, giant, etc.), people cannot engage in many activities until it is approved by government. They are not permitted to do so until they have applied for a license, much as the person in the game has to ask permission to take the steps. And just as the captain can whimsically refuse the request to move forward, a bureaucrat can deny an application to engage in a lawful activity – sometimes quite arbitrarily. When I played this game as a child, we called it *Captain, May I?*, but I have since heard others call it *Mother, May I?* Perhaps making the comparison with that name is more appropriate, since government has been increasingly taking on a mother's role by trying to nurture us and care for our every need – much like a mother does.

A barber or hair stylist poses no real threat to a client. In general, the worst thing they can do to you is make you look dreadful, but even that is for a short time. Possibly the application of some chemical could harm the hair – particularly if repeated for a long period, but such cases certainly don't happen often. A person shaving a man's neck could possibly cut him badly enough that he would bleed to death. I don't know if that's ever happened, and it would certainly be very rare.

But what about occupations where a mistake could be much more serious – such as medicine? Doctors often have their patients' lives literally in their hands. Surely, you say, you wouldn't allow them to practice their profession without a license? Well, yes, actually. The reality is that a person who didn't have a certain level of competence would be unable to stay in business. Word of mouth spreads quite fast about those who haven't performed well. Plus, doctors would still have to demonstrate a great degree of competence to graduate from medical school. Prospective clients would consider which medical school a doctor attended as a criterion for choosing a physician. People would be free to go to a doctor who didn't have a degree from such an institution, but realistically the only way that would happen is if a person were somehow able to gain medical experience in another way. What would almost inevitably happen is that private medical certification boards would appear to evaluate physicians. Patients would use them to aid in their choice of doctors.

In fact, this type of certification happens today. A good example is the various ISO certifications given for meeting standards set by the International Organization of Standards. Such accreditations would likely be used much more in industries and professions if licensing by governments was less prevalent.

So, without licensing there would still be evaluation of the providers of various services; it just wouldn't be controlled by government.

It is proper for governments to require prior approval for things like the building of structures that have the potential for harming neighbors or which will house equipment or processes that could threaten them.

A few go so far as to say one shouldn't need a license to drive on public roads. I disagree with that for a couple of reasons. First, since entities of government operate our roads, it is appropriate for them to establish minimum competency for driving on them. More importantly, one can choose who he has cut his hair and to whom he entrusts his medical care, but cannot control who is out on a road driving with him. There needs to be some system for preventing drivers who will be a danger to others from operating on our roads.

Government Should Not Try to Impose Fairness in a Fallen World

Christians realize that, because people are flawed, conflict between different interests in society will always exist. These are often based on differences in economic status, sex, race, ethnicity, etc. Such conflict is exacerbated when government tries to base policies on those differences. Efforts to ameliorate grievances of a given group (either real or perceived) is seen (sometimes justifiably) by others as coming at their expense. Those who believe they have been harmed then seek some type of compensatory action to equalize the situation. No group is ever happy – always believing others have a leg up on them. These actions by government are often promoted by those who claim they are needed to make some situation fairer.

But fairness is inevitably subjective. Rarely does everybody agree about which outcomes are fair on a given issue. The objective of a political entity should be to promote freedom – not fairness. When people have an expectation that government will take care of any perceived inequities in their lives, they will often be discontented – believing others are being dealt with in a preferred manner. The only really fair thing government can do is not take any action itself which treats one segment of society different from others. If government would end its attempts to implement fairness among its citizens, I believe it would go a long way in reducing conflict in our society. If people no longer expected government to fix their problems or make them more equal to others, they would be less likely to be envious of others. Whether government restricts itself in this manner, Christians should not have an attitude of expecting it to assist them personally at the expense of others.

Frequently, the state deals with people as part of subsets or classes. Many people have come to expect government to promote fairness or equalize situations within groups of which they are a part. They are often not satisfied with the results, and then develop bad feelings for those in another group they believe have been treated better. This leads to what has been called class warfare – involving attitudes like envy etc. that are actually sins. Christians should never let their experiences cause them to have such feelings. These types of conflicts are caused when a government that should be impartial takes sides – thus pitting various segments of society against one another as they become rivals for receiving taxpayers' largesse or gaining special attention.

The role of government in society should be like that of a referee in an athletic event; it should enforce the rules of the game. One can imagine the ire of players and fans if a referee were to give preferential treatment to one team or individual participants. Yet that is what government has been doing when it gives subsidies and other advantages to segments of society – be they certain social classes, categories of business, etc. We can certainly see why this practice has resulted in much dissatisfaction and even anger among our populace.

When those running for office promise to give certain subsets of the population subsidies of some type with the hope of getting their votes, it is little better than engaging in extortion. In one sense, it is worse since a self-respecting extortionist will at least use his or her own money rather than the taxpayers.

Certainly, one key change to improve this situation would be to eliminate all government subsidies – whether they are guaranteed loans to businesses, research grants, welfare, etc. The role of government should be to protect its citizens, punish lawbreakers, and adjudicate differences among constituents – not to support them financially.

Much concern has been expressed about how polarized our country's citizens have become. We do seem to be split into a red state/blue state dichotomy. The closeness of most recent presidential elections would seem to suggest that the two sides of the divide have about equal numbers. That could be somewhat misleading, since those who vote for the same candidate disagree on many issues, and those voting for different candidates may have much on which they agree. And we have had very poor choices who often don't well represent the views of many Americans. Therefore, people find themselves voting for a candidate they don't really agree with as the lesser of two evils.

It is, nevertheless, true that we have substantial differences among our populace regarding the direction our country should take. This political polarization has been exacerbated because of the insistence of statist politicians on trying to implement one-size-fits-all solutions for the whole nation (or at least for a given state). A good example is the setting of educational policy from Washington. When that is done, there is a good possibility half (or more) of the country's citizenry will be unhappy with a given directive. If we would return to making decisions for schools at the local level, less dissatisfaction would result with the likelihood of more agreement on values within a given community. If, likewise, in other policy areas higher levels of government would stop trying to impose their decisions nationwide, our people would not be as divided.

A slogan used during the French Revolution was "Liberty, Equality, Fraternity." Only one of these – liberty – is a legitimate object of government. In fact, equality and enforced fraternity are incompatible with liberty. People are not, by nature, equal in their abilities, temperaments, and personalities. As such, their positions, status in life, etc. will vary. Any attempts to try to equalize them through the law must, of necessity, involve the curtailment of freedom. Fraternity also cannot be achieved by legislation unless the state takes away the right of individuals to choose with whom they can associate. It is no wonder that trying to impose equality and fraternity in the French Revolution ended in a bloodbath.

Some arsonists have started fires that killed hundreds of people. Others have set off explosions that killed over a hundred. But most killers – even mass murderers – number their victims in the dozens. Contrast that with governments like those of Mao, Hitler, and Stalin that killed millions of their own citizens. Their homicidal binges were all enabled by allowing government to gain too much power.

Where Should Stewardship Decisions Lie?

A large part of being obedient to God is being a good steward of the resources with which He has entrusted us. Every dollar we pay in taxes is a dollar over which we have lost the stewardship decision. When government adopts policies that require the use of our time, we have less to use as God wishes. This can happen in a variety of ways. We can spend time filling out tax forms or doing detailed reporting for our businesses etc., to meet government requirements. Government also does things (including establishing high tax rates) which make it difficult to earn enough to provide for our families such that we have to work longer hours or take a second job – robbing us of time we could use to serve God and spend with those families.

Individuals vary in their ability to manage their financial resources. But, in general, they do a better job than the government does, because it is their own possessions for which they are caring – unlike governments that use the funds of taxpayers. This is a reason for keeping as much money as possible in private hands.

Government as a Problem Solver

We, as Americans, have come to think of government as a problem solver. When some difficulty arises a common response is "The government ought to do something about that." Really? Actually, the responsibility for addressing most situations should be primarily with the people involved. And others often will volunteer to help. The government should just provide an environment where people are free to take care of problems – not try to solve them.

In situations such as flooding which affect a large segment of population and/or a lot of land area, it is necessary that government does get involved, but these are exceptions. Too often government action becomes the method of first – rather than last – resort. Problem solving should not be considered one of the main functions of the state. There are many situations where government really is the problem. In such cases it needs to solve the problem by stopping its involvement.

Christians' Positions Shouldn't be Driven by Fear

Because Christians put their faith in Christ, and should actually place their lives in His hands, we should not allow our views on issues to be controlled by fear (*For God has not given us a spirit of fear, but of power and of love and of a sound mind* – II Timothy 1:7 NKJV). Many people throughout history have willingly traded freedom for security. As a result, they have enabled governments to take on additional powers because they believed it was necessary to provide them with protection from economic, physical, or other threats. In the process, they lost their freedom. Believers whose security is in God should be very wary of proposals that purport to give them security – but which take away their rights. As Benjamin Franklin said: "Anyone who trades liberty for security deserves neither liberty nor security."

Those who prefer security over freedom are like those disobedient Israelites who expressed their desire to return to Egypt. They preferred the security of a known situation – which was *de facto* slavery – to the unknown life in the Promised Land. Their problem was they didn't trust God with their futures. If believers are willing to trade our freedom for security, we are also demonstrating our lack of trust in God.

No doubt a person's worldview impacts his beliefs on what the role of government should be. Believers should recognize that, due to the fallen nature of mankind, people have a tendency to assume power over others and will use government to do so when possible. Thus, the role of government should provide very limited opportunities for gaining such power and have checks against its use.

In general, government should not impose a set of values associated with a particular religious belief system. However, if a particular religious body does not believe in protecting freedom then its views will be in conflict with others like Christianity that value individual rights. An example would be Islam which believes the state should mandate the practice of its religion. Or if a religion believes in polygamy, it would not be compatible with most other belief systems. There has to be some very basic religious beliefs on which a government is founded. They can either be the tenets of a given religion, or common ideals upon which a preponderance of religions agree. It is instructive to note that while the United States was, to a great degree, based on Christian assumptions, it has provided an environment where people have been free to practice many and varied religions.

Voting and Democracy

Much dismay is expressed over the number of people who do not exercise their right to vote. However, one could make the case that what is truly tragic is the number who actually do vote.

Many voters do not even know who the incumbents are. Nor do they know what either challengers or officeholders stand for – except possibly what is dispensed in very general, self-serving campaign slogans. Their votes are not grounded on thoughtful, objective analyses of accurate information about a candidate's positions. Rather, they are subjectively based on feelings, which are influenced by images created by slick campaign literature and a few seconds of radio and/or television commercials.

Many voters have little appreciation for the concepts which are the basis of our American form of government. Often, they have no consistent beliefs about what the role of government should be.

The belief that merely *to vote* is in and of itself a positive public good is largely based on a misconception that what makes the United States a free country is the right to vote. We are a free people not because we can vote, but because we can make decisions about our daily lives with a minimum of interference from government.

Our country's founders recognized we are free naturally, by being humans who, as the Declaration of Independence states: ".....are endowed by their Creator with certain unalienable Rights." They set up a system with a constitution to guarantee the rights we already possess. To prevent the loss of those rights and freedoms, they provided various safeguards such as three separate branches of government, balance of authority between national and state governments, and direct voting for members of the House of Representatives.

Voting is an important part of the safeguards they provided. However, we should not confuse voting – a mechanism for preserving freedom – for freedom itself. It would be possible to live very freely under a government which guaranteed rights with methods that did not include voting. However, our founders very wisely recognized that freedom would not likely endure unless the people had the ultimate power of electing their representatives. What is a reality are countries where the residents are virtual slaves with the right to vote for their slave masters. To call the people of such a country free because the people can vote is to mock the very concept of freedom. In a jurisdiction where residents merely have the right to vote, but no protection of rights, it can be decided by the majority to take away the rights or even the property of others.

The confusion about voting and freedom has caused the general, but wrong belief that our system is a democracy and which has held that system up as the political *summum bonum*. People are truly free not when they can vote, but when they live in a polity where rights are guaranteed in the basic law of the land and where safeguards are in place to keep them from being infringed. That basic law in the United States is our Constitution. Such a system is properly called a republic – not a democracy.

The general public at the time of the adoption of our government had a high level of understanding of these concepts. What we now know as "The Federalist Papers" were published in regular newspapers to argue for the acceptance of the Constitution, and were read by the average citizen. Our founders were counting on a continued high level of awareness and understanding among voters to ensure good government, and to preserve freedom and the institutions they had set up. This level of awareness and understanding is just not present in the public of today.

Should people with such a lack of knowledge be making decisions for which they are so ill-equipped? Are their votes helping to elect those who will do the best jobs in addressing the issues and preserving our form of government?

In the United States, a certain percentage of people always vote for Republicans and another percentage vote Democratic. In the middle are those who go back and forth between the parties or split their ticket in various election years. Some of these (a minority, I believe) study the issues and candidates and make their votes based on their own personal philosophies (which may be a mixed bag of ideas). But many in the middle are swayed by media campaigns and/or vote based on subjective feelings and don't actually have much of a grasp on issues or any consistent views. These are the voters who might potentially vote for candidates of either party. The sum of their votes often determines who gets elected. So, we have a situation where the most uninformed, politically unaware people frequently decide elections.

Why is there so much concern shown about low voter turnout, and so little concern about the low level of political understanding on the part of those who do vote? There is a much greater threat to our nation from the choices of ill-informed voters than from non-voters.

Each person should ask herself whether she has the proper understanding of the candidates and issues. If she cannot honestly say she does, she has an obligation not to vote. If this were truly done by a significant portion of the electorate, we would have considerably lower voter turnouts and our country would be the better for it. Our officeholders would be much more accountable – knowing people could not be easily fooled by candidates who tell them one thing and act quite differently once they are elected.

However, if sufficient numbers of those who found themselves deficient in political knowledge and understanding would commit to studying about the founding of our nation, current issues, and the records and positions of candidates, we could once again come to a point in this country where we could justifiably hope for a larger voter turnout.

A Christian has a responsibility to not only vote, but to educate herself enough on issues and candidates so she is making informed choices. If she has a consistent philosophy but has not learned about the candidates in a given race, I think it is proper for her to rely on counsel from others who share their views and vote as they advise. If she is neither informed nor able to get reliable counsel, I believe a Christian has a responsibility not to vote.

A Word About Political Labels

I am addressing in this section:

1. The various ways labels have been used to describe political philosophies and which ones I believe to be most appropriate.

2. The views of those who have used such labels.

Where should persons calling themselves Christians find themselves on the political spectrum? What, if any, labels should we use to classify ourselves? In recent years, a majority of evangelical Christians with an interest in politics have adopted the views of what has been called "conservatism." But what does "conservative" mean, and how should we relate to it and other labels used to designate political philosophies?

What should really matter for Christians are the political philosophies or policies in which we believe. That is more important than what terms we use to describe our beliefs. However, in politics perceptions are very important. So are the impressions people get from the words used to describe groups and ideas. So, a description of such names is in order. While, as Shakespeare said, it may not matter what we call a rose, it does make a somewhat significant difference what terms we use to describe our politics.

Throughout this book, I very definitely espouse a limited role for government. Such views fall at least generally within what has been known as a conservative philosophy of government. I will address the questions that follow from the perspective of a person with that philosophy.

When one places people and ideas on a political spectrum, certain terms are used to identify their position on it. But such placements are misleading and/or can be confusing since not everyone assigns the same meanings to the terms being used.

Should We Call Ourselves Conservatives?

Words used as political labels lead to a couple of problems. The first is that some – like conservative, liberal, etc. – are used to describe a person's lifestyle and religious perspective as well as her political philosophy. This can lead to confusion since a person might be conservative politically, but not personally or religiously. Or they may be a liberal politically, but be quite conservative in how they live and/or in their religion.

The other problem is that many terms have a more literal, base meaning and a secondary implication that attaches itself more to how it has come to be used over time. The literal meaning of conservative refers to an interest in conserving existing values in a society and a reluctance to make many changes in its structure or practices – particularly rapid ones. So, political conservatives in the United States have tended to work to preserve our country's founding principles. These have included a belief in limited government, lower government spending, a strong national defense, and local control. Such views can be considered conservative in that they are consistent with the preservation of ideals, and I believe they are generally consistent with a Christian worldview.

Confusion can arise with the term "conservative" since it has other connotations when used outside of politics. A conservative Christian is thought of as being one who has orthodox theological views. It can also imply a person has a quiet, steady lifestyle. Such people are often political conservatives, but not always. It is even more likely they at least follow the conservative line on what have been called social issues. But to refer to someone as a Christian conservative when speaking of politics can be misleading. They may be conservative in their religion, but not at all in their politics. When speaking strictly of their political leanings, it would actually be better to refer to a person as a conservative – rather than a Christian conservative or conservative Christian.

Since we have deviated so far from our founding principles, is it even proper to refer to people who still believe in them as conservatives? Do we really want to conserve what we now have – which is a gargantuan national government, massive deficits, etc.? The problem with the literal meaning of conservative is that it relates to where a society is at a point in time. A term that describes better what we wish to do currently is "restore." We want to restore our nation to how it was conceived by our founders. So, possibly, we could call ourselves "restoratives." However, if we, *mirable dictu*, were actually successful in returning our nation's government to one close to the original form, the term "restorative" would no longer apply.

Another problem with the use of "conservative" is due to the influence of neo-conservatives; the meaning has changed in recent years. The best indication is the fact that many on both the left and the right refer to George W. Bush as a conservative, although his policies followed very little of the traditional conservative philosophy. Further discussion of neo-conservatism can be found in Chapter 17.

Some Other Possible Labels

A political label should describe what its adherents believe about the role of government. Those on the right should use labels that pertain to our belief in limited, constitutional government and the promotion and preserving of liberty or freedom. Let's look at a couple that might fit those criteria.

The term "constitutionalist" seems like a reasonably good term at first blush. It well describes those who believe in the original US concepts as embodied in our Constitution. One problem is that others construe that document so differently. Many on the left often cite the Constitution (frequently inaccurately, I believe) in support of their positions.

Liberal is etymologically related to liberty and would actually be a literally proper word to describe those who believe in freedom and limited government. It has the advantage of not having a relation to the current state of affairs, and it was used in the past to refer to believers in economic and political freedom. The problem with using it would be overcoming the baggage attached to it from decades of its use to describe promoters of big government. Another problem is the negative connotations associated with it when used to describe a person's lifestyle or religious views.

What About Libertarian?

Libertarian is also related to liberty and is another more literally correct word to describe freedom lovers. Some of those currently called conservative are fearful of that term. Particularly Christians, I believe, shy away from its use – associating it with an "anything goes" philosophy of life. They likely think of it as a synonym for libertine, but we shouldn't confuse its use to describe a person's lifestyle with its political application in relation to the role of government. Some libertarians seem more interested in having a limited government to allow them to live a looser lifestyle, than being concerned about preserving liberty to maintain a free and prosperous society. That fact helps create an association of the term libertarian with a liberal way of living.

I like the term "libertarian" because it incorporates "liberty" which I believe should be the primary focus of government. It also has the advantage of not being tied to a current political situation – a belief in liberty should be timeless. I also, in general, agree with a good deal of those who have used the label – but not all. As with any political appellation, disagreement on various issues arises among those who use it.

Some libertarians who do not recognize the fallen nature of man are somewhat naïve about the need for a strong national defense or to gather intelligence information about our country's enemies. And some do not recognize threats to the traditional family.

While we can agree with many of the ultimate political positions of some libertarians, believers often arrive at those positions from different philosophical starting points. Some libertarians are atheists – although many more with those religious views are on the left. While atheists can believe in the same concepts of individual freedom as Christians do, they do not have a solid philosophic basis for those beliefs. Most atheists are materialists; that view is certainly consistent with a belief that there is no God. In fact, one cannot really account for anything other than physical matter without some type of God (actually I don't even know how one could explain even the material in the universe without God!).

If matter is all that exists, there can be no mind independent of the brain; mental activity is merely a physical thing; and our thoughts and actions are just randomly determined. Many atheists acknowledge this. This belief does not allow for free will without which liberty is meaningless. It is the existence of a mind and soul independent of our physical bodies that is the basis of free will and the justification for political freedom. This is why we, as believers, can say we have been endowed by our Creator with inalienable rights. So, Christianity provides a philosophic warrant for libertarianism – atheism does not.

One can arrive at a correct political philosophy from a theology that is not Christian. That philosophy can even be implemented into government policy. However, unless the underlying political ideas are grounded in a proper view of the world and the humans who live in it, any political structures based upon them will not endure – they are built on sinking sand. Actually, it is being charitable to say they rest on a foundation of sand; in reality, in a world that consists of only matter that randomly occurs, there can be no foundation for anything at all.

One of the people that many libertarians cite frequently is Ayn Rand. While even many conservatives who don't consider themselves in any way libertarians agree with much of her defense of free enterprise, she arrives at her views from an atheistic starting point. She also rails against altruism. Christians are commanded by the Lord to be selfless and help others. The problem comes when government tries to enforce altruism. But to be against all effort and concern on behalf of others is to throw the baby out with the bathwater. The bottom line is the Christian view of the dignity of humans who have been created in the image of God and gifted with freedom is an infinitely superior basis for libertarianism than the atheism of authors like Rand.

Those who currently call themselves libertarians vary in the policies they advocate. Some carry the concept of limiting government so far they could almost be considered anarchists. But I think most who adopt that appellation have views consistent with the limited government upon which our nation was conceived.

Really, the principles of our Constitution and the limited government under which we lived as a nation for our first century and a half are pretty close to the ideas of today's typical libertarian. Likely, a clear majority of Americans who lived during that period would not have a problem with much of what they advocate, so we should not look upon most of their ideas as something radical or far-out.

We suffer in this country from too much government – not a lack of it. Our goal needs to be to reduce its size and scope. It is better to err on the side of working for too much freedom – rather than too little. Many countries and civilizations have been destroyed from too much government. I'm not sure any have gone under because of too much freedom. If I had to choose between a libertarian and a modern liberal (or a so-called "moderate") for office, I would certainly prefer the libertarian. I consider myself a conservative with strong libertarian leanings, but if someone calls me a libertarian, I am not offended. A strain of libertarianism has always been in the modern conservative movement. The libertarianism of a Christian will, however, vary somewhat from that of a non-theist.

I believe the term "libertarian" is appropriate to describe the views of those who advocate limited government. I am not necessarily saying conservatives should become libertarians as they are defined today, although I do think our views are often not that far from theirs. Some who choose to start using that name to describe themselves may have to deal with some misunderstandings about what they believe on certain issues. But that is true of any label persons give themselves.

Is "Compassionate Conservative" a Legitimate Political Label?

In recent years, some, like George Bush, have started referring to themselves as "compassionate conservatives." Those who use this label may be trying to communicate different things. Yet it seems they include a willingness to use government to ameliorate social problems. This is not in accord with what conservative has meant as applied in the past. When some people use this term to describe themselves, they are not really defining a conservative at all.

The problem is that users of the label combine one word "compassionate" which describes a personal characteristic and another "conservative" which has come to denote a political philosophy, then attempt to use the resulting compound term to name a new political designation that implies a conservative who is compassionate will have a somewhat different political philosophy from other conservatives, but that is not necessarily true.

Without any context "compassionate conservative" would describe a person who is sensitive and displays a lot of pity for others in unfortunate circumstances, and who happens to believe in the political precepts of conservatism. There would not be a presumption that, because of her concern for down-and-outers, she would try to take care of their problems through government programs. In fact, the opposite should be assumed, since that is not the approach conservatives generally take.

One would expect a person's political philosophy to be independent of his or her emotional predilections, although they could be influenced by them. Uncompassionate persons could be conservatives because they do not really care about other people. However, they could also be leftists who want government to take care of people, so they don't have any personal responsibility for helping them.

Compassionate persons might be on the left and really want to have government programs to aid the needy because they believe this is a way to help them. But they might also be on the right because, although they care deeply about those with problems, they don't believe such programs are effective, and/or infringe on the right of taxpayers to choose their own charities, and/or realize government involvement causes other ancillary problems.

It should never be assumed that because one doesn't believe in forced contributions to reduce poverty, he has no sympathy for the unfortunate, or that one who believes in such methods is necessarily compassionate. Willingness to spend public money on something doesn't prove one's solicitude. The true test of a person's concern for others is how she personally responds to and treats her fellow human beings, and how willing she is to use personal time and resources to help them – not on what her political beliefs are.

To use compassionate as a modifier to try to come up with a new category of political philosophy which implies that those conservatives without the qualifier are somehow less compassionate is spurious. All people, particularly Christians should be compassionate, but that doesn't mean they should advocate or work for statist solutions.

In actuality, one shouldn't let his compassion or lack thereof influence his political views – rather he should be dispassionate by not letting his feelings determine what he believes. A political philosophy should be based on solid thinking – not emotions.

What Should We Call Those on the Left?

There is also the question of how to refer to those on the left. Liberal has been the primary term used for some time. However, as previously noted, that term is really more appropriate for freedom lovers. It comes from the Latin word *liber* – which means free or unrestricted. Today's liberal does little to promote freedom. In fact, the policies they advocate usually call for action that takes away freedom. As has been aptly observed, the only thing a modern liberal is liberal with is taxpayers' money, although one could make a case for using "liberal" to describe those who would interpret the Constitution in a manner that would allow greater power to the federal government (loose constructionist).

The problem with confusing the political and non-political usages of the word is also an issue. Socially liberal is used to describe those who adopt a more relaxed application of morality to their lives. The term is also used to refer to those with a less rigorous and literal interpretation of Scripture. Most often those who are socially or theologically liberal are not political conservatives.

Progressives, You've Got to be Kidding!

An appellation that a segment of the left has commandeered is "progressive." This term implies that those claiming it believe in policies that promote progress. However, advances in society through the centuries have come as freedom of the individual has increased and the role of the state has decreased. The greatest progress has resulted from the growth in the influence of Western (Christian) Civilization as it culminated in our American experience.

Self-styled progressives invariably promote policies that enhance the power of government. Those are directly contrary to what has provided progress throughout the ages. They are not progressive – they are regressive. In fact, self-styled progressives could more properly be called atavistic. Those who believe in liberty should assume this label, as we are the true progressives.

The so-called "progressives" also like to call those on the right "reactionaries" and say we want to repeal the twentieth century (and now the twenty-first, I presume). However, many of the policies we properly react against are those that they themselves have implemented that have had the effect of repealing the advances of several centuries prior to the twentieth.

Other Terms for the Left

I have no problem using statist to refer to those on the left. They certainly work to enhance the power of the state over individual and private interests. They usually see government as the first resort in addressing societal problems.

Another very appropriate term for a person of the left is "collectivist." It is important to be clear not to confuse its use in a political context with non-political applications. Nothing is wrong – in fact it can be quite noble – for individuals to voluntarily organize to collectively promote a common goal. It is forced collectivism through government, as sought by the left, that is objectionable.

I recommend phasing out using "liberal" to refer to those on the left. Due to its root meaning "free," such a use is a gross misnomer. Although we should discontinue using the word in this way, it is still the most frequent term used to describe the left. You will note I still use it occasionally myself in this book.

Defining the Spectrum

Right and left are good ways to distinguish the two different philosophies if one properly defines their meanings. References to a person, group, or philosophy being farther in one direction or the other imply the existence of a continuum along which something varies. What should distinguish the two poles is the amount of government in which each side believes.

Those on the extreme left believe in total government, and those on the farthest point on the right would opt for no government. Those who have been known as conservatives would be on the right, libertarians a little farther in that direction. Socialists and communists would be on the far left – social-welfare statists somewhat more toward the port side. Also, on the far left, would be the fascists and Nazis. It makes no sense to place them on the right as some have tried to do since they, like communists and socialists, believe in strong, centrally-controlled, authoritarian states. Nazis were really national socialists and the Soviet Union's full name was "The Union of Soviet Socialist Republics." Many who have tried to place fascists and Nazis on the right have done so in an attempt to discredit advocates of limited government by associating them with distasteful ideologies. In reality, some who have tried to make this faulty connection themselves advocate policies that can accurately be described as fascist. It is amazing so many people would actually fall for such a nonsensical, illogical thought that fascism and Nazis are opposites of socialism and communism.

The booklet and DVD entitled "Overview of America"[8] provides an excellent and much more in-depth explanation of this topic which also includes definitions of the various types of government such as republics, democracies, oligarchies, etc.

Isn't it Good to be Moderate?

Before leaving this discussion of political labels, I want to address one more category – the increasing number of people who choose to call themselves "moderates" and who claim to occupy a spot on the spectrum between left and right. Again, we encounter a term that can be confusing depending on whether one uses it in a political context or for another purpose. However, unlike "conservative," "liberal," and "libertarian," which have legitimate political definitions, I'm not sure "moderate" is even a proper term to describe a political personage.

When used of a person, it refers to character and behavioral traits. It normally applies to attributes like tastes, attitudes, temperament, etc. It is generally considered a positive in that the person being described is eschewing some extreme. In political usage, it should refer more to the methods a person or group uses – not their views. It certainly could indicate views that are not extreme, but a term used to describe a political philosophy should tell us something about what a person believes. However, those who call themselves "moderates" seem to adopt a hodge-podge of positions that has little consistency.

Self-described moderates often accuse those on the left and the right of being ideological. Dislike of ideology seems to fit well in our current society that tends to express disdain for anyone with strong beliefs. That is consistent with postmodern thought which asserts there are no absolutes (how then does one assert anything at all?).

Those with an ideology usually have a political philosophy and evaluate policies based on how it stacks up against that philosophy. The philosophy is based on some core set of beliefs about the world. A

8 *Overview of America* (DVD) (Appleton, WI The John Birch Society; 2007)

believer should be able to have an ideology deeply rooted in the Christian worldview.

Those who say they don't have an ideology (such as self-proclaimed moderates) often are pragmatists since they claim to be for whatever works. However, they tend not to exclude any potential solution they believe might be beneficial – and that would include those that require a very heavy hand from government. So, their claim not to be ideological is disingenuous since their willingness to use government as an option really makes them statists – although they may not elect to use it in every instance.

It is proper to evaluate another's ideology and make judgments regarding its correctness. However, merely having an ideology should not be seen as a negative. Although those with ideologies may try to adopt positions on issues based on their political philosophy, we, as Christians, know it is impossible in a fallen world for anyone to be one-hundred percent consistent. Ideologues at least make sincere attempts to justify their views from their basic beliefs. This often requires difficult thinking. It can be hard work. Those who identify themselves as non-ideological can avoid reconciling their views with a philosophy. For some of them, adopting the "moderate," non-ideological position is just due to intellectual laziness, since it releases them from the obligation to develop a philosophy of government, much less adhere to it consistently.

Christians should believe in absolute truths. These truths should be embodied in a worldview, which in turn should be the basis for our political philosophy. It is hard to see how a Christian could justify being a political moderate. Those who believe in absolute truth should have consistent guidelines to evaluate political ideas. Of course, the methods we use to espouse and attempt to implement our ideas should not be extreme.

Who Isn't for Good Government?

A political category I call "good government" involves people who are, personally, very moral and civic-minded, and have a servant attitude. They are people one would like to have for neighbors. They may be Democrats or Republicans. They generally don't have any firm political philosophy. Such people are particularly prevalent on school boards and city councils. They see only the good government can do and have visions of all the possibilities it can accomplish. They are generally pragmatists who tend to evaluate proposals only on the basis of whether they see them as likely to work. They do not look much at secondary impacts or long-term effects of laws.

Some Christians are counted among their ranks. Such people have lost sight of the damage government can do to our freedom. Particularly the believers in this group should recognize the potential for abuse of power due to the flawed nature of humans. That view of human nature has fallen out of fashion in most churches, and even many Christians look upon people as basically good. For many, the long period of prosperity and relative freedom in the United States has lulled them to sleep regarding the threat to liberty. Very possibly, the fact that most pastors rarely preach against sin anymore has caused them to become inured to the corruption of humans that results in the abuse of power.

Unfortunately, these "good government" types can migrate to state legislatures and the US Congress where they can do even more damage by carrying their naïve views with them. People are likely to vote for them because of their character (which may or may not remain intact if they serve long in Washington D.C.!). However, they often lack knowledge of history, any discernibly distinct political philosophy, and wisdom. They prove being a good person does not necessarily make one a good public office-holder.

There is a term of which we should beware. When anyone talks about reforming something in a political context, it most often involves an expansion of governmental authority. "Reform" and "reforming" are further examples of what were once perfectly good words being hijacked by the left to disguise further encroachment by the state.

So, What is the Right Term for Believers in Limited Government?

The problem we have in distinguishing between the two poles of political philosophy is that the base meanings for "liberal" and "conservative" – the most common terms used today – are not really antonyms. It is possible for a person to call themselves both a liberal and a conservative if they believe in conserving what remains of our freedom. That would have been particularly true in the 19th and early 20th centuries when we had a lot more freedom to conserve.

The bottom line is that any appellation used for the right has been misconstrued to the point it would be difficult to use it in the sense of its literal definition. If we were starting from scratch with our definitions, "conservative" is not a term we should use to describe believers in limited, constitutional government since it is inadequate for all the reasons mentioned in this section. It does nothing to define the proper role of government. But, in evaluating a label, we have to consider how it has been used historically. I think it is still proper to use the term "conservative" because enough understanding remains of how it has been used in the past to make it a helpful definition. I do think whether one uses "conservative" should depend somewhat on his audience and that one should not refer to neo-cons as conservative without using the "neo" prefix.

However, I also like the term "libertarian." As a label, it does accurately describe our focus on liberty as the political *summum bonum*. Since it is solidly grounded in the Christian view of man, believers should not be afraid of calling themselves "libertarians," even though we may not share all the views of others using that name. In a sense, what I am advocating in various places in this book could be part of what might be called "Christian libertarianism." I think it appropriate to use that term since we would expect the libertarianism defined by believers to vary some from that promulgated by secularists. Whatever label a person uses, they will find others claiming it who have some beliefs with which they do not agree. I see no problem in calling oneself both a conservative and a libertarian. Perhaps if more liberty-minded people start calling themselves "libertarians," that term will gradually replace "conservative" in the political lexicon.

I have assumed in the past few paragraphs that the right is the proper site on the political spectrum for evangelical Christians to be. I believe that and provide justification for that opinion throughout this book. This does not mean I agree with all opinions of the so-called "Christian right" or with all their political strategies. I deal with that topic in Chapter 17.

CHAPTER 5

God, Morality, and Government

> [1]*Every person is to be in subjection to the governing authorities. For there is no authority except from God, and those which exist are established by God.* [2]*Therefore whoever resists authority has opposed the ordinance of God; and they who have opposed will receive condemnation upon themselves.* [3]*For rulers are not a cause of fear for good behavior, but for evil. Do you want to have no fear of authority? Do what is good and you will have praise from the same;* [4]*for it is a minister of God to you for good. But if you do what is evil, be afraid; for it does not bear the sword for nothing; for it is a minister of God, an avenger who brings wrath on the one who practices evil.* [5]*Therefore it is necessary to be in subjection, not only because of wrath, but also for conscience sake* (Romans 13:1-5).

> [1] *First of all, then, I urge that entreaties and prayers, petitions and thanksgivings, be made on behalf of all men,* [2] *for kings and all who are in authority, so that we may lead a tranquil and quiet life in all godliness and dignity* (I Timothy 2:1-2).

Christians are often accused of attempting to legislate morality. Sometimes it is stated more inelegantly as "trying to shove your morality down my throat." Both believers and non-believers often ask whether it is appropriate for government to pass laws outlawing acts deemed immoral. However, the larger question believers should ask is: "What is the relation of morality to law and politics?" To be moral is to be in accord with the standards of right conduct. Morality also denotes a particular system of such principles. Most people will agree on general standards, but beyond that, morality does involve different codes of behavior based on one's theological and philosophical perspective.

Christians should be concerned about morality in all aspects of life. Since we are dealing with politics in this work, I will primarily address it as it applies to government. The question for believers is broader than just whether there should be legislation against immorality and, if so, which kind of behavior should be illegal. Hence, this chapter is entitled "God, Morality, and Government" – rather than "Legislating Morality."

Certainly in carrying out its functions, government itself should not engage in immoral or unethical acts. Here we have a possible problem since ideas of morality vary. But all political systems must be based, at least to some degree, on moral assumptions, which are often associated with one or more sets of religious beliefs. I believe Christianity has the best and most consistent system of morality in history, and it has the most respect for the individual because of our belief that we are made in the image of God. Most people, whether believers or not, should recognize this and not have a problem with a government being based on Christian morality, since atheists and non-Christian religions have had almost complete freedom to practice and promote their religious views in America.

Should Morality be Legislated?

Although any government should be based on moral principles and should itself act morally, it does not necessarily follow that it should attempt to prevent its citizens from performing actions simply because they are immoral. Some Christians believe in trying to prevent all moral infractions through laws. I believe they are in the minority. Many believers have certain pet sins they would like to see outlawed, and we certainly vary in how far we would like to see government go in suppressing immoral acts.

There has to be some objective standard used when applying morality to a discussion of politics. The position that used to be taken by many conservatives is that government should not legislate morality. This was the view of many of those who supported Barry Goldwater for president in 1964, when they defended his vote against the Civil Rights Act. They said this bill was about legislating morality.

The response often given by Christian conservatives today is that all law should be based on morality. That is true, but doesn't answer the question as to whether everything that is immoral should also be illegal. I guess I will stick my neck out and declare that morality should not be legislated, that no activity should be banned merely because it is immoral. Most Christians are reluctant to say that directly. They likely believe that by doing so they are in some way condoning unrighteous conduct. That is not true. Such a statement simply says it should not be the business of government to regulate morality.

Some areas of human activity that relate to morality have justification for legislation. However, that takes into account other considerations such as the involvement of children. What I am asserting is that merely the fact that something is immoral should not be a sufficient reason in and of itself to outlaw it.

Christians should definitely be a moral force in society. We do this, first, by personal example. We should also work to ensure the government itself acts morally toward its citizens and doesn't actually promote immoral behavior. And it is the duty of Christians to teach the Word of God which definitely declares many human activities to be immoral. Believers as individuals, as the church, and through Christian ministries, should publicly address moral issues in our society. In fact, we should be the strongest voice promoting moral behavior. Certain segments of the church have been quite lax in speaking out on morality due to their concern about not offending anyone. This includes congregations that adopt a seeker-sensitive model to draw people into the church.

When believers speak against immorality, we should be using the Bible and making it clear that it is God who is declaring certain activities sinful and/or immoral – not us. Nevertheless, we can expect to be attacked when doing this since it is often the messenger who is blamed for the message. This should not deter us from presenting God's word to others, since what God says about sin will have convicting power. It is one of the primary things that will bring people to God for forgiveness.

However, outlawing immoral practices has no convicting power. It is the government speaking against an activity – not God. While it might stop a few from engaging in a proscribed activity, it does not bring people to God. If the given law has been enacted at the behest of believers, it just makes people mad at the Christians who pushed for it – driving them farther away from God. We should not use government to punish immorality. It is not necessary since God does a good job of penalizing those who commit immoral acts. If we, as Christians, wish to correct moral problems, why would we seek to do so through the government? It has historically been very ineffective in solving any problem.

Another reason for not enforcing morality with law is consistency. If we believe in freedom, we must acknowledge some people will do things we don't like. We, as Christians, want to be able freely to proselytize. Many secular people would prefer to curtail that action. They certainly are not going to buy into the idea that we should have such freedom, and they should be denied the freedom to live their lives in a way we know to be immoral. We may have gotten by with this in an earlier, more moral, America, but it certainly isn't going to fly today.

If government is to enforce personal morality, that which it will impose will be based on the values of those who have the most influence in the current regime in a given jurisdiction. It is far from certain that what will be enforced will be morality based on Christianity. We can certainly see, for instance, the way in which humanists are increasingly imposing support for homosexuality in our country.

Those on the left accuse conservatives of trying to impose our morality on others. With immorality being so rampant today, it is hard to imagine anyone who desires to commit immoral acts is being prevented from doing so by government. What quite clearly is happening is that liberals are using government to push their morality. This is particularly true in the public schools when they follow policies and curricula that promote the idea that homosexuality is normal. They have also advocated a loose attitude toward sex in various classes. Government also encourages immorality by subsidizing it with programs that give money to those having children out of wedlock, etc. The left seems to have no problem with imposing their immorality in these ways.

Is it Even Possible to Enforce Morality?

There is a sense in which it is impossible to legislate morality. We humans are moral agents because we are free to make choices – either to be moral by doing what God judges to be right conduct or to be immoral by disobeying His ethical laws. We have been given this ability by God to choose right or wrong. Animals, although they can make some decisions, are not capable of moral choices.

A legislative body can pass a law prohibiting an immoral activity. If they make the penalty severe enough, some will refrain from committing the outlawed act, although their preference is to engage in it. But if their only reason for obedience is to avoid the penalties, they are not really making a moral decision. Hence, the law has not enforced morality. A truly moral person will not commit wrong actions because he wishes to do what is right. That is not the same as avoiding something due to negative consequences.

In the movie *A Clockwork Orange,* Alex, a juvenile delinquent, has been jailed for various acts of violence. In prison, he is used as a guinea pig to test an experimental program called "Aversion Therapy" which is to cure him by making him sick of violence and sexual aggression. Alex is drugged and forced to watch violent films and is tempted by a provocatively-dressed woman. The drugs make him sick during the sessions. The "treatments" are repeated several times until the person administering them declares Alex "cured." However, the prison chaplain rightly says that Alex's humanity has been corrupted because his capability to actually choose to do right instead of wrong has been removed. The program is intended to have the subject discontinue criminal activity by associating it with sickness. He is to get ill when tempted to participate in inappropriate behavior. The therapy is based on humanistic, behaviorist psychology.

Subsequent portions of the movie indicate that Alex has not really been cured. Even if he had been, would we say he was then a moral person? No, because his ability to make a moral choice would have been taken away. He would not be doing what is right by a mental decision, but merely because his body had been programmed in a Pavlovian manner to react negatively to the thought of crime. Without the freedom to choose, morality is meaningless.

Violating God's Laws

It is clear we are responsible first to God for our behavior – not to government. He has laid down some very specific laws in His word. To violate them is to sin against God. It is ultimately to Him we must answer for any disobedience of those laws. He is the one who will administer the punishment for any infractions. It is also clear that no person is capable of keeping His rules perfectly. Should we be trying to have government enforce laws that the Creator of the Universe has said are impossible to keep? (*All have turned aside, together they have become useless; there is none who does good, there is not even one* – Romans 3:12).

We should distinguish between sins that are external and those that involve our internal thought life. I believe most Christians would not want to pass laws against sins that are purely internal. But some sins deemed to be among the most serious involve our thought lives. It is really quite difficult to punish someone for pride, for instance. What would be the criteria for proving guilt?

Of course, some internal sins are also immoral – for example, lusting after a person of the opposite sex. Again, proof would be difficult. Interestingly, the left does at least verge on punishing people for their thoughts with legislation like anti-discrimination laws. Such laws attempt to objectively judge people for making decisions which in reality are very subjective. In effect, they are punishing people for what they think.

This would also be true of proposals like the so-called "hate crimes" legislation. In such laws, people are not being judged merely for their actions, but also for their motives. Motives, of course, involve our thoughts.

We, as Christians, certainly believe someone who worships a false god is sinning. But most of us believe in freedom of religion and would not seek to outlaw such practices. Unlike the adherents of some other religions, we realize a decision to follow Jesus Christ needs to be an act of the heart, mind, and will. One cannot become a Christian through force. Does it make any more sense to say a person can become moral by passing laws against immoral behavior? Yet, some believers think the state should enforce morality. That would include believers in what has been called Reconstructionism which asserts that earthly governments should be ruled in a theocratic manner by the laws of God as described in the Bible.

What about the sin of gossiping? If we start passing laws against things like that we'll have more people behind prison walls than outside them. The point is that it should seem obvious that not everything against God's Law should be legislated against by humans.

It seems that quite often items that get thrown in the moral category are sexual in nature. Certainly, these seem to be the ones discussed the most, and about which the greatest differences in opinions are expressed. By doing so, we often adopt too narrow a definition of moral. Many infractions of God's Law should be considered immoral acts although they don't involve sexual thoughts or acts.

There should be some reasonably consistent criteria for determining whether actions should be prohibited by law. If something should not be deemed illegal, just because it is immoral, what should be the basis for deciding an activity should be against the law? The primary criterion used to decide if something should be illegal should be based on whether a person is using coercion on another, or if they fraudulently and/or deceitfully get them to participate in a transaction, although some exceptions and situations exist where it is difficult to determine if conditions fit these criteria.

Rewarding Wrong Behavior

Some will say we should outlaw certain behavior because the problems that result involve expenditures borne by taxpayers. An example would be a drug user who is being treated by a government-subsidized facility. The problem is that we have passed laws that provide government care for self-imposed problems that shield offenders from the full consequences of their actions. The answer is not to outlaw the wrong behavior, but to stop using government to soften the negative results of the decision to engage in such behavior.

Liberals want freedom in moral matters, but they want everyone to pick up the tab for the consequences. This is, in effect, subsidizing immorality and contributing to the growth of such behavior in society. Freedom that doesn't involve suffering the consequences for one's acts is not true freedom. When a person has to live with the results of what they do it creates a built-in incentive to do what is right. True freedom promotes self-discipline. Our society's social welfare policies have largely removed that restraint. It also isn't right to force others (i.e. taxpayers) to pay for the consequences of another's moral failures. To do so is asking others to effectively be an unwilling accessory to his immorality.

Morality of Taxpayer Subsidies

As previously mentioned, government itself should not carry out its activities in an immoral way or promote immorality. To evaluate that in more detail we need to look at what government really is. It is basically legitimized force. Ultimately, it has the power of life and death over its subjects. If a person does not obey it, its agents will seek to apprehend him, and if he resists or flees, they will pursue him and, if necessary, kill him. A quote attributed by some people to George Washington said it well: "Government is not reason, it is not eloquence, it is force; like fire, a troublesome servant and a fearful master." Whether he or someone else originated that comment, it well states the fact that government is a powerful force.

Because government has such potential for misuse, we should be very cautious about what powers we give it. And those powers should be very explicitly stated, as we have done in our Constitution here in the United States.

In determining these powers, a good rule is only to allow government to do things we would legitimately do as individuals or in a group. It would be proper for a person to defend his person, family, home, and property from those who would harm him or deprive him of his possessions. It would also be acceptable to gather others to help him with such a defense. When we assign this function to policemen, we are really bestowing on government the authority to do for us collectively what we would justifiably do for ourselves.

However, when government is given the authority to take something from one person and give it to another as it has been doing with welfare and so-called "social programs"; we are conferring on it the right to do something we could not morally do ourselves: expropriate others' resources for our own use. Neither would it be right for us to band together with our neighbors and decide that the person down the street has something we want and gang up on him and take it. The fact that the victim may have more than he needs does not make it any more right to deprive him of what is legitimately his.

Yet, this is what government has been doing. Economist Frederic Bastiat referred to this in *The Law* as "legalized plunder" (see bibliography). The fact that such actions are deemed legal does not make them moral. This immoral practice should be stopped, and Christians should be in the forefront of those calling for its termination since we should have higher standards than others.

Many, if not most, Americans (including Christians) probably believe it is fine for governments to engage in such practices. Let me suggest several possibilities why this may be the case. One is the fact that it has been going on in this country for so long. Time seems to legitimize things in many people's minds. They become inured to such practices similar to the way humans become hardened to sin after an extended time of engaging in it.

Another possibility for Christians is that they have confused the commands of Jesus regarding helping the poor with the actions of government. As a result, they believe it is legitimate for the government to force people to follow His commands. This will be discussed more thoroughly in Chapter 16 on the Christian Left.

Two other possibilities are related. One is that they just have never really thought about the whole idea. The other is their view of government. Many people believe government is an entity with ultimate authority and should be able to do whatever it wishes as long as it follows democratic procedures. However, simply the fact that something was voted on does not make it right. Would we say it is okay for the residents on a block to steal from one of their neighbors – even if everyone except the victim voted for it? No! Morality is not about majority rule – it is about doing what is right and not doing what is wrong.

It is actually worse for a government to engage in such activities since the authority they have gives their actions an aura of legitimacy. If a person steals from you, you have a recourse. The government will try to find those responsible and bring them to justice. However, where does one go when the government which is supposed to be protecting your possessions is actually confiscating your assets on behalf of others? Such government thievery is also worse in the way it is more wrong for a group of people to gang up on someone than it is for one person to beat up on them.

Christians' Attitude Toward Getting Government Aid

It is also important that Christians have the right attitude about the potential actions of government. We should not expect that we will gain something at the expense of others through government mandates. Lobbying for a law we believe will benefit us personally takes that a step further. Even hoping for the implementation of policies that will enrich us at the expense of others is coveting. This would not include a desire for lower taxes which is moral since it is merely wishing to keep more of what we have legitimately earned. Taxes do not involve a desire for something owned by someone else. But to expect to have government transfer wealth to us from others is not an appropriate motivation for believers. Coveting is sinful (a violation of one of the Ten Big Ones).

It is possible to support such programs without coveting; one might just believe it is good public policy for our society regardless of whether he personally expects to benefit from it. In some cases, the person may actually believe he will not profit from the program and that his taxes will help pay for it. But I think, more often than not, a person who adopts a favorable position toward a program involving wealth transfer believes he will come out on the long end of the bargain. Each person must examine his own heart to determine whether his motives in advocating a government aid program are to gain a personal advantage. If so, he is coveting.

No one who has taken advantage of a government program should be condemned for doing so. With the spate of such programs available, it would probably be hard to find anyone in our country who has not availed himself of some government benefit. But we need to be asking whether such programs are good public policy and more importantly (particularly for Christians) whether it is moral for government to use its immense power to transfer assets from one party to another. While it should be apparent, I want to stress that it is just as morally inappropriate to take taxpayers' funds and give them to business entities as it is to give them to individuals. That is true regardless of whether the program disbursing the funds is called a bailout, subsidy or whatever.

Certainly, God has used government programs as a way to take care of His people. It has undoubtedly been a method He has used to provide for Christian individuals and families in need – at least on an *ad hoc* basis. Some believers can point to situations where, based on the circumstances, it appears likely or almost certain that the meeting of a need in this way was an answer to prayer. However, this should not be seen as proof that the program meeting the need was a good one, or one that God would endorse.

God has achieved his purposes by using things that are of themselves not necessarily good. He used Assyria and Babylon to punish Israel and Judah, respectively, for instance, although He did not approve of these nations themselves. Any government policies should be evaluated on their overall merits and consistency with a Christian worldview – not based on anecdotal citing of instances where they may have been a tool God used to accomplish His will and/or to answer prayer.

Another attitude believers can develop when government provides a high level of social welfare is that of looking to the state as their provider – rather than to God. If carried too far, one might actually make an idol of government or have it serve as their god. Of course, it is also possible for a person who receives no government aid and works for everything he has to trust more in his own talents, abilities, work ethic, and perseverance to meet his needs than he does in God. Ultimately, the believer needs to put his faith in God to provide for him and recognize that He uses different methods to do so. However, God has mandated in His Word that we are to provide for ourselves and our families by working. No evidence supports the idea that we should seek to meet our needs with public subsidies.

A moral problem also associated with welfare policies occurs when office-holders or candidates promise beneficiaries some benefit that will increase the amount to be received, or when they commit to supporting some new give-away. Such statements are often made while asking for votes of constituents. This is reprehensible! It is little more than bribery – using taxpayers' money.

Mischaracterizing Issues as Strictly Moral

Christians often bring up laws against things like murder or abortion as examples of moral laws. They do so to argue that it is proper to legislate against immorality. Of course, murder is immoral – few of any political bent would question that. But it is not against the law because it is immoral. It is legislated against because it takes away the rights of another human. In fact, it takes away all their rights by negating their very person.

Liberals will try to say that, in advocating the outlawing of abortion, we are imposing our morality. That is not true. We want to prevent abortion because it takes away the right of the unborn – not because it is immoral. Of course, if one believes the unborn are truly persons, as most believers do, then killing them is also immoral.

Homosexual Issues

Another issue that is miscast as a moral issue is that of homosexual marriage. Sodomy laws would be considered legislating morality. But that isn't really the main issue today. Virtually nowhere in the nation are violators of such laws being prosecuted. Nor is there any great cry from any quarter for them to be enforced. Homosexuals can engage in pretty much whatever activities they wish. Some will say they want the right to be married so they can express their love for each other. There is nothing stopping them from doing that. They don't need a marriage certificate to express love – in either a legitimate or an immoral way. So marriage questions are not really moral issues since a certificate from the state is not required to perform an immoral act. Neither are they really freedom issues since the presence or absence of a marriage certificate does not impact the liberty to commit sodomy.

A commonly cited reason by homosexuals for needing the legal protection of marriage is guaranteeing the right to visit a partner in a hospital. The first problem is that this should not be considered a right. Medical institutions, like all organizations, have policies. If anyone does not like a given institution's rules they are free to lobby to change them. Too many people today believe that if they don't like a policy set by an establishment, a law should be passed to force that organization to adopt the policies they wish.

In reality, in this age of acceptance of homosexuality, it is likely most hospitals will soon, if they don't already, consider a homosexual partner the same as a family member. If some don't, people will just have to live with that. Most of us in a free society frequently encounter policies we don't like. If it bothers us enough and other options are available, we may choose to go to another business or organization. The response is too often to attempt to get a law passed to force the parties involved to adopt the policy desired.

Homosexuals have chosen to live in a manner that flouts the norms of society and that many people find offensive. When one does that, he has to be prepared to live with the consequences – one of which is that people may not accept his behavior and discriminate against him in some way. In a free society, people want to be able to live the way they wish, but they also need to acknowledge that others should have the freedom to reject their actions. Many homosexual activists, however, want to live a deviant lifestyle and force others to accept it.

Unfortunately, the right to engage in the immoral practice of sodomy has been conflated with the granting of the status of marriage to homosexuals. These are two separate issues and should be treated as such. A good indication that the two questions are confused is that supporters of homosexual marriage, when defending it, will talk of the freedom of people to engage in certain sexual activities. This is not the issue with marriage since one does not need to be married to perform those activities. And marriage is not a right. It is a legal definition used in a society primarily to provide for families, inheritance law, dealing with children who have lost their parents, etc. So, homosexual marriage has been miscast as a rights issue. It is important that conservatives stress that it is not. I believe one of the main reasons support for homosexual marriage has increased in recent years is that so many think not allowing such legal unions is denying a right. If this continues to be the way the issue is seen, we will lose this battle.

For many homosexuals, the real reason they seek government recognition through marriage is they want to get an official stamp of approval on their relationships. Already, many schools discuss homosexual relationships as though they are just another legitimate family option. If same-sex marriages are legalized, the depiction of families consisting only of heterosexual couples will likely become taboo – even in Christian schools (certainly in government schools). If a homosexual union has been given the imprimatur of the state, how can it be considered wrong? Although we know, as Christians, that everything legal isn't moral, it will be argued that to speak against homosexuality is wrong because it has legal status. Prohibition of preaching against homosexual practices will likely come with same-sex marriage. We need only look to other countries to see where we are going.

An incident in England illustrates the trend and indicates where our country could be headed. A pastor there who was involved in street evangelism, at some point mentioned to a woman bystander that homosexuality was a sin. This was not part of his public presentation, but merely a private conversation. Nevertheless, a policeman who overheard the conversation threw him in jail.

Jerry Falwell had to revise the broadcasts of his programs aired in Canada to leave out statements about homosexuality due to their laws. The question we have to ask as Americans is: "How far are we behind such countries in losing our right to the freedom of speech?"

Homosexuals talk a lot about tolerance, but it is apparent that what many of them, if not most, want is forced acceptance. They have no intention of tolerating anyone even speaking against their lifestyles. It isn't only their sexual practices that are perverted, but they also have a perverted view of freedom of speech.

Advocates of homosexual marriage often proclaim that their having this "right" will have no impact on straight people or their marriages. Most of those saying this are being quite disingenuous, since they know very well that it is likely to change what can be preached in churches and the right to speak out against homosexuality. It most certainly will force all to conduct business with homosexual couples – including those who believe doing so is contributing to iniquity. In fact, I think for many such supporters, this is one of the results they hope to achieve by granting homosexuals the ability to marry.

Christians need to be proclaiming loudly and clearly (and frequently) that homosexuality is wrong. When something is stated only rarely or spoken about in hushed tones, it is much easier for opponents to make the case that such thoughts are extreme. It then becomes more acceptable to actually outlaw speech about the issue.

Part of the reason the movement toward same-sex marriage has gone so far is the fact that the church and Christians have not been speaking out against homosexuality, allowing supporters of such legislation to portray our views as out of the mainstream.

While homosexual marriage is not a rights issue, the practice of sodomy is. Many Christians have favored the retention of laws against such activity. In the past, I adopted that position also. I didn't really believe the state should try to prevent two consenting adults from engaging in a behavior just because I considered it very sinful. However, I thought we should keep such laws because we were increasingly being denied the right to discriminate against those committing these acts. For example, a Christian landlord may be sued if he or she refused to rent to a homosexual couple. If sodomy were illegal, he might have at least the argument in his defense that he is denying the prospective renters a place to practice an unlawful activity by not renting to them.

I'm not certain that legal argument has worked often anyway. I believe the proper philosophical position is to not legislate against homosexual practices, but to allow complete freedom to discriminate against those involved in them.

Another reason for eliminating sodomy laws is that they are virtually never enforced. There really never has been good justification for outlawing a voluntary act which takes place between two people. When a minor is involved, of course, the same legal prohibitions should apply as they do for heterosexual sex.

By advocating the continuation of laws against sodomy, we cannot say we are not attempting to take away homosexual rights. This will make us appear to be anti-freedom and weaken our position against homosexual marriage – which should be our most important emphasis. There have always been people who engaged in a variety of sexually immoral behaviors and that will continue to be the case. But just because society does not outlaw these activities does not mean it should give its approval to them by enshrining them in the law.

Rather than trying to retain such laws, we should focus on preventing same-sex marriage. We should just as strongly oppose laws allowing civil unions between same-sex partners. Implementation of those laws would go just as far in taking away the rights of private parties by forcing them to deal with homosexual couples as though they were married.

In our opposition, we should stress that such marriages and/or unions are not about homosexual rights – that they, in fact, take away the rights of citizens. We should also cite the fact that such relationships go against nature and have been accepted in almost no cultures in history. Even in this country a very few decades ago, a homosexual couple who wished to marry was covered in the news of the weird. I think a majority still recognize, instinctively, that for society to acknowledge such aberrant behavior as natural and give it its stamp of approval is wrong.

Some libertarian-leaning people (including some Christians) believe the solution to the controversy regarding who can marry is to remove the government from the situation altogether. Churches would, as they do today, marry people, and Christians could consider only those who had such a ceremony as actually married before God. The libertarian in me initially reacts positively to this suggestion.

However, this does not address situations where it is important that there be a formal, legal recognition by government of marital unions. One is where a person has died intestate. It can be hard enough as it is to sort out the issues in inheritance cases, but with no legal recognition of a relationship between spouses, a person who may have lived in a conjugal union with the deceased person for years or even decades could be left with no legal standing to receive an inheritance they may have helped create.

In disputes over children, it is also necessary in some cases to have a formal recognition of marriage to determine who has a legitimate claim on custody of such kids. It is likely that, in most jurisdictions, that would mean a homosexual pair would not be able to adopt a child. This would be a case where homosexuals might say they are being denied a freedom. However, government involvement in custody cases is to act on behalf of a child who is not able to care for himself. It must do so in the best interest of that child, which would not be served by being in a homosexual home. Although couples – including those who have been unable to conceive – may fulfill a desire by adding a young person to their family, adoption isn't really about the parents; it is doing what is right for the children's welfare.

I don't think a lot of homosexuals would be happy with a hands-off policy by government. If it would be instituted, it could then be said they weren't being discriminated against because the government isn't recognizing any marriage – gay or straight. However, I believe what many of them want is the stamp of approval conferred on their relationship by the state. So, they would see a policy of no recognition of marriage as lacking.

This is an issue where Christians with libertarian leanings will have differences with some others of that persuasion. Most believers will not want the government to give any legitimacy to a homosexual union, nor will they want those in such arrangements to be able to adopt children.

I think that if libertarians would think this through and see how homosexual marriage would force people to deal with such couples and would restrict their rights to speak out against such relations, they would have misgivings about granting them the right to marry.

One of the problems with some libertarians is that they see a situation where all laws conform to the ideal of liberty. But in the real world, one set of laws may follow that ideal, while others related to it are far from it. So for some issues one needs to look at how making a particular change will work in the current political context. For example, many might agree with libertarians that the government should not be involved in education. However, since that is not likely to happen for some time, we have to deal with a situation where government is still heavily involved. I believe working for local control of schools is a good intermediate goal. However, in that situation, policies will be set by school boards and administrations that involve values with which not all in a particular district will agree.

More pertinent to the immediate discussion, libertarians should agree that people should be able to form their own views about homosexuality and speak out against it if they believe it is wrong. They would also believe one should be able to elect to do business with whom they wish – including not, for instance, renting a room to a homosexual couple in a hotel or bed and breakfast. However, as long as we have anti-discrimination laws and an anti-discrimination mindset in the courts, such freedoms will likely be taken away if homosexuality is given the legitimacy that comes with a formal recognition of marriage by the government.

I'm not sure I like the current system where a couple has to get a marriage license, since that implies they need to get the government's permission to wed. A simple requirement that they register their marriage should be adequate.

Supporters of homosexual "rights" accuse their opponents of being hateful. I personally know no one who hates homosexuals – certainly no Christian. I think most of those advocating for homosexuals know few, if any, of those on the other side hate them. They just accuse them of being hateful as a strategic way of portraying themselves as victims. Accusing conservatives of "hate" is one of the key *ad hominem* attacks by the left (along with calling us "racists"). Christians don't hate alcoholics – we hate the destruction it brings to their lives. In the same way, we hate the sin of homosexuality for the way it harms those practicing it. In both cases, hating the activities is really an indication of love for the individual, since we don't want them to hurt themselves through such practices. If one truly hated alcoholics or homosexuals, they would want them to continue in those lifestyles to their ultimate ruin.

Activist courts have, in some cases, implemented same-sex marriage through their rulings. They justify such decisions by saying laws requiring marriage partners to be of opposite sex are discriminatory and/or do not provide equal protection of the law. But at the time when the federal and all state constitutions were passed, no one would have even thought of placing any statements in their documents regarding gender in marriage. Marriage had been assumed to be between a man and a woman for centuries. The joining of a man and a woman was the very definition of marriage. It still is, regardless of laws that say otherwise. It would have been totally unnecessary to define marriage in any constitution.

When courts rule that requiring a marriage to be between a man and woman is unconstitutional, they are clearly not following the original intent of the constitution they cite, since the drafters of those documents would not have, in their time, had any other intent than a man/woman marriage. This is another example of courts using the words (or lack thereof) to say what they want them to say rather than what they obviously would have meant at the time of their insertion in a constitution.

Another aspect to this issue is that the public should in no way be responsible for correcting any physical or emotional problems resulting from homosexuals' destructive lifestyles. For government to provide programs addressing such ills is really to subsidize immorality.

I believe enough people still believe in traditional marriage that our response to calls for same-sex marriage should be, "You've got to be kidding" and "Are you serious?" We should not even consider such proposals to be legitimate in any way.

The decision on marriage should be made at the state level. Some may want to create a federal law or constitutional amendment to define marriage as between a man and a woman. However, having the national government decide the issue means they could also pass legislation approving homosexual marriages. It is better to leave it at the state level to ensure the people in a state are not forced to accept such marriages. The only law at the federal level should be one that says one state is not required to accept a homosexual marriage performed in another state.

Government Control of Drugs

Before embarking on a discussion of the legality of mind-altering drugs, I want to clearly state without doubt that God disapproves of them, and no Christian should engage in their use. That is not the issue. The question is whether it is wise or right for government to try to control them.

One of the most controversial issues with moral connotations is the question of the use of such drugs. I will deal with this since many more people are questioning whether government should be outlawing such activity. It has been one of the questions I have wrestled with the most. It has been a dilemma for me since, philosophically, I do not believe in legislating against activities carried out voluntarily. But I also have had this nagging thought that maybe it should be prohibited, because it is such a big problem and often has such terrible results.

I think the fallacy I followed was that government should be a problem solver. Government really should ensure an environment where citizens can individually and collectively work to solve problems. And, while government is quite good at creating problems, it is notoriously poor at solving them.

While one cannot dispute the tragic consequences of using narcotics, those supporting the continuation of drug laws have made some assumptions that might not be valid. The first is that how bad something is should be the criterion for whether it should be illegal. Second, they have assumed such laws have really helped the situation and that, without their presence, the problem would be even worse. Third, they have not considered the possibility that the collateral effects of such laws may actually be greater than the direct consequences of drug use itself.

Problems Related to the Increased Price of Drugs

What has happened with the banning of drugs is what always happens when the supply of anything is restricted: prices have escalated dramatically. This has greatly increased the incentive to engage in the production and distribution of prohibited drugs. This, too, is economically what one would expect. Those contemplating the participation in an illegal activity will weigh the potential penalties against expected rewards and benefits. The lucrative gain to be made from selling drugs has convinced an increasing number to decide the possible punishments are worth the risks involved.

The great rewards of their activity have turned the drug trade into a high-stakes game. Participants are subject to very serious penalties so they are willing to do anything to avoid detection and apprehension by the authorities, including the things criminals do: steal, cheat, and kill. This activity can get so bad that it totally disrupts society as in the case of Mexican border towns. And because drugs became so expensive, many who are hooked on them resort to stealing to maintain their habit.

Because of the potential for obtaining large profits, many ghetto youths see selling drugs as a way out of lives of hopelessness and despair. It brings them status as well as money. Due to the huge profits, everyone involved with distributing drugs has a major incentive to get others hooked on them. As a result of such pushing, it is possible the problem is much worse than it would be if drugs were legal, although we can't really know for certain.

Another negative of the artificially high prices is that land in countries in South America and Asia gets used to grow crops for producing drugs. This is land which would otherwise be used to grow food and raw materials to use for beneficial purposes. Further damage is done when this leads to shortages of such crops and the consequent increases in prices. This most often happens in poor countries where obtaining the needed crops is difficult enough without this added burden.

The War on Drugs Empowers Government

Ancillary effects of our drug policy relating to how it empowers government also come into play. Civil liberties have been curtailed in the effort to apprehend drug dealers – things such as "no-knock" search warrants. Such practices set precedents for law enforcement abuses in general. At the federal level, the only constitutional authority for dealing with drugs is the possible function of restricting entry of drugs into the country.

And how just are some of the drug laws? Some jurisdictions have very severe penalties for a person consuming even a very small amount of a drug and/or for first-time use. The rationale is usually that drugs are such a bad thing in our society that there must be harsh penalties for any use to prevent it completely. But punishment should be commensurate with the infraction committed. A young person who uses a small amount of a narcotic may just be experimenting as youth do, or it may only be a one-time experience. They aren't hurting anyone but themselves. Is it really fair or just to apply a severe punishment if they are caught? Such a person is then a criminal and this could start them down the road to a life of crime.

From a pragmatic standpoint, drug laws may well produce more problems than they solve, by actually causing those who would not otherwise do so to use narcotics. But, as has been pointed out throughout this book, the prime determinant of an illegal activity is whether the person performing it is taking away another's rights. Based on that criterion, I do not believe using drugs in itself should be illegal. We need to have a view that is as consistent as possible about what should be against the law.

That being said, it doesn't mean there should be no laws regarding narcotics. For instance, when I was in Amsterdam a number of years ago, the smell of marijuana permeated the air in their main downtown shopping district. Non-users should not have to put up with having to breathe such smoke in public areas. It is essential that laws against being under the influence on highways, streets, and roads apply to drugs as well as alcohol. Laws against getting minors hooked on mind-altering substances could also be put into place. But if drugs were legal and no longer so expensive, such pushing would not likely be as much of a problem since the incentive for creating new users would be greatly reduced.

With this issue, we again see the government taking a problem that primarily affects a small number of people who participate in an activity and, by legislating against it, creating additional problems that affect all of society. If drugs were legal, it would mostly be drug consumers who would be impacted by their use. But since they have been outlawed, it has led to increased theft, murder, etc. Some will say a person's drug use does affect others – like their family and friends. That is true. No one is so isolated that their actions do not impact others. A husband and a father who becomes addicted may neglect his family and fail to provide for them. That is also true of a man who is lazy and won't work or spends too much time away from his wife and kids. Consequences for poor life choices often affect others, but government cannot monitor all aspects of our lives to see if we are living up to some standard.

Billions of dollars have been spent by various levels of government in recent decades to eradicate drugs, yet their use is greater than ever. The main effect of these efforts has been to give greater power to government.

If drugs were legalized, their use should never be a mitigating circumstance when convicting or punishing a person of any crime. If a person freely decides to place themselves under a mood altering substance, they must take full responsibility for anything they do while in their impaired condition.

No government agency should take any responsibility toward rehabilitating people who become addicted to any drug. With freedom comes responsibility. It is not right to saddle taxpayers with the costs of anyone's unwise decisions. Of course, Christian ministries should work to help people in this situation. It also has to be acknowledged that if drugs were legalized, all the problems caused by the laws would not immediately go away since the large number of people who have become addicted would still be hooked.

When Can a Christian Disobey Government?

I have posited that governments should be moral toward their subjects and that they should not generally enforce morality among citizens. However, what about the moral obligations of residents of a jurisdiction to its government? In general, they should be expected to obey its laws, but there are exceptions.

Government is an institution ordained by God. The Scripture that most directly addresses this is Romans 13:1- 5. In it, Paul tells us to be obedient to government authorities. Yet, when Peter and John were told by authorities to stop preaching, they disobeyed. Peter told them, *We must obey God rather than men* (Acts 5:29), indicating we should obey direct commands of God – even if forbidden by government. By inference, we can also say, conversely, that if we are directed by government to do something prohibited by God, we should also disobey.

Most Bible-believing Christians would agree with that, but when it gets beyond such clear cases, answers don't come as easily. It takes some further analysis to determine what is proper.

What About Disobedience to Prevent Abortion?

If believers regard abortion as murder, is it proper to try to prevent others from terminating the lives of the unborn? Since government has mandated abortion is legal, we would be disobeying the law if we made such an attempt. The effort would quickly be quelled by authorities. Some have actually murdered abortionists and justified it by saying they are defending the rights of the unborn. The Christian should reject such rationalizations since two wrongs do not make a right. If such methods were to be sanctioned by Christians and engaged in widely, they would turn many people against the pro-life movement. The reduction in sympathy for the cause would decrease the likelihood that legislation preventing or restricting abortions would be passed. It would also seriously dissuade many from considering a commitment to become a Christian.

It is proper for a person to take action to prevent the murder of another human. It is considered both morally and legally right to go to the length of killing another to stop a murder. So, some might say that if abortion is murder, it should also be justifiable to take action against an abortionist (up to, and including, killing him) to prevent him from killing not just one human, but many. The difference in the two situations is that abortion is considered legal by law enforcement agencies whereas murders of others are not. Although Christians may believe abortion to be murder, it has been deemed to be legal and thus illegal to prevent someone from engaging in it.

An important distinction needs to be made between laws that mandate we disobey God or prevent us from doing so, and those that merely allow a person to disobey God. If government eventually commands health care professionals to provide abortions (and this could happen), a Christian doctor would have to refuse to perform an abortion and believing nurses should not participate in the procedure. However, it is not acceptable to try to prevent others from taking part in an action like abortion which the government has been deemed to be legal – even though we know it to be wrong.

God Raises up Governments

The form and boundaries of various governments have changed over the years. The methods whereby they have changed have involved rebellions, coups, etc. If we believe God raises up all governments, then when a major change in the rule of a given country occurs, we must believe God raised up both the old regime and the one that replaced it. So, if Christians participated in an effort to replace one set of authorities with another, they would have been helping God to raise up a government.

But how did these believers determine in advance of their decision to help overthrow a government, that this was God's intention? If the effort failed, does it mean it wasn't God's desire to create a new government? Were the Christians who participated in the attempt then being disobedient? That would not necessarily be true, since we know doing God's will does not always result in what we consider a positive outcome. Success is not always a good criterion to judge whether an action performed was in God's will.

Part of the difficulty in sorting such things out is caused by the way some biblical commentators have encouraged us to look at God's working, His will, and how He achieves His purposes. God ultimately does accomplish His goals, but, in the process, men and women, both individually and collectively, do things He does not desire them to do.

Those actions cannot be said to be His will. He certainly would prefer to realize His goals through those acting in obedience to Him. However, because sinful man rebels against God and His laws, He is forced to work within that reality to arrive at the situation He desires. He could squelch the evil actions of men, but He often allows them to proceed to facilitate His larger purposes. But to believe He actually wills the existence of corrupt governments means a believer working against those governments would be opposing the will of God. It would also mean God wills the existence of governments like Nazi Germany, the Soviet Union and Communist China which murdered millions of their own citizens.

Since we really cannot know whether God wishes a set of rulers in a given country to remain in place or to be supplanted, a Christian considering possible involvement in overthrowing a government needs to use criteria to determine if such action is proper. A government murdering its own citizens would be one situation that qualifies as a valid reason to attempt to remove it. Another is when no provision exists to make changes through peaceful, legal means. A government that severely threatens the spread of the gospel is also a candidate for replacement.

God does ordain the concept of civil government, but that does not mean He approves of all the specific governments that exist at a particular point in time. Nor does He favor all of their leaders. Some governments were established by evil men and women asserting their free will to oppose God.

What about Evil Governments?

In the last century, the world saw the rise of a diabolical system called communism which ruled over many nations. These governments were, in fact, a cause for fear for even those on their best behavior – in contrast to the government Paul describes in Romans 13. These governments used fear and terror – not as a deterrent for doing evil – but rather to maintain their power and prevent any dissent from their rule. Their authority was not used as a minister of God for good and against evil. Their rulers were actually themselves personifications of evil.

Governments like this should not even be considered legitimate based on the criteria in Romans 13. They were more of a criminal gang than a government. However, while they were in control they did also provide the police powers any government uses to fight crimes like robbery and murder. A Christian living in such a place is obligated to observe the laws covering those crimes. They could not, for example, say that because the government is evil, it is okay for them to steal from their neighbor. It is apparent this is the type of law we are told to obey in Romans 13. In that way a government – even one that is otherwise evil – is a minister of God for good as stated in verse 4. These verses are not intended to give *carte blanche* for government to ride roughshod over its citizens. This is confirmed by 1 Timothy 2:2 where it says we are to obey government so we can lead tranquil and quiet lives. Subjects of a jurisdiction cannot have such lives when their government actually terrorizes them, as some have done.

When a movement such as communism or nazism seizes control of a country, a Christian should in no way cooperate in its evil ends. It should be appropriate to actively oppose it as did Dietrich Bonheoffer in Germany when he participated in a plot to assassinate Hitler. And Corrie Ten Boom and her family were certainly justified in hiding Jews from the Nazis. There really isn't any way to reform a government like this. The only way to prevent it from carrying out its wicked program is to overthrow it or thwart its efforts.

Obedience to Constitutional Law

In the United States, we operate on the basis of being a government of laws – rather than men. That idea is embodied at the national level in our written Constitution – which is really the law for the rulers. So, what about a situation where rulers disobey this law that governs them? This is not a hypothetical situation. Our Constitution clearly limits the purview of the Federal government. It is further constrained by the Tenth Amendment which states: "The powers not delegated to the United States by the Constitution, nor prohibited by it to the States, are reserved to the States respectively, or to the people."

Yet, Congress continually passes laws clearly outside these constitutional boundaries. The courts have allowed such legislation to go unchallenged by not construing the Constitution as originally written. Therefore, the "laws" they have passed are illegitimate in that they were passed in contravention of the ultimate civil law. It is these legislators and judges who are really the law-breakers and renegades. Are citizens bound to obey such illegitimate laws? Would a Christian who disobeys them be violating God's command "to be in subjection to the governing authorities" if the ultimate authority is the Constitution?

Is it more right to be obedient to those in power even though they themselves are disobedient to the ultimate law, or would it be more proper to follow that law even if it meant defying the authorities who are thumbing their noses at it? In a nation with a government of laws rather than men, one could make a case that a Christian's loyalty and obedience should be first to the ultimate law (the Constitution) rather than disobedient men.

In some of these situations, rulers are reprimanded by the court system for overstepping their authority. One of the ways to contest unconstitutional laws is by bringing cases to court. This happens when laws are challenged by a person or party disobeying them to test their constitutionality. Is such an action justified for a Christian if the intent is to rectify an infringement of the Constitution? I don't believe it would be wrong to do so to preserve the integrity of the Constitution – the ultimate governmental authority.

In Revelation, we are told people are not to take the mark of the Beast. Yet, this is a requirement made by the Antichrist who is a ruling authority – actually the highest on the earth at the time. What he requires is not something that would cause a person to disobey one of God's laws laid down in Scripture. It is really an economic rule – a mandate that one bends to his authority to be able to buy and sell. It appears what God is opposed to here is anyone cooperating in any way with an evil authority. This is a very specific command for a particular situation at a given time. Yet, it does seem to indicate that when a government becomes obviously evil and opposed to God (like communism), He would not want us to cooperate with it. As we see the growth of the world system prophesied in the Bible, at what point do we actively oppose it? There may not be easy answers to such questions, but Christians need to be asking them.

Chapter 6

Life and Health Issues

Protection of Life

I will not have too much to say here since this is one issue Christian commentators and activists have covered quite thoroughly. Among conservative believers, we find a great deal of agreement about what protection of life entails, although some differences exist regarding the strategy of how to approach the effecting of the desired outcome.

Protection for Murderers?

Self-styled pro-choicers often say one of the reasons killing pre-born babies should be legal is to prevent back-alley abortions where some pregnant women would die from complications. They claim this happened when abortion was illegal. I'm sure it occurred occasionally. Whether it did frequently is debatable.

However, the frequency of such incidences is not the most important issue. A woman who decides to have an abortion intends to kill another human being. Before this practice was made legal, she would have been committing a crime when submitting to the procedure. The rationale by pro-abortionists is basically that abortion needed to be legalized so it could be done safely. It makes as much sense to say that since so many armed robbers are getting killed in the process of committing their crime, we ought, therefore, to legalize armed robbery to keep the act safe. It is actually worse than that since what the woman who terminates her pregnancy is doing is killing her baby. So legalizing abortion to protect such a woman is equivalent to legalizing murder so killers can do it safely.

Abortion Will Remain an Issue

Prior to the Roe versus Wade decision, there was a push for legalization of abortion through legislation. If that decision were to be overturned, it is likely abortion would be legalized in some states. The problem with the Supreme Court decision is that nothing in the Constitution indicated this is an issue that should be addressed at the national level.

Virtually all Americans believe murder should be outlawed. However, other than some exceptional cases like those involved in killing a federal officer, the laws against it have always been limited to those enacted at the state level. That was also the case with abortion laws prior to *Roe vs. Wade*. The ideal solution would be to have that case reversed by another Supreme Court ruling. However, that depends on a change in the composition of the court. There is an easier way. Article III, Section 2 states that the court has jurisdiction with such exceptions as Congress makes. This means Congress can remove any cases regarding abortion from the Court's bailiwick. Congressman Ron Paul introduced a bill to do just that, but it surprisingly got little support from pro-lifers. The passage of such a law would effectively allow states to legislate once again in the area of abortion without interference from the federal courts.

If the courts would no longer prevent abortion legislation, I'm sure some would attempt to get a national law passed that would outlaw abortions. However, we as conservatives – particularly those who are Christians – need to be consistent. We can't cite the lack of authorization in the Constitution in opposing laws with which we disagree and then turn around and seek a law on abortion for which no federal authority exists. Another problem with such an approach is that if a national law against abortions can be enacted, then one permitting them for the whole country can also be passed.

It is better to pass state laws against abortion wherever possible once the judicial roadblocks have been removed. Congress could pass a Human Life Amendment recognizing an unborn baby as having legal standing as a human being. However, battles would flare up in many of the states over ratification of such an amendment. It would take a considerable amount of time before three-fourths of the states would approve it. It is likely this would never happen. It is better to get as many states as possible to pass laws and at least save the lives of some babies.

We, realistically, need to recognize it is unlikely all states would do this. So, babies will continue to be killed, as much as we would like to completely end such murders. The reason is the great moral and spiritual darkness in the land and a severe lack of respect for life. The judicial issue has allowed the taking of a huge number of God's creations since 1973, but removing that hurdle will not stop the bloodshed completely due to the great moral deficiency in this country.

It is proper for states to pass laws against abortion, but the killing likely won't be completely stopped until the United States experiences a revival and/or a major moral reformation.

Health Care

Health care is a hot topic as this book is being written in 2013. Legislation has been enacted by Congress that substantially increases the federal government's role in medicine. Since it was passed during the administration of Barack Obama with his strong support, it has become known as Obamacare. Provisions of the bill were being challenged in court, but the Supreme Court ruled it is constitutional. So, I will address the issue based on what I believe is philosophically correct, how I believe Christians should approach it, and what we could expect the results of certain policies would likely be, based on past history.

A Health Care System?

Most who deal with this issue make references to our nation's healthcare "system." This implies medical care is one organic unity and is something that can be directed and should be addressed as a whole. We don't look upon the delivery of other services as part of a system (with the notable exception of education). For example, the establishments where we go to get our vehicles repaired are not generally referred to as "the automobile service system." Neither should we do that with medicine.

I don't know when or how it started being applied to medical care, and it is likely most people use the term out of a habit developed from hearing it so often. However, I believe it is purposely being used by those who wish all medicine to be controlled by government, so others will get used to thinking of healthcare as being one "system." We need to go back to thinking and speaking of medical care as part of a marketplace that offers all types of services and products – not as a "system."

In a sense, it already has become a system because of steps government has taken that have standardized many aspects of care and which have inhibited competition. This interference with market forces that should be in play with the delivery of medical services, along with the large percentage of costs paid by third parties like insurance companies and government programs, have been the primary culprits in the dramatic increase in costs.

Healthcare Costs are Too High

The one thing most will agree on is that medical costs are too high. But many people try to address that situation without a rigorous analysis as to what is driving up the costs. There seems to be more concern with trying to come up with programs that allow the rising costs to be met by everyone rather than with identifying their source and bringing them down. Most proposals just deal with treating symptoms and are not really getting at the factors causing the problem of high costs. It is likely any programs implemented will drive up the total cost of US healthcare – even though subsidies may, in fact, reduce what some are paying. These increased costs would be consistent with what we have seen happen with programs like Medicare and Medicaid.

When products and services are allowed to be sold freely, competition drives down costs and increases quality. In fact, competition is normally the only thing that actually minimizes the cost of anything sold in the marketplace. The amount of government regulation in our country has some impact on the ability to sell all products competitively. However, markets for most items are still relatively free. Not so with healthcare and health insurance.

If government were drastically to reduce its regulation of healthcare and health insurance, there is no reason to believe costs would not go down dramatically as happens with other products and services allowed to be sold competitively. Some say things like healthcare (and education) are too important to be operated on a for-profit basis. In reality, they are actually too important not to be run that way, since it is the profit motive that drives down costs and increases quality.

Currently, a major area of government intervention in the medical field is the Medicare system. The program dictates how much can be reimbursed for given medical procedures for a Medicare recipient. This is frequently less than the amount normally charged. Healthcare institutions then increase charges to other patients to make up for revenue lost through Medicare clients – driving up overall costs.

The fact that most patients have insurance has contributed to cost increases in various ways. Medical personnel who know a person is covered will more readily prescribe various tests and procedures. Many nonessential procedures are performed. A patient who has insurance is less likely to question whether a course of treatment is really necessary. When they get their bills, such patients are not as concerned about whether charges are correct. The amount of administrative overhead is also substantially increased with insurance.

I once had a cholesterol check which the insurance I had at the time would likely have covered. I received a bill within a short time with a note that instructed me not to pay it since it had been submitted to my insurance company. I believe the charge was $59 (it could have been $69). I continued to get this bill for several months with the same note regarding the insurance. Concerned it had not been paid, I called the clinic and was told the reason for the delay was that the person who administered the procedure was not in the insurance company's system and had to be added. When the bills kept coming, I called again several months later and was told the claim had expired and they were going to re-submit it. So, the bills kept coming. Then they stopped. This also concerned me since I had received no notice that it had been paid, and I wanted to make sure it somehow didn't show up as a blot on my credit standing. So, I called again. They told me they had cancelled the bill and were writing it off.

That means the clinic never got paid for the cholesterol check, plus they spent who knows how much in an attempt to get the payment. It was probably considerably more than the charged amount. Such situations likely happen fairly frequently. Some of them might involve much more costly procedures. Charges that are written off end up being covered by increased charges to cover losses. And the amount of effort required to track such incidences increases the cost of administration. It all adds up to greater medical charges, which in turn increases insurance premiums.

Until recently, I had a high-deductible health policy, so I ended up paying a lot of medical bills myself. Naturally, I didn't want to pay for anything billed incorrectly, so I looked closely at each line of the bills to make sure the charge was proper. The description is often incomprehensible and doesn't match the language used by medical personnel when they discuss services with a patient. Sometimes I could figure it out, but, on other occasions, I called to verify the billing. Once I was told the insurance company had to use standard billing codes and descriptions by government edict. That figures! Trust the government to come up with a system with descriptions difficult to decipher. And all the calls that medical facilities get from people like me add to their costs also. The other problem with the government-enforced code standardization is that it is one more step toward making our healthcare a system controlled by the government.

Who Should Pay for Healthcare?

Insurance companies expect to make a profit. If they don't, they will go out of business. The current belief of many is that all their medical costs should be covered by insurance. This attitude tends to remove incentive for either the user or provider to control costs. This forces insurance companies to raise premiums – which then eventually become a burden for individuals and families.

If government pays, funds will come from one of these sources: taxpayers, borrowing, or by printing more money. If the funds are borrowed, taxpayers will still ultimately be responsible for the bill as they pay off the debt accumulated. Printing more money to cover costs creates inflation which everyone pays for in reduced purchasing power and erosion of savings.

If health care is considered a right, then everyone will be entitled to it whether they contribute anything to its cost or not. If some people pay little or nothing, then others will cover them either through taxes, increased insurance premiums, or inflation. Those other people need to work to be able to take care of those costs. This means some are forced to take actions to maintain others' health care. Nothing which requires an action by another party can be a right (see discussion of rights in Chapter 4).

In this country, up until the early 20th century, everyone paid for their own medical bills. In the 1920s and 1930s, Blue Cross organizations started offering hospital and medical expense insurance. Everyone then had a choice. They could either purchase such insurance or, if they believed over time their costs wouldn't exceed the price of premiums, they could continue to pay their own way. For a number of years a great number of people elected to do just that.

Insurance was a product on the market that people could choose either to purchase or not purchase. As medical costs rose and more people started choosing that option, it began to be viewed by many as essential and by some as an entitlement everyone should have – even if it meant someone else had to pick up the tab.

My grandfather died in 1964 – just before the Medicare law was enacted. Prior to his death, he was hospitalized for about a week. His total bill for everything was $141. There has been considerable inflation since then, but certainly not enough to account for what such a bill would be today. My grandparents didn't have insurance, but this bill didn't break my grandmother. The two of them did not have much income or savings. If they even got Social Security, it was a very limited amount. If they didn't need a Medicare system, I don't believe anyone did. The reality is that the system was not established due to great need, but to get the government camel's nose into the healthcare tent.

When HMOs (government-created entities) entered the scene, people started thinking in terms of what they called insurance as pre-paid healthcare. More wanted to pay a fixed amount and have everything covered. Although it is still called insurance, it really isn't in the same sense as policies that cover things like our houses and cars. Those types of insurance cover extraordinary events – not our ongoing repair costs. The number of people covered by insurance also expended greatly due to tax policies that encouraged companies to cover a good portion of the premium cost for their employees.

The costs even for medical check-ups and the correction of minor problems have risen so dramatically that they can be almost like disasters to the financial budgets of many people.

Should Everyone Have Health Insurance?

It is assumed when addressing healthcare that all should be covered by insurance. That assumption is based on the fact that due to very high medical cost all but the wealthy need it to pay large medical bills without being broken financially. The reason we assume all need insurance is the high cost of medical care – which is the root problem. If that problem were alleviated, it would no longer be necessary for all to have insurance and it would no longer be an assumption that everyone needed it. Trying to come up with a solution that ensures all are covered actually prevents the addressing of the real problems causing escalating costs. If we freed up the medical marketplace so its services were once again provided competitively and reasonably, many people may elect to forego insurance or carry only policies covering catastrophes.

Of course, the increased cost of medical care has also caused the price for health insurance to rise dramatically. Government has also contributed to the increase in such insurance by mandating standard policies cover virtually everything. This is tantamount to enforced subsidization by making all pay for coverage they may not really want, and which only benefits others. For instance, all policyholders pay for the great medical expense incurred by AIDS patients.

Without such mandates, companies could offer tailored policies in which a person only pays for the insurance they want. Many might elect not to have coverage for AIDS and their premiums would be less – possibly considerably. Of course, those who wished to include coverage for AIDS would have to pay more since they are no longer being subsidized by those who have elected not to get such coverage. This is only proper and fair.

In the case of AIDS, policyholders are not only paying for others' healthcare, but actually being forced to subsidize immoral behavior, which is a factor in some cases of AIDS infection. If government would remove mandates, insurance rates would likely be a lot lower for most people.

Another issue is the inability of those with pre-existing conditions to obtain insurance. As much as one can sympathize with that dilemma, the proper solution is not to force insurance companies to provide them coverage. If one looks at the situation logically, it would, as someone has said, be equivalent to forcing a company to write a fire policy on a home when it has already started burning.

If we truly had a free market in medicine, the costs would be greatly reduced, and not being able to get insurance wouldn't be as great a calamity. It is also likely that, with freedom, policies would be available to those with existing conditions – with a higher price tag, which is appropriate.

The purported aim of getting government more involved in medicine is better care for more people. But, as is the case whenever government gets involved, other unfavorable consequences surface. As there is more intrusion into health care, many doctors are likely to get frustrated with having to deal with the bureaucracy. Some, possibly many, will retire early or just quit and go into some other type of work. It is also likely fewer men and women will enter a so highly regulated medical field. If those things happen, it will result in less care, rather than more.

A Christian View

How should Christians look at the issue of healthcare? First, being aware of the fallen nature of man, they should realize people will take advantage of any system that government subsidizes. Those paying little or nothing for medical care will overuse the available services.

This causes an increase in demand for those services. That has been the experience with places that have installed socialized medicine. The greater demand causes backlogs and waiting lists for those requiring critical care. Ultimately, for some, this causes complications and even death. Christians should also acknowledge the serious moral problem of using the power of government to force some in society to subsidize the health care of others. As with other types of benefit programs from government, believers should not expect that their costs will be borne by others.

CHAPTER 7

School and Work Issues

'Tis Education forms the common mind, Just as the Twig is bent the Tree's inclined. – Alexander Pope, *Epistle to Cobham, I*

Education

Education is an issue about which Christians should be very concerned – particularly if they have children. Many believers have elected to teach their children at home or send them to a Christian school. Those who have chosen to use one of those options, as well as those with no children currently being formally educated, should still be concerned about what takes place in the public schools.

All taxpayers should certainly be interested in how the public schools spend their money. They will want to make certain educational funds are not being used in a wasteful manner, but are spent in a wise and efficient way. But more importantly, they should be concerned with what is being taught in schools and the educational methods being used. Students of today will be running our businesses and institutions tomorrow. They will be voters and some will be involved in aspects of our political system. As such they will ultimately determine the direction of our country and our civilization. So, education is something all citizens have a stake in and with which they should be concerned.

What Should Be Taught in the Classroom?

When thinking about curriculum, the starting point for a believer is that what is being taught is consistent with a Christian worldview. The way one looks at the world will impact how one approaches most subjects. The degree to which that is true will vary for different disciplines. For instance, the teaching of math would not generally depend too much on the worldview of the instructor.

In today's United States, it is doubtful whether a majority agrees with the basic tenets of a Christian worldview. Indeed, many believers themselves do not even consistently apply a Christian worldview to the affairs of life. In the past, much more agreement with the basics of Christianity existed – at least from an intellectual standpoint. The teaching in public schools was directed primarily from local levels. And at least within individual communities there was a fairly broad consensus about the values that should be part of education.

Those who misconstrue the First Amendment today claim that religion must be totally separated from government. Therefore, they say this must apply in schools. However, Christians will not want the teaching of most subjects to be separated from religion. We believe that those subjects are intimately intertwined with a religious perspective. In some cases, leaving out a reference to religion by default is assuming an atheistic view – which is just as much a religious perspective as is that of Christianity, Islam, or Buddhism, etc.

Since it is impossible to separate religious beliefs from education, it should really be separated from the state. No good philosophical reason supports education being a function of government. Since the separation of schooling from government may not happen for some time, or possibly ever, a way of handling such issues for the present must be addressed. The first requirement is that teaching must be truthful. To teach school students about the Pilgrims and the first Thanksgiving without a mention of God is patently dishonest. To teach about the founding of our nation with no mention of the Christian influence is very misleading at best. If education were to be controlled at the local level, it would be less likely to have such an anti-Christian bias. However, in recent decades, schools have been increasingly controlled by the state and federal governments. So, even where substantial agreement still exists on education in a local community, decisions have been taken out of the hands of parents and school boards at that level.

What About School Funding?

The trend of more control over education passing to higher levels of government is related to where it gets its funding. Ideally, if we wish to have local control over education, it should primarily be funded at that level. The problem is that property taxes are the main source of revenue for local government, but such taxes should be used primarily for property-related services like roads, police, fire protection, and parks. It really isn't fair to saddle seniors and those without children with higher taxes to cover a service for which they get no direct benefit. If all education were to be financed by property taxes, they would likely be so high they would force many elderly and others on fixed incomes from homes in which they have lived, in some cases, most of their lives.

In most cases, a substantial portion of school funding ends up coming from state tax sources. And what the state funds, it also has a tendency to regulate. Thus, local control is substantially reduced. When the rules from the state touch on curriculum, they are usually not favorable to a Christian outlook in today's society.

Since no good local source for school funding exits, and because it is hard in a pluralistic society to get agreement on what should be taught and how it should be taught, education really should be separated from government.

Absent that reality, another possibility would be to finance schools with a local income tax (at a city or even school-district level). This should only be done if there is a corresponding reduction in state income taxes. With such a funding system there would be less justification for trying to control school policy from the state government, since they would not be providing the financing. Since a good share of most states' budgets goes to finance public education, it should result in a large decrease in taxes from that level. And a statewide educational bureaucracy would no longer be needed.

Teaching About Our National Values

The main justification for making education a public concern should be to instruct children in our country's heritage to create well-informed citizens. But this really isn't being done today anyway. In general, even by the time they have completed their secondary education; many students in the public schools have little understanding of what went into the founding of the United States. What may be worse is that what they do learn about civics gives them little appreciation for the Christian underpinnings of our founding institutions, or the concepts of limited, constitutional government on which our nation was founded.

To ensure all students learn about our nation's heritage and institutions would require a national mandate. Even if this would start out with the information being conveyed in an accurate manner, as time goes by the teaching would likely be subverted, so a distorted view of our political system would be presented. And the national effort to transmit this information would conflict with both the Constitution and the idea of locally-controlled education.

I believe if control of education were actually returned to the communities, in most localities much more accurate information would be taught about our political system than there is today, or would be likely with state and/or federal mandates.

The Constitutional Issues

The issue of what is appropriate or constitutional to be taught in public schools has entered into many court cases. The American Civil Liberties Union (ACLU) has been the instigator of a good portion of them. Most of them have been initiated on the basis that something is being taught or promoted that putatively violates the First Amendment – predicated on the assumption that it calls for a stringent separation of government and religion.

The key point here is that the US Constitution does not mention education as a role for the federal government. The Tenth Amendment clearly states that those powers not delegated to the federal government are reserved to the states and the people. Since education is not mentioned in the Constitution, according to the Tenth Amendment, the federal government should have nothing to do with what is taught in public schools. Such lawsuits should be summarily rejected and not heard by federal courts (where most are filed) because they are not within their constitutional purview.

Many of these cases have been ruled in favor of the ACLU and its cohorts. Conservatives have tried to remedy this situation with federal legislation mandating that certain things be allowed in schools. Many Christians have supported such bills. But such laws are also unconstitutional since they, too, violate the Tenth Amendment by directing educational policy.

Conservatives can't have it both ways – protesting that the Feds shouldn't be involved in our schools when we don't like what they are pushing, and then turning around and promoting legislation that dictates school policies that we favor. We must be consistent in our advocacy. Either we should try to get to get federal legislation to specify what we want and then not complain when the left also gets laws passed, or we should fight their attempts at controlling education from Washington on a constitutional basis and not try to influence education from there ourselves.

I believe the latter approach is the proper one for several reasons. First, if the left gets its laws passed at the federal level, we have no recourse (except to repeal the law). But if we can prevent any federal influence on schools, we will stop the worst infractions. We may still have to fight bad educational policy in some states and localities, but at least it won't be imposed on the whole country. Second, schools should be locally controlled. We should not dictate these policies from Washington. Third, and probably most important, the proper construction of the Constitution mandates that education not be addressed by the federal government. To attempt to mandate a conservative agenda for schools is wrong. Christians should never advocate a course that corrupts the basic law of the land. We can see what has happened with the Constitution as this has been done in the past. As we have ignored and misconstrued it over time, it has lost its meaning and effectiveness. If we continue this process, it will become little more than a meaningless piece of paper. If we ignore and bypass it in this area, how can we justify trying to use it to preserve our rights in other areas? A constitution where portions are ignored becomes a worthless document.

However, something can be done at the federal level. Article III, Section 2 states: "In all the other Cases before mentioned, the Supreme Court shall have appellate Jurisdiction, both as to Law and Fact, with such Exceptions, and under such Regulations as the Congress shall make." Congress should restrict the federal courts, since they have refused to acknowledge the Tenth Amendment and allowed federal interference with education. Congress should use this power to remove all educational cases from the jurisdiction of federal courts. Such legislation would direct them not to take any cases related to public education.

The other thing that should be done is to legislatively get the federal government totally out of education. Conservatives have talked a lot about eliminating the Department of Education, but there hasn't really been much effort expended toward that goal. That would be a good thing, but if agencies under its umbrella are merely transferred to other cabinet jurisdictions, we will have gained nothing. It is more important to terminate all federal programs that deal in any way with education.

Action at the Local Level

We must realize that if we were to remove the federal government totally from the field of education, the fight would not be over. In some states, similar battles to repeal mandates that prevent local school districts from setting their own policies would be fought.

Many school administrators currently adopt policies that unduly keep out anything even hinting of Christianity since they are aware of legal actions in other districts and wish to avoid them. If the Feds are taken out of the picture, administrators need to be informed this is no longer necessary (although it is possible that the ACLU et al. may try to file suits alleging infractions of some states' constitutions). Where administrators personally favor a policy of severely restricting Christianity, then conservatives should go to the school board. If they get no action from them, those members who are problems need to be replaced at the next election.

Most school board elections have very poor turnouts. They are often held at times other than general elections which have higher numbers going to the polls. Often activist teachers and school employees who do turn out are able to get the people they want on the board. An organized effort by conservatives in a given district often has a good chance of attracting enough voters to elect good people. Certainly, if a substantial percent of the Christians and conservatives in many districts voted, they could have boards that reflect and implement policies based on our values. It is likely that few today make much of an effort at getting the right people elected, because they know so much is decided from state and federal levels, and those on local boards have their hands tied as far as what they can actually do.

If the federal influences were to be eliminated and the states' seriously curtailed, more citizens might be involved in attending school board meetings, lobbying members, and electing those sharing their values. A system with true local control, of course, imposes more responsibility on parents and other citizens. Reducing government always means more responsibility falls on private individuals, but it is certainly better to have it rest there than with bureaucrats.

If there were local control, there would still be a problem with the educational establishment. Whether a school is private or public, teachers should be looked on as those who have been hired by parents to teach their children what they wish to have conveyed to them. Unfortunately, many teachers and administrators believe society should determine what and how children should be taught. They consider themselves in the vanguard of those who should be directing educational content. What is taught in schools inevitably involves values. The values of educators – not those of parents – often have been imposed on students. This has been done through mandates from federal and state governments. But if those mandates stopped, there would still be attempts to continue to impact values through teachers, administrators, and school boards.

Many of the educational activists who have been influencing curriculum are antagonistic toward Christianity. Ironically (and hypocritically), they are also often the ones who are the most vocal in complaining about Christians imposing their values on others.

The Teaching of Human Origins

One educational issue very important to many Christians relates to the teaching of human origins. I do not intend to make a comprehensive case for creationism or intelligent design. Many others have done in-depth studies about such topics and this is a book about politics. However, before addressing the teaching of human origins in schools, I have a few things to say about the theory of evolution itself.

If a person were truly seeking for the truth about how humans came into being and were totally unbiased (which no one is), and had no preconceived ideas about the topic (also very unlikely), they would consider all evidence. However, those scientists who have set the agenda for studying the origin of life have determined that only scientific data can be used and no spiritual ideas can be part of the discussion. Requiring such criteria tells us that they are not really interested in finding the truth since they have ruled out some possibilities before even starting their search. Another assumption the scientific establishment has made is that only a highly-technical life scientist is capable of addressing the issue of evolution.

In fact, evolution can be refuted by those who know some basic scientific principles, are capable of logical thinking, and address probability. For example, if evolution were true, we would expect to find the material world populated by an infinite number of intermediate forms of life. We actually see only very distinct species.

It seems obvious that an organ (like an eye) could not evolve when it requires all its pieces to be in place before it can even function. Evolutionists claim organisms have changed to adapt to their environment, but none of them started with an intelligent control system like a brain. So, how did the organism determine what changes to make before it had any intelligence? How did it detect the need for a given adaptation?

One thing that is rarely mentioned, but which is a huge problem for evolution, is the development of different sexes. How did asexual organisms develop into two versions with different reproductive organs? It would have had to happen in one of two ways.

One possibility is that a particular strain of a life form developed male organs while another added female ones. But how would one know in what way the other was evolving so it could develop in a manner compatible with its ultimate sexual partner. Remember, the evolutionists' system provides for no outside intelligence to coordinate such separate developments. Also, the creation of the sexual organs would take a considerable amount of time. One would assume other parts of the two eventual partners would be changing over such a period also. Without coordination, how would there be any assurance the two life forms would even be the same type of animal by the time they had fully developed sex organs and were ready to mate? Without something common controlling their changes, maintaining compatibility would be virtually impossible.

The other way sexes could develop would be for one organism to evolve both male and female organs, and then later split in two. The question then would be why would it do so? What would be the reason for needing this adaptation? Also, when the split occurred, the original organism would have had to develop all body parts in duplicate so the two resulting offspring would have all they need. And if they did not immediately have fully formed sex organs, there would also be a problem of maintaining compatibility until they were capable of having intercourse.

Bringing the discussion back to educational policy, one key question is: "Why is it necessary to teach about human origins in science classes – particularly at primary and secondary levels?" In other disciplines (the exception being history), there usually isn't much time spent going into how that subject developed. For instance, there may be an occasional reference made to Euclid in geometry, but generally a detailed history of the subject is not included.

Even at the college level there seems to be no real need to teach those studying zoology or botany about how the life forms they study came to be. Advocates for evolution have said students will be lacking in their education if they are not taught what they consider the most advanced science of origins. But is that true? Does a doctor or nurse need to know evolutionary theory to practice medicine? Hardly. It really seems the insistence on teaching the theory of evolution is more about humanists wanting to discredit the idea of a God than it is for meeting any real need of students.

It could well be that a college or university might offer courses that study the various theories of life origins. But as previously mentioned, if they were really interested in finding the truth, they would be open to all possibilities – including spiritual ones.

These are just a few of the problems with evolution that should be discussed. In reality, humanists who control the biological scientific agenda insist the theory is established fact and will brook no thoughts that question their suppositions.

Those on the left claim public schools should be neutral regarding religion, but that is not really possible. Human origins is a good example of a subject area where the same people who purport to believe in such separation support the teaching of a theory which undermines the beliefs of Christian students.

The real answer, of course, to this question is the need to have curriculum decisions determined by local schools that teach subjects desired by parents in a manner consistent with values of the community. This would not sit well with the educational establishment that wants to impose uniformity on the populace by indoctrinating children with their values.

Other problems with public education exist. Since it is perceived to be free, it is not valued as it should be. It also promotes the idea that it is the state – rather than the parents – that is responsible for training offspring. If each family had to pay for its own education, parents would likely be more concerned that their children apply themselves in school. Church ministries could assist those families that have a financial problem paying for their children's schooling.

Employment Issues

In recent years the government has gotten more involved in employer/employee relations, so such issues have become more political. Most Christians and/or their spouses have jobs – so there is a very real possibility they will be confronted with some aspect of one of these issues.

Job Requirement Disagreements

Situations which have come up recently include those regarding whether employees should have to carry out activities that conflict with their faith. One example concerns the question of whether a pharmacist should be expected to dispense the RU486 abortion pill or birth control medicine if she is opposed to their use. In the case of the RU486, there is the question of whether it should even be lawful to sell it. But since it currently is deemed to be legal, I will address the issue with the assumption it will be sold.

For starters, no drugstore should be forced to sell them (or any other items). Such retailers are private businesses and can sell or choose not to make available whatever they wish. If a store or chain has elected to carry these products but is willing to provide some type of accommodation, so employees who object to them do not have to personally sell them, then it really becomes an issue between the merchant and any dissatisfaction the policy may cause by inconveniencing some customers. If he is unwilling to allow employees to refrain from selling the products, and such sales are part of the employee's job description, a Christian who believes it would be enabling or abetting evil to sell those products should quit his job. They should not seek legal redress since an employer has the right to set the terms of employment. A drug store owner who has elected not to carry items he doesn't believe should be used or who allows employees not to sell them may get customer complaints. He then has a decision to make – will he accede to customer demands or stick to his principles? If a retailer is a Christian who believes selling a given product is providing for the use of something he believes is wrong, he should certainly not sell it – which he has every right not to do. Government should never tell a business they have to sell anything.

Another situation has arisen where Muslims who are cashiers at grocery stores have refused to touch pork. If the store owner is willing to allow employees to ask customers to ring the pork up and/or bag it themselves, then it is a question again of dealing with customers who are unhappy with the policy. If they are unwilling to accommodate the employee, he or she needs to seek another job. There should be no legal intervention to allow an exception for the employee – since handling pork is part of the job. It will be very likely that an employer making an exception for a Muslim in this case will get customer criticism. The employer then makes a decision as to whether to ignore or put up with the complaints or possible loss of business, or to change her policy and require all employees to handle pork.

Behavior in the Workplace

An area of employment that impacts Christians is the issue of witnessing and proselytizing on the job. People talk with their fellow employees about all sorts of things. They will also solicit one another to purchase things like raffle tickets or items sold for a child's fundraiser. So, why should a discussion of religion or even an attempt to convert another to one's own beliefs be any different? Usually, this is not a problem. But sometimes a person may be quite heavy-handed in his evangelism, talk about religion too much, or do so to others who don't appreciate the topic. However, people also talk about other subjects to the point where others weary of them.

The best scenario is that the offended person just tells the speaker they do not wish to talk about a certain topic. A believer should certainly honor such a request. We really should only speak of our Christianity in a work setting when it seems pretty clear a listener is okay with our doing so. We should never be overbearing in our proselytizing at our places of employment.

There will be cases where a person complains to a supervisor or other authority in the company about a person discussing her religion. If this results in a reprimand, the person should desist from the activity. If this should happen to a believer, or an employer has a policy forbidding such discussions, the Christian should abide by it or find a job where she is free to talk about her faith. She should not assert a right to practice her religion, because an employer should be able to set the rules for the workplace.

We have freedom of religious expression in this country. However, when we take a job, we agree to do the work we were hired for and to follow any rules the employer has established.

I believe, most often, Christians will not run into problems when talking about their beliefs if they are not overbearing, don't talk incessantly about such matters, and don't speak on topics with which another is uncomfortable.

Discrimination in Hiring

There is a question as to how Christians who are employers should approach having homosexuals as employees. I believe they should treat them as any other applicants and hire them if qualified – with some exceptions.

It should go without saying that they should not be hired for ministry positions with Christian organizations, and they should definitely not be employed for working with children or youth. They should be released if they flaunt their sexuality in a way that makes other employees uncomfortable (as should any heterosexual person who acts in a similar fashion).

I believe employment has become too institutionalized in modern society. Essentially, it should be viewed as a trade of an employee's time and abilities for compensation. Too often a job is looked upon almost as a position one obtains, and a job opening is seen as a prize for which all must have an equal and fair chance to compete. The government's primary roles should be ensuring trade is undertaken by mutual agreement and that the parties adhere to any signed contract. This means a person cannot be forced to work for any individual or company. That would be slavery. It also means an employer's choice of who they hire should be just as free from outside interference as is the employee's regarding his or her choice of a particular job. Government should not try to impose any standards on who an employer hires.

If one looks at a job as a trade of labor for compensation, it changes the way one views hiring practices. Currently, laws against various kinds of discrimination exist regarding who is hired. A white person who receives an offer for a job may decline it because he finds out the person he will report to (or the owner of the company) is black. Why shouldn't there also be laws outlawing a person making a job decision on that basis. They are inappropriately discriminating just as surely as the person who decides not to hire someone based on the color of their skin. Since a job is a trade of service for pay, it would make as much sense to outlaw discrimination on the part of the one offering his labor as the party offering the compensation.

The problem really starts with the false idea that discrimination is bad. Actually, it is to make a decision – to choose. It, in itself, is morally neutral. What one chooses, and in some cases how one goes about choosing, can be value-laden. It depends on the values of the person making the decision. A believer should make choices consistent with biblical principles. When hiring people, employers should choose based only on factors that have an impact on the ability of a potential employee to do the job. It is certainly wrong to choose or not choose someone based on their race or ethnicity. The Bible clearly teaches we should not choose in such a manner.

But there are problems with making such decisions a matter for the law. One is that it takes away freedom. If freedom is to mean anything, it must allow the ability to make wrong decisions as well as right ones. It is not always clear in such cases what is right and what is wrong.

Hiring is often a very subjective process. Job seekers are not just resumes; they are flesh-and-blood humans. It usually isn't just the number of years an applicant has done a particular function. Circumstances relating to one's experience can vary considerably. Rarely will two or more candidates for a position have work records that can be quantifiably compared on an apples-to-apples basis. It often comes down to a sense that one or the other will fit into the position and the work environment better than others – what some call a gut-level feeling. Admittedly, such feelings can include prejudices against a person which may relate to their being part of some ethnic or racial group. But those feelings can sometimes be so subtle that even the person experiencing them does not realize they are influencing their evaluation of a potential employee. Should we be passing laws where a third party such as government judges what a person is thinking and tries to identify prejudicial feelings that the accused person themselves may not be aware they have?

What may be worse is the type of penalties often assessed. A person who is determined to have been passed over for a job or a promotion for prejudicial reasons is likely to be awarded pay for the time they would have worked if they had been selected for the job. Such a judgment makes a total travesty of the concept of compensation. A person normally receives remuneration for providing a service or helping make a product. A job isn't some sort of prize to be awarded to someone for having the right qualifications – particularly when the entity making the award is a third party that cannot truly understand the qualifications necessary for a position as well as those operating the company or doing the hiring. A person receiving back pay has contributed nothing in the economic equation and yet is given compensation.

Such actions by government seem to make the assumption that a person has some sort of claim on a given job and helps engender the attitude of entitlement in society. All one should have in a truly free society is the right to offer one's services and talents in the marketplace and to use them when one finds a willing buyer.

The greatest justification cited for laws outlawing discrimination has been to rectify the situation where blacks often were not hired due to their race. This was a real problem, and there is no doubt this was wrong. It was particularly bad for Christians to have made such decisions. However, this does not mean the correct way to address the problem was to take away the rights of people to choose with whom they will make economic trades.

A great example of how it should be done, and how, in fact, it was, is the case of the integration of Major League Baseball. In 1945, Branch Rickey, president and general manager of the Brooklyn Dodgers courageously signed Jackie Robinson, and he was assigned to a minor league affiliate. In 1947, Robinson started playing for the Dodgers as the first black man in the major leagues, and within a few short years, Major League Baseball was fully integrated. Robinson had some rough times his first few years as he was the target of verbal abuse and various humiliations, and that was very unfortunate. It is certainly true that blacks should have been playing in the majors much earlier. Nevertheless, without any law being passed, a situation where there were no blacks in the majors was completely turned around in a relatively short amount of time.

While anti-discrimination laws were enacted primarily to address prejudice against blacks, they have had additional ramifications. One is the perceived need to extend such "rights" to other groups. So, it has been a slide down a slippery slope that has brought our society to the point of giving such privileges to homosexuals.

Another result of such laws that is arguably even more substantial is the way it has changed the way so many have looked at rights. Instead of rights involving the ability to freely engage in mutually agreeable relationships, many now believe such rights are entitlements which effectively deny individuals and parties to use their own criteria in selecting with whom they will carry on transactions.

What About Labor Unions?

The key activity unions are involved with is negotiating with employers wage rates and benefits for their members. This is known as collective bargaining; it is perceived by union supporters to be a right. But in a free economy, individual parties negotiate and reach agreements on any market trade. This holds true also for a job where an employer and a prospective employee agree on terms – including pay. A person considering a job may elect to ask an agent to represent them in working out the details of compensation, benefits, etc. This is often done in some fields of employment such as professional athletics and acting. An employer should have no obligation to deal with such a representative if they do not wish to. To require the employer to accept a surrogate in negotiations would be to impose a condition on one party in what should be a freely transacted agreement.

A union also acts as an agent for its members. If an employer agrees to negotiate with them on behalf of employees, fine. However, laws have been passed that require employers to deal with unions. When this is done, people start referring to this as a right to collective bargaining. This is a result of a misguided idea of what a right really is. Employees and employers have a right to discuss freely and come up with terms for a job. But when government steps in and imposes a condition on either side of a transaction, it is not a right. Laws that provide for such mandates have no place in a free market. If a law has to be passed to provide it, it is likely not a right – it is a government grant of a privilege. Rights occur naturally; they don't have to be legislated, although laws may be passed to protect them.

When public jobs are involved, a government entity is the employer and the legislative body that governs it will decide whether they will bargain collectively through unions. If they choose to allow that, it should not be considered a right, merely a decision on how they will handle employee relations.

Unfortunately, when people have experienced the benefits of a special privilege granted by government for a period of time, they come to think of it as a right – something to which they are entitled.

Do Unions Really Help Their Members?

It is believed by some that unions have been a great boon to workers, but I question that. Collective bargaining that treats all workers as part of a class or job description promotes mediocrity. The more capable person has no real incentive to show initiative and is denied the opportunity to be paid more for being more productive.

One of the misconceptions of those who trumpet the fact that union wages are higher is that pay rates are ultimately determined by employers. In reality, they are set by the law of supply and demand. While it is true they can be higher if government grants some power or privilege to one side or the other, it always causes distortions as a consequence. When an employer is forced to engage in collective bargaining and faces the possibility of a union calling a strike, they may be coerced to pay on scales that go beyond free-market rates. However, this ultimately results in fewer jobs as the employer has less to pay for them. While it may be good (in the short-term) for workers in the union, the end result is fewer jobs.

Unionized jobs have often been those that have involved repetitive, assembly-line type of work. For many, such jobs provide little job satisfaction or sense of achievement. The natural tendency would be for such people to work in these jobs for a short period while they pursue more meaningful positions. But the union's ability to obtain wages beyond what the market would pay – in many cases more than they might find in more potentially rewarding jobs – promotes staying with a job that is less fulfilling due to the higher wages. Many feel trapped and remain in jobs with which they are unhappy for years or even until retirement.

And society loses the contributions these talented people could have made. The unions, in this manner, hold back people and discourage them from reaching a higher potential.

Without the power unions have been given to deliver wages and benefits out of proportion to the value provided by jobs, much of this work would likely be done by those just starting their working life and who are on the way to bigger and better things – not those making a career out of what may well be considered by many to be transitional work.

Unions also overinflate the value of the workers they represent – particularly unskilled factory laborers. The relatively high wages paid for their labor are only possible because automation has enabled them to be more productive; they can turn out more widgets in a given amount of time with highly-efficient machinery. Such equipment – often very sophisticated -- has been developed by others using scientific principles and engineering techniques financed by the company and its investors. The employee who uses such tools has contributed nothing to their development unless he has bought stock in his employer's company. The person using the equipment can still only put out a limited number of products in a given timeframe. But those who invented the machine have enabled the potential for the manufacture of an unlimited number of them, which may continue to be used to produce widgets for a considerable amount of time. This allows many laboring men to increase their output and receive much greater wages than they ever could if they had to make the items with their hands or rudimentary tools. The value of the tools provided by financers and developers is much greater than the value of the labor of those who merely use those tools.

There has been much glorification of the working men and women in recent years. Often it is implied that those who aren't doing physical work are not putting out as much effort. Certainly, nothing is wrong with earning a living with honest, manual labor. It is essential to have some people doing such tasks. And many who do, work very hard – sometimes to the point of exhaustion. But many overrate the contributions of such employees. Their use of "the working man" and "working class" implies those who use their minds or funds for the manufacturing process are of less importance. In reality, it is those who develop the tools used to make products that really drive the creation of wealth. Everyone in a society benefits by the lower prices enabled by machines that create consumer items more inexpensively.

The unions' ability to obtain unrealistic wages for employees makes its members dependent on them and gives its leaders a lot of power. One wonders how many of those leaders are more concerned with keeping that power than of promoting the interests of union members.

One of the tools the union uses is the strike and the threat of calling one. When a person agrees to work for someone, a mutual understanding exists; they will do the specified job and the employer will provide the agreed-upon pay and benefits. The employee has a moral obligation to fulfill the agreement. To walk off the job is to violate that agreement. This too, is now deemed to be a right. It is not a right – it is a wrong. A Christian should always keep his commitments – it is a matter of integrity and keeping one's word. So, I consider it wrong for a believer to participate in a strike.

I believe it would be fine to have employee organizations that designate representatives to discuss concerns workers may have with employers. That would include safety issues, workplace rules, fairness in promotion policies, etc. Such discussions should be done in good faith – not with the adversarial attitude taken by today's unions. However, the current system of unions with the power they have been given by government does a great disservice to employees and employers alike.

Working Conditions

Non-monetary employment factors like the environment in which jobs are carried out are part of the supply and demand equation. If the number of available workers is abundant, an employer need not have great working conditions. However, if there is a shortage of qualified employees, companies will find it necessary to offer a more pleasant, clean, and safe workplace. The amount of compensation offered by various firms for comparable jobs will usually be quite similar due to economic laws. When that happens, working conditions may be the consideration that causes some applicants to choose one position over another.

As such, the best answer to improving conditions on job sites is not government requirements. Rather, it is removing barriers to job growth that will increase the demand for workers and force employers to provide workplaces that attract employees from a short supply.

CHAPTER 8

Financial Issues

For since the creation of the world His invisible attributes, His eternal power and divine nature, have been clearly seen, being understood through what has been made, so that they are without excuse. (Romans 1:20)

He is in this, as in many other cases, led by an invisible hand to promote an end which was no part of his intention. – Adam Smith, *The Wealth of Nations*

In the Carboniferous Epoch we were promised abundance for all, By robbing selected Peter to pay for collective Paul; But, though we had plenty of money, there was nothing our money could buy. And the Gods of the Copybook Headings said: "If you don't work you die." – Rudyard Kipling, *The Gods of the Copybook Headings*

Free Market Economics

I will be talking here about what is generally referred to as capitalism. I never use that term when referring to our American economic system. It is almost impossible to do so without conjuring up the image of greedy businessmen exploiting people. Capital is that which is used to produce wealth (the means of production) and all economic systems employ it – be they be free, communistic, or somewhere between. The difference is in who owns and/or controls the capital. In a communist or socialist system, governments own the major means of production.

In a fascist economy, private individuals have the actual title to those means, but the government largely controls them. Since they use capital, these systems are just as capitalistic as are the free market economies to which the term has been applied. An excellent comparative discussion of various economic systems can be found in *Overview of America* mentioned in Chapter 4.

Whatever one chooses to replace the term capitalism, it is important that its name emphasize it is based on freedom. Free enterprise and free market system are two I believe are particularly good. In defending free enterprise too much emphasis is often put on how affluent a nation becomes when it is implemented. It is okay to point that out, but when we speak of the wealth that results from a free economy, the left will use our arguments to try to demonstrate how it leads to inequalities. They will say such a system enables many to be greedy. We should focus more on the fact that such a system is based on personal freedom since that is what makes it just and right. Greater wealth is not the most important reason for advocating such a system – it is merely a byproduct.

Freedom in Economics Works

I will not spend a lot of time talking about how or why freedom in the marketplace produces such good results. Many who have studied such issues for years have written about the benefits of allowing prices and wages to be set uninhibited by government rules. They have also documented the deleterious effects of interference in the free pricing system. I have included several books that cover these topics in the bibliography.

The suppositions of free market proponents that economies prosper most when left unfettered from controls have been demonstrated countless times in history. Certainly our experience in the United States has proven the best example of the success of such a system.

From a pragmatic standpoint, leaving the marketplace free is the right policy. From a logical perspective, it just makes sense that in a centrally-controlled economy without freely floating prices it is almost impossible to determine how many end products or component parts will be needed. It also should be clear to a Christian, who knows about the selfish nature of man, that a system based on self-interest where each party seeks to maximize their gain will work the best. Since participants in the marketplace attempt to buy items at the lowest price possible and sell at the highest level they can, prices and wages will achieve the optimum level. The knowledge of the selfish nature of man should itself be sufficient to cause believers to be supporters of a free market system.

Other Reasons a Free Economy Is Important

However, two other reasons exist for Christians to support freedom in commerce – both of which are more important than its effectiveness. First, if production and distribution of items is determined by government, those in charge can use, and have used, the resulting power to control people. Believers know that, based on the frailty of humanity, some people will use such authority to benefit themselves and to tyrannize others. Those who direct a centrally-planned economy can decide who eats – which ultimately means who lives and who dies. With this power, they have the ability to control the actions of any individuals or groups they wish. We observed such a system in action throughout the communist world where governments completely repressed their people by managing (mismanaging, actually) their nations' economies.

They used that power to suppress Christianity. One cannot prove that Satan is directly behind evil movements like communism. However, it makes sense that he would use indirect methods to impede God's people from furthering His kingdom. To cause God's enemies to use an economic system to control believers would certainly be the type of thing he would do. Christians usually recognize direct efforts, such as laws, that specifically restrict their activities. It makes sense that the Devil, master of deception that he is, would try to restrict our efforts through placing our ability to meet our economic needs in the hands of authorities who can use it as a tool to get us to obey them rather than God. Of course, communists used both direct and indirect methods against Christians.

Second, the most important reason for freedom in an economy is that it is morally correct. A person or group creating a product should have the right to sell it for what they wish. Only they know the effort put into the creation of the item and the value they place on it. The same is true when a person goes into the market to sell his labor. A person should have the right to decide how much they are willing to pay for a product or service. Only they can know the value they assign to it vis-à-vis other ways they might opt to spend the money.

Values and Prices Have Subjective Values

A real misunderstanding about the concept of prices and values exists. I believe many tacitly accept the labor theory of value advanced by some economists – notably Karl Marx. This view holds that the amount of work that has gone into a product is the main or even sole determinant of its value and should be used to set its price. Some carry this so far that they assert that it is illegitimate for anyone to charge a price for an item beyond its labor costs and that it is robbing those who actually made it when they do so.

However, this idea is easily demonstrated to be false. I could spend a great deal of time nailing a bunch of boards together in a haphazard manner to come up with a product of no practical use and no aesthetic appeal. Its value to most sane people would likely approximate zero. No one would be willing to buy it at any price despite the fact it has a lot of "labor value."

In actuality the economic value of anything is not an objective amount, it is entirely subjective and can only be determined by those who possess a thing or who are contemplating purchasing it. This is why items like collectibles – be they art objects, antiques, etc. – often are sold for extremely high prices even when they have limited or no practical utility. One can speak of a market value, but that is only determined by the aggregate value fixed by all buyers who desire a particular product.

The idea that the value of an item is determined by the labor put into it is increasingly less true as the process for making it becomes more mechanized. When cobblers made shoes by hand, it was mostly one person's effort that created the product. He might price the shoe based on the cost of the materials he put into it, and a per hour value he placed on his time. But if no one wished to pay that price, he would have to reduce it to the level where he would find a willing buyer. Even then, it was true that labor did not solely set the value or price. However, when shoes are made on an assembly line, the people who run the machines represent a much smaller amount of what it takes to produce them. While they may be the only ones of whom it could be said are laboring, those who financed, designed, and built the machinery the worker uses contribute considerably more to the product.

Morality and Freedom in the Marketplace

It is simply morally wrong for a third party to dictate to someone what they must ask for their goods and services or what they can pay for those they wish to purchase. In a like manner, it is right to allow a party in society to set their prices, even if such a system were not to result in the greatest good. We know a seller is constrained by the willingness of a buyer to pay the price he is asking, and that a purchaser may not find someone willing to sell to him for what he will pay. These limitations are part of the impersonal operation of the laws of supply and demand. That is quite different from the action of a government authority that often will prevent a transaction at a price where both buyer and seller are willing to make an exchange. Wage and price controls and minimum wage laws are two of the most obvious infringements of this right.

A person or group who makes an item develops the plan, obtains the raw materials, purchases components, and assembles the final product certainly has the right to dispose of it in any way they wish, including selling it for any price, since no one else has contributed to its manufacture. The product would not have existed had they not gone through the many steps to create it. Yet some people seem to believe they have some type of claim on such products at a price they want to pay and think the government should be involved in its pricing. Of course, the manufacturer could set an outrageous price on items they make, and they should have that right. In reality, no one who wants to sell them will be able to do so unless they price them at a level attractive to willing buyers. Had I not heard others talking in this manner, I do not believe it would have ever occurred to me that anyone other than the creator of a product would have any say in how it is priced.

Allowing buyers and sellers to freely transact trades at mutually agreed prices results in the greatest good for the greatest number of people – which is actually the criterion used by utilitarians to judge actions and systems. However, that is not the primary reason why we should favor this policy. We should advocate for it because it is morally right; that should be the main justification Christians use to defend free enterprise. This means that even if such freedom resulted in only the most responsible in society benefiting from it, we should still favor that type of system. And if it could be demonstrated that a centrally planned economy actually did provide the most benefit to the most people in society, we, as Christians, should nevertheless oppose that type of system because it has taken away the moral right to buy and sell. The ends do not justify the means – which should always be the position of a Christian.

This would mean also that if a highly-controlled, collectivist rule were based on the right moral principles, we should advocate for it, in spite of the fact we know such systems have caused misery for countless millions throughout the centuries. However, as Christians we know God wouldn't create a world where following the right principles would lead to such conditions.

A clear parallel exists here to the way we are to live our lives as Christians. We are to obey God's Word and His specific directives for our lives – not because we, or even others, will realize some benefit from our obedience – but simply since it is the right thing to do. In fact, we may find, in some cases, that severe trials and travails may occur as a consequence of our obedience to God – although we know, ultimately, *God causes all things to work together for good to those who love God, to those who are called according to His purpose* (Romans 8:28).

Thankfully, we know that what is right in economics (allowing freedom of action) is not only what is logical, but also what has historically benefited the most people. If we believe God is good, that is exactly what we would expect in a world He has designed – that following His principles would generally result in the best outcome, although there will always be those who individually do what is right and nevertheless suffer in some way.

However, too often, the free market system is advocated and justified merely for its results. Not enough attention is paid to the fact it prevents government control of people and that it rightly and morally allows us to use our God-given free will to make economic decisions. Although we have prospered greatly as a nation by allowing the free exchange of goods and services, we should not be focused on the benefits of such a system. The issue is not primarily about financial rewards; it is about being able to maximize our responsiveness to God. The wealth that results is just a fortuitous byproduct.

This does not mean we, as believers, should not point out the pragmatic reasons the free market economy is superior. This is particularly true when we are involved in a political campaign. However, we should always be mindful of the greater reasons for a belief in allowing free exchanges of goods and services. And we should be ever alert for opportunities to present the ultimate reasons why such a system is moral and proper.

This right to buy and sell freely can be infringed by government in ways other than the most obvious: wage and price controls. They include: minimum-wage laws, subsidies, and tax credits to certain categories of business, etc. All are interferences in the free market, mess up the law of supply and demand, and lead to misallocations of resources and a loss of wealth to society. The government setting of interest rates is too often forgotten, since this really interferes with the price of obtaining credit. This will be dealt with more later in this chapter.

Laws of Economics Are Part of God's Revelation

When you saw the quote from Romans 1 at the beginning of this chapter, many of you may have thought it was misplaced. Surely, a reference to acknowledging what God has created is out of context in this discussion. I must have really meant it to be in some other location. But, no, its placement in this chapter is entirely intentional.

In this passage, Paul speaks of the fact that God has revealed Himself in the world He created. This refers to the visible things in nature. However, it is not only the wonders of the world which we behold with our eyes that testify to God. The scientific and mathematic principles and formulas behind them also point to a grand designer; they reveal that a God exists. They are things that He made just as much as what we visibly observe. They are also "clearly seen" – although not with our eyes. What we see would not be possible without the orderly, unseen laws that enable them.

There are other evidences of God's creation. One is the fact that notes, scales, etc., allow for the composition and performance of music. Without the regularity and precision of tones, no melodies could be created – all sound would be irregular and cacophonous. This fact surely points to a designer of the universe, although it involves what is not physically seen. So, too, economic laws like that of supply and demand are parts of what has been termed general revelation. We see them in operation in the world around us.

Paul says these marvels are obvious, and one who rejects them is without excuse. The implication is that these things are so apparent they testify to having been designed by an all-powerful being. Economic laws may not be as obvious as visual creations or musical concepts. Yet, a person who truly observes the economic interactions of men and women should be able to recognize them in operation.

We discover mathematic and scientific laws as we observe nature and the physical world, and we discover economic principles as we observe men and women interacting in the marketplace. If one looks at how the law of supply and demand works, there is evidence of design – just as when one looks at any of God's physical creations. The fact that it is based on the fallen nature of man is also a clue that it comes from God. It works so beautifully well when allowed to operate without interference that it could only have been created by an all-knowing being. In fact, free-market principles should be part of a Christian apologetic. We, as believers, should use it as a proof of a creative, orderly God, just as we use scientific principles for that purpose.

Economic laws are not as exact as scientific and mathematical ones. For instance, a person could point to incidences where the principle of supply and demand has been violated by an individual or company. That is because these laws involve human decisions and God has given us free wills. So, one can, for his own reasons, use his will to act contrary to the norm and, for example, sell something for less than what the market would bring. However, since people normally act in their self-interest, these laws work reliably in the aggregate as men and women participate in an economy.

We know our perfectly designed physical universe is not operating flawlessly since it has been marred by imperfect humans. Yet, the design of God is apparent; that is what we should point to as an apologetic. So, too, economic laws have been hampered by the interference of men and women. We see this in the way humans, through their governments, have placed so many hindrances on these laws that they prevent them from working as designed. Consequences result – some quite dire – from interfering with their workings. A good example is the busts that happen when the Federal Reserve pumps funds and credit into the economy by creating artificially low interest rates rather than allowing them to float based on supply and demand.

The system as designed is what should be used for an apologetic – not the crippled one we often see in practice. Although there never has been a society that allowed economic laws to function completely freely, by comparing nations where they largely operate without interference with those where they have been prevented from working, we can see the design and superiority of economies that follow these laws.

The fact that the design in economic laws is so obvious and should be recognized by all should not be a reason to take anything away from the free market advocates (some of whom are not Christians) who have developed elaborate economic thought systems. They have gone beyond the fact that freedom in the marketplace works, to describe how and why it works. They have also detailed how the varying interferences have impaired the effectiveness of its workings.

Humanism and Collectivism

There seems to be almost a symbiotic relationship between humanism and collectivism. As a nation rejects Christianity in favor of materialism, it has a tendency to adopt a centrally-controlled economy and start dispensing more benefits. Conversely, it is also true that as a country starts providing more social welfare for its residents, they tend to put more faith in government than in God. This in turn leads to more acceptance of collectivism. As the process continues the whole society devolves into a very secular, statist entity. Nowhere is this example of humanism and collectivism feeding off one another more evident than in Europe where increasingly socialistic regimes rule nations which can only be called post-Christian.

The atheistic scientist, though he may be very brilliant, ignores the obvious evidence of design in the universe. Similarly, many who reject God also do not accept principles like supply and demand. In both cases, *they have become futile in their speculations and their foolish hearts were darkened* (Romans 1: 21). Because they do not acknowledge God, they foolishly deny the design He built into His creation. It is interesting that atheistic scientists, who deny the fact of the physical design of the universe, nevertheless use the resulting principles, mathematical formulas, laws, etc., in their work. However, many non-theists don't even recognize the validity of economic laws or apply them – much less give credit to God for them. Of course, just as some people acknowledge that God created the world, but will not allow Him personally into their lives, there are those who recognize God's sound economic laws although they haven't accepted Christ.

Supply and demand operates naturally without any need for man's interference. This is likely why so many non-theists find it inadequate. They believe in the goodness of man and that there are no limits to what can be accomplished through human effort. It makes sense that those with a humanistic worldview would want an economic system built on man's ideas – one that can be engineered, and for which they can take credit. They are likely to believe man's ingenuity can construct a better system than what just happens spontaneously through the actions of buyers and sellers. Adam Smith attributed this to an invisible hand. That hand is the hand of our invisible, invincible God!

In addition to a constructed economy, many want one which can be centrally controlled and which they can have a role in manipulating. Their pride in their own intelligence and that of their colleagues convinces them they can run a system – even to the point of determining how much to produce. They consider man's direction as superior to what they see as the vagaries of a chaotic, uncontrolled market. Even those who generally believe in the market believe they can make it better by applying human intelligence to tweak it – essentially trying to improve upon the system God gave us. Such efforts have always failed and will continue to do so. This is a fact Christians should realize. In fact, if the laws of supply and demand are truly designed by God, even the smallest attempt to improve them or interfere with their workings will produce deleterious effects. Laissez Faire!

Free Commerce Is Part of God's Provision for Mankind

Not only are economic laws part of God's revelation to man, they are a gift to us. They can appropriately be considered part of what has been termed "common grace" – those things He gives for the use and enjoyment of all men and women, both believers and non-believers. It is certainly true that many who have no use for God have benefited greatly from the application of free-market principles. As is true of any of the gifts of God, the free economy must be preserved and protected. We need to be stewards of it as we would of the physical parts of God's universe which He has given us.

The free market is part of God's way of providing for the needs of the world. God's primary method for meeting our material requirements is that we should work to provide for ourselves and our families. Because of the fall, He says in Genesis 3:19 that we would do this in the sweat of our faces. Although it appears God always intended that men and women would labor, the effort required was magnified after the fall. Due to the curse placed on the earth that, and many other travails, became part of life in this world.

God, in his graciousness, also left us a world with the capability of mitigating the curse's effects. These include the scientific principles that allow for developing labor-saving devices, treatment of plant diseases, etc. These capabilities had to be discovered by men and women. In doing so, we also follow God's command to work, since such discoveries involve considerable effort.

Some of the more rudimentary tools like the wheel were discovered fairly early and decreased the effort required to get the earth to yield its bounty. However, many other aids to production that have helped us in modern times lay buried for centuries. In fact, the way life was lived did not really change all that much from biblical times up until the Nineteenth Century when the treasures of God's world started to be unearthed in a major way.

In addition to all the physical blessings God has placed in His wonderful world, various principles have greatly aided and improved life when applied. Among the greatest is the concept of the free economy with the laws of supply and demand.

The precepts of the free market have also been the key to unlocking many of the other gifts God has built into the earth. It is instructive to note that real progress in the improvement in peoples' lives and in their ability to harvest earth's riches using God's uncovered mysteries did not occur until the application of the free economy. This really accelerated with the emergence of the United States, which allowed freedom in its commerce far beyond what any society in history had done to that time.

This is not to say that every recognition of the capabilities God hid in His world was made by Americans. But while the underlying scientific principles may have been recognized earlier by those in other countries, it was often not until the United States came along with its freedom that the economics were there to take those principles and apply them to practical uses that would improve life.

Our American experience was really the culmination of an increasing recognition of God and His precepts as Western Civilization developed. It surely is no accident that such a remarkable use was made of God's marvelous resources to greatly overcome the results of the curse and to improve life here in a country where He and His ways were acknowledged to a great degree. It was through the recognition and implementation of His economic laws and the incentives they provided that such a transformation was enabled. To think, it is the antediluvians who seek to cripple the free market (and its astounding results) with many laws that prevent its effective operation, who have the unmitigated gall to call themselves "progressives"!

It is not surprising that, as American society has increasingly rejected God, we have also turned from the free economic principles He gave us to a statist, controlled market. Nor is it surprising that it is often those who do not acknowledge God who also do not recognize the marvelous economic principles He has given us.

Although God does intend men and women should labor to earn their keep on this earth, there are those who can't provide for themselves in this manner for various reasons. God's intention is that these individuals be taken care of through voluntary giving. But when men try to substitute other methods for meeting their needs through government redistribution programs, they are trying to take a shortcut to earning their living. This involves enforced charity – which is very much an oxymoron. Those who try to enrich themselves through such methods are being disobedient to God's ways.

Voluntary aid is much more effective in getting help to those who truly need and deserve it. Prospective donors tend to look closely at organizations that help others to make certain they are using their contributions wisely. So, an accountability is attached to such giving. Government, conversely, has a strong tendency to create programs that are not very selective in passing out their largesse. They are often set up on the basis of recipients getting help based on entitlement – rather than merit or true need. As such, these programs promote dependency.

Private Property in the Bible

In looking at economic issues, we must recognize a key component of a free market is private property. While it would be hard to come up with a passage in the Bible that expressly advocates private ownership, the concept is assumed throughout both the testaments.

Examples abound in the Old Testament from Abraham and Lot's dividing of the land, Abraham's purchase of a burial site, to the comparisons of Jacob and Esau's flocks. It is covered in the law with the eighth commandment's prohibition of stealing and the tenth's regarding coveting another's belongings, and in many other rules laid down by God. This includes the idea of gleaning which assumed an owner of the land would leave the grain in a field's corners for the needy.

The parables of Jesus refer often to property owners in a way that shows He assumed it was proper for individuals to hold land, animals, etc. For example, in the parable of the laborers in the vineyard in Matthew 20, Jesus tells the story of a farmer who paid the same wages to various men, although they had worked differing amounts of time during the day. He justified this by saying, *Is it not lawful for me to do what I wish with what is my own*? The lesson Jesus was teaching was not that an employer could pay whatever wages he wished. However, Jesus cited the man in such a way that it was obvious He believed (and assumed His listeners would agree) that his action in paying different rates was appropriate and consistent with his property rights.

Free Enterprise Promotes Civility in Society

In a free market system, businesses attract and keep customers not just by offering the lowest market prices, but by giving good and pleasant service. "The customer is always right" is more than just a cliché – it is the description of a model for good customer relationships. Often, the actual prices for comparable products and service don't vary that much due to the law of supply and demand. If prices are the same as, or close to, competitors', people often buy from an establishment where they are treated well – where sales clerks and marketing reps are pleasant, not disagreeable or arrogant. Employers insist their employees act in this manner. There is an incentive for being cordial and fair. This introduces a civility in society that extends beyond commercial transactions. Although, they may not do so initially for noble motives, fallen people who act courteously toward others realize they feel good about being nice. And they realize when they treat others well they often receive similar treatment themselves. This instills a habit and attitude of wishing to please.

When government sells services and products as a monopoly, the incentives for being nice to customers is missing. I think, in general, you will find most civil servants in this country are polite and accommodating. But that is in a nation where examples of pleasant service abound in private industry. Public servants who interface with those in the private sector are treated well and their experiences there tend to carry over in their own jobs. The general civility that results from free commerce impacts the whole society. Where a system is so socialized that there aren't many private models to emulate, one is more likely to experience the coldness of a bureaucracy. In these places, few are in a position where they need to be nice to keep customers' business.

Christians should, of course, always treat people respectfully and be pleasant whether in business, civic affairs, personal relations, or as government employees. However, we should also support the free market system because it promotes these positive personal attributes among the population at large.

What About Corporations?

Here I will be venturing into philosophical territory where my views have not been fully formed – that is the propriety of government granting corporate liability. I haven't really studied the history of how corporations came to be. Neither have I heard or seen much discussion about their legitimacy; it just seems that most assume their existence is proper.

However, as I have thought about the question in recent years, I have been troubled by what I see as an inconsistency between the corporate system and the basis for rights. Government has allowed individuals to create an entity, and then treat it, in many respects, as a pseudo person. In doing so, it limits the liability of those who form or join that entity.

Throughout this book, I have maintained that we, as individual humans, have rights because God created us in His image with volitional free wills. Our rights are based on the ability to exercise these wills with our minds. This gift of God is inherent in our very beings; it does not come from government. In marked contrast, corporations are not created by God; they are contrivances of man. They do not have minds and do not, in and of themselves, exercise a free will. Yet, they are, in some respects, given "rights" by government. But the definition of a right that I believe is correct is that it is an ability we have naturally – not something we are granted by government. However, government deals with them in many ways as though they have the same rights men and women have as individuals.

Another thing I have been emphasizing is that people should have the ability to act freely, but they should then be responsible for the consequences of their actions. This includes liability for any impact on other parties. A corporation also has responsibility for the actions it takes as an entity, actions which are determined by its officers, directors, boards, and stockholders. The corporation itself is liable although it cannot make decisions itself. Those who make decisions on its behalf, however, have limited liability if the corporation is unable to fulfill its financial obligations.

It seems such a system is likely to, and has, led to irresponsible activity. I wonder how many of the problems in our economy have been exacerbated by the existence of the corporate system. If we would as a society decide to stop allowing the creation of these fictive persons, we would still be able to combine our resources and efforts in enterprises by forming partnerships as we have always done. But there would no longer be the diluted liability.

I have not by any means dealt with this question definitively. I am not ready to say flatly that the corporate system should be discarded, although I have misgivings about it. I do hope to give additional thought to the issue and study it more. I believe there needs to be much more discussion and examination of the issues surrounding this question.

Monetary Policy

Monetary policies and those surrounding money constitute some of the most important issues in today's America. Yet, for many years they have rarely been mentioned as campaign issues, nor have they been topics addressed by political commentators – even those on the right. An encouraging development is the increased attention being paid to such issues in recent years, primarily due to the emphasis placed on them by Ron Paul in his runs for the presidency in 2008 and 2012.

We will be talking here about things like inflation, the Federal Reserve, true money etc. Since this is not an economic treatise, I will not deal with these items in detail. My main objective is to provide enough background, so I can discuss what is a proper Christian view of such matters. A number of sources provide excellent detailed information on this topic, and I will point you to them.

Development of Money

Money has two primary purposes – it serves as a medium of exchange and a store of value. A variety of items have been used as money including salt, shells, and cattle. All of these had some intrinsic value in the societies where they were used. Before the development of money, goods were traded in a barter system.

The problem with such a method is that a person wanting a certain item had to find another who desired something he had. This probably worked fairly well in a simple economy where people lived at a subsistence level. The things most people needed were the basic items required for life and didn't vary that much from person to person. A man who raised corn and wanted a sheep would likely quite easily find someone who had one and needed some of his crop. But as society's needs (and wants) expanded and people became more specialized in what they produced, it became more difficult for a man or woman to locate a person who had what they wanted and who also desired his products. People began trading by using items that could, in turn, be bartered for what one really wanted. As people in the society started using these standard items for trade, they became their *de facto* money.

Many of the things used as money had shortcomings. Over time, civilized societies began using precious metals for exchange. They had definite advantages and were relatively rare, so they had intrinsic value. They were durable and, therefore, could be kept for long periods of time without deteriorating, and they could be divided, allowing various sizes to be used to represent different values. The most important attribute was their value, since that would allow for them to be saved and used for future purchases. Such money systems developed naturally – they were not created by, nor were the values of coins manipulated by, their governments.

Debasement of the Money System by Governments

Eventually, paper money was also used. Initially, the bills that were printed were like receipts and could be redeemed for the amount of metal specified. Later, governments started issuing unbacked currency that had no intrinsic value. Since its only value was what the government declared it to have, it came to be called fiat money. It does not really qualify as true money, but still served as a medium of exchange.

Its use as a store of value was severely compromised due to being subject to control by the state.

Importance of Monetary Issues

Monetary issues are important for several reasons. First, the Federal Reserve's practice of monetizing debt and creating money and debt allows Congress to spend huge amounts of funds beyond what they extract in taxes. If our representatives had to actually go to taxpayers for everything they spend, there would likely be a massive citizen revolt. It is very probable many of the largest give-away programs would not be politically tenable without the ability of government to inflate the currency. Our monetary policies have thus become the great enablers of the welfare state.

Second, by making credit more easily available through the setting of artificially low interest rates, the Fed causes major maladjustments of investments in the economy. Interest rates are the price paid for credit. So, it is important they fluctuate as dictated by the demand for borrowing in the economy. When rates are determined artificially by the Federal Reserve, it creates distortions in the allocation of credit in the same way that is done when government interferes with wages and prices for products. Setting the country's base interest rate is really establishing a price control for credit. This is actually more harmful than those imposed on specific products and types of labor, since it affects the cost of everything purchased with borrowed funds.

Inexplicably, many conservatives who are properly convinced that government should not do anything to affect supply and demand of goods and services seem not to be bothered by the same type of actions in the marketplace of credit and funds. At the very least, they have minimized what is a major problem in our nation.

Third, closely related to number two is that such policies create bubbles in our economy that eventually break – resulting in recessions and depressions.

Fourth, the inflation caused by these policies robs the value from the savings of some of the most productive and responsible of our citizens – those with the foresight to prepare for the future. It also impacts some of the most vulnerable in society, notably retired people on fixed incomes or those who are relying on their life savings – which they have assumed would retain its value.

Fifth, inflation promotes excessive borrowing. When the value of money is going down, people realize if they borrow a given amount today, they can pay their loan off with tomorrow's dollars – which will be worth less.

An issue our government deals with on an all-too-frequent basis is the increasing amount of debt it is allowed to accumulate. If we had money backed with precious metals, a natural maximum would be in place on how much could be borrowed since a finite amount of those metals exist on the earth. Governments could not increase their debt limits beyond a certain level since there would be no more money to borrow. Therefore, the amount they could spend would also have an absolute cap. However, as we have seen with unbacked currency, the sky's the limit.

Personal Lesson on Inflation

I had an early introduction to inflation. I enjoyed playing *Monopoly* when I was growing up. In that game, the bank has a fixed amount of money, and a specified amount of it is issued to each player. It is then used to buy properties. The first person landing on an unsold property has the option of purchasing it for a set price and can later place buildings on it. Once a property has been purchased, a player landing on it has to pay rent to the owner depending on how many buildings it has. After properties are initially purchased, players are free to buy and sell them to each other for any mutually agreeable price. When a person loses all her money, she is out of the game. If there are only two players, the other one is then the winner. If more people are in the game, those remaining continue until only one of them has money.

Quite often, I would play with two or more other kids. If one lost his money, he would have to sit and twiddle his thumbs while the rest of us kept playing. Since *Monopoly* games tend to be quite lengthy, he might have to wait for some time. If he was a neighbor kid, he might just walk home, but often players were part of a family visit. Sometimes they were from the country and dependent on their parents for a ride home, and the visiting family might stay for a long time. Plus, if the game was being played in your home, it wasn't considered hospitable to leave children who were your guests out of your activities. So, we often allowed the one losing all their money to continue to play by borrowing from the bank. We did this by writing IOUs with various amounts on pieces of scrap paper. The borrowing player then spent these as though they were "real" money. As time went on, more lending would occur, and the amounts of created money could sometimes end up being quite substantial. When that happened, the amounts that the properties sold for escalated dramatically.

We had effectively expanded the money supply while the amount of available property remained the same. This caused prices to increase greatly. This really is what inflation is – artificially increasing the amount of money. Just as in the game of *Monopoly*, in the game of life the result of money manipulation is escalating prices.

Inflation Causes Higher Prices

Often, in the media, inflation is referred to as "rising prices" and those who increased them are blamed. However, if the supply of money isn't increased, the prices of all items in an economy cannot go up. If some prices rise, there will be less available to spend on other goods, and some prices will have to be reduced accordingly. This is not inflation, but merely price changes reflecting the shifting priorities of purchasers in the economy. It is only when the amount of money is increased that there can be a general increase in the price level of all products and services. The increase in money is the inflation – the rising prices are the result. Generally rising prices are a symptom of inflation – not inflation itself – which is the increase in the money supply.

And prices do not necessarily go up when there is inflation. In a productive economy, where technology and increased automation allows for creating products less expensively, the prices will tend to go down over time. However, if inflation takes place, the additional money may prevent some or all of the price decrease that should have resulted from decreased production costs. The consumer then has, in effect, been robbed of the benefit of the reduced prices he or she should have received. What results are prices that are not necessarily higher than they were, but, rather, higher than they would otherwise have been without any inflation.

Another way people are defrauded by inflation is that it results in a transfer of wealth. When new money is introduced into the economy it does not immediately result in higher prices. The higher prices will start to occur when the funds have rippled through the economy. This means those who initially get the created funds (like banks) are able to use them before they lose any of their value. They gain at the expense of those who lose the value of their money after the rise in prices occurs.

How should a Christian look at monetary policy as it has been practiced in recent decades? The creation of new fiat money is inherently dishonest. The practice introduces bills that look like the ones already in circulation and are purported to have the same value. However, they are not only worth less, but cause all the other bills already in circulation to have less value. This is equivalent to using dishonest measurements as condemned in Scripture. (*You must have accurate and honest weights and measures, so that you may live long in the land the LORD your God is giving you. For the LORD your God detests anyone who does these things, anyone who deals dishonestly.* (Deuteronomy 25:15, 16))

The deceit continues when Congress funds its programs with created money – rather than tax revenues. The honest way would to be to propose a tax increase if they want a new program or increased funding for an existing one. Christians should thoroughly reject the dishonest policies associated with fiat money. It is not incorrect to label them as theft. And the deceitful, fraudulent way this is done makes it proper to call it a scam.

Money can be inflated in a limited number of ways. One is by allowing an entity like the Federal Reserve the power to authorize the issuing of fiat currency. A second is through a fractional reserve banking system which allows financial institutions to lend out more funds than they actually have by keeping on hand only a percentage of the total amount loaned to customers. However, if the currency is redeemable, a check is in place on how much inflation the banks can cause, since they need to consider the possibility that more depositors will ask to redeem their bills than what they can cover with metals.

With unbacked money though, the only check is the reserve limit. However, there is no limit on the amount of inflation that can be created by an agency like the Federal Reserve with a fiat currency system. With the Fed and a fractional reserve banking system, we have the worst of both worlds in the United States. The Federal Reserve is not really a government entity. It is a private institution owned by investors. Some Fed opponents make a big issue of that fact, but the important thing is that it has been empowered by Congress to increase the nation's money supply. There is absolutely no Constitutional warrant for their powers.

The Fed could, through its actions, inflate the money supply such that it could wipe out the savings of a substantial portion of Americans rather quickly. Our founders set up a limited government with checks and balances to prevent any body from exerting too much power. Can you imagine what they would think if they saw the kind of power a small group of individuals in the Fed has been given? It is entirely accurate to refer to that system as a fascist monetary system.

Some tout the system of manipulating the value of money as promoting stability, but it is more important that interest rates are allowed to be fluid to adjust to changing supply and demand of credit.

We need to return to an honest money system – one in which all currency is backed by precious metals. And we need to abolish the Federal Reserve since it is exerting power in an unconstitutional manner, and in a way totally incompatible with a free society. It is morally equivalent to fraud. This is a corrupt system no Christian should support.

CHAPTER 9

Foreign Policy

What is the source of quarrels and conflicts among you? Is not the source your pleasures that wage war in your members? (James 4:1)

When the Cambrian measures were forming, They promised perpetual peace. They swore, if we gave them our weapons, that the wars of the tribes would cease. But, when we disarmed They sold us and delivered us bound to our foe, And the Gods of the Copybook Headings said: "Stick to the Devil you know."
– Rudyard Kipling, *The Gods of the Copybook Headings*

Gentlemen may cry Peace, peace -, but there is no peace. Give Me liberty or Give Me Death – Speech, Patrick Henry

They have misled My people by saying, 'Peace!' when there is no peace. (Ezekiel 13:10)

The Military

Foreign policy issues have become increasingly important as the United States has expanded its role in the world in recent years. It is also a place where we have been spending more funds. These realities mean all Americans should be concerned about such issues. Worldview applications come into play heavily in discussions of foreign policy. I will first discuss military issues and then talk specifically about the recent wars in Iraq and Afghanistan.

War is Part of the Human Condition

The Sixth Commandment tells us not to murder. It is clear from other sections of Scripture that this does not apply to killing done by soldiers in the legitimate use of a nation's military. That does beg the question of what is the proper use of military force by a nation. I will address this later.

Believers know men and women are imperfect beings. James 4:1 says that quarrels and conflicts come as a result of our self-centeredness – we want something we cannot obtain. This is due to our fallen nature. We know disputes among people are inevitable, and it usually happens between two or more individuals and/or parties when each wants his or her own way. This is part and parcel of the human condition. If you have never been involved in such squabbles, you are a rare person indeed!

So, should we be at all surprised disputes also occur between nations? Countries whose leaders are also imperfect will have disagreements with each other. Although they may talk these over, it is inevitable that their diplomacy will at times fail, and one country will invade another in an attempt to impose its will. In some cases, no real issue exists between nations; the leaders of one will just decide to use military aggression against another to impose their will and/or take over some, or all, of the other's territory. This should be expected in a fallen world. The bottom line is we know there will always be wars. All nations have found it necessary to have a military capability to defend themselves against attacks. In fact, having a national defense force to protect its citizens is perhaps the most legitimate function of a national government.

For anyone to believe, as some peace advocates do, that if a nation will just scrap their weapons, others will follow suit and peace will ensue, is naïve. Christians who know the condition of the hearts of people should be the last to believe this is possible. We know peace will prevail only when Jesus Christ rules.

What About Arms Control Agreements?

So, countries shouldn't just throw down their arms unilaterally. But how about two parties agreeing to eliminate or reduce certain armaments? This was done in the Cold War between the United States and the Soviet Union. There were several problems with such pacts. The most important was that the Soviet Union was not sincere in working to reduce arms. This was admitted by Lenin who said, "Treaties are like pie crusts; they are meant to be broken." They used such agreements merely as tools to gain an advantage over their enemies.

The response to this situation by peace advocates is that reductions could be monitored and verified. But it is virtually impossible to confirm that a country has eliminated weapons covered by a treaty. There is just too much territory where weapons can be located and too many ways they can be concealed. And if it were determined that such a country had violated a treaty and maintained banned weapons, what could be done to enforce the treaty at that point? The other country would be justified in abrogating the agreement, but if they had followed the treaty themselves, they would find they are now at a great disadvantage.

If both parties follow the terms of the agreement and disarm, another problem with bilateral disarmament pacts is that those parties are still potentially vulnerable to the designs of any other nations who were not part of the agreement.

The hard-core disarmer might acknowledge these problems and say the only solution is a disarmament arrangement involving all the nations on earth enforced by an organization like the United Nations. But that would magnify the problems of monitoring and compliance. The central controlling agency would need a very powerful military capability to be able to enforce the ban. In that case, weapons will not have been banned – they would just be concentrated in an organization that is now a threat to impose its will on all the nations of the world.

In reality, Christians should realize none of these disarmament accords will ever work in a world filled with sinful, power-hungry people. A nation should not rely on any kind of agreements to lessen their need to defend their interests in a hostile world. Rather, they need to create an arsenal strong enough to dissuade any other nation from invading them. This is surely a legitimate and necessary function for all governments.

When Should a Nation Go to War?

Much has been written regarding what is called "a just war theory." Those who address this issue (including Christians) have attempted to define the conditions under which it is morally proper for a nation to invade another country. I will not fully discuss such theories. However, I think it is important to recognize situations exist where it might be justifiable to launch an attack, but it is not wise to do so. National leaders should look beyond the question of justice to determine if an aggressive action is prudent.

When should a government move beyond a purely defensive status and go on the offensive to attack another country? One situation where such action is justified is when a nation's intelligence-gathering apparatus has determined the existence of an imminent plan by another country to invade them. Making a pre-emptive strike to stop such an impending attack is technically an offensive action, but from a practical standpoint, it is being done to defend the country.

The big question being debated today concerns countries (primarily the United States) trying to enforce peace in the world by engaging aggressive nations which pose no substantial or immediate threat to them. Such actions have included replacing disreputable regimes. This has aptly been described as playing the part of the world's policeman. The rationale in the United States is usually that we are so powerful and capable of helping smaller nations, and, therefore, since we can do so, we should replace undesirable leaders and/or institute democracy.

This involves an implicit comparison with an individual who encounters someone needing help like the Good Samaritan did. That person is morally obligated to come to the other's aid. Christians take this a step farther: we believe it is an act of obedience to God to help such a one whom Jesus describes as being our neighbor. I believe it is likely this is the line of thinking that has caused so many believers to be advocates of the activist foreign policy our country has pursued in recent years.

They have, in effect, taken the parable of the Good Samaritan relating to individuals and transferred its teaching to nations.

There is a problem with this rationale. The Good Samaritan committed himself personally to the injured traveler. He took any risks associated with helping him, and bore the cost of lodging and feeding him. This is also true of any individual who makes a decision to help another. He assumes any negative consequences he may experience due to his decision to get involved, including, in our litigious society, the possibility of being sued. This would still be the case if several people joined in an effort to help others, or if an organization does so – as long as the efforts and contributions of all participants are voluntary.

When a nation takes a military action, it is committing all its residents to its costs and any consequences. All taxpayers will certainly share the financial cost. Some will have to engage in actual fighting; some will suffer loss of life or health. And all inhabitants will experience the potential of blowback resulting from retaliatory action that could be taken against the country.

Some may say: "Isn't using our military to help other nations similar to committing taxpayer resources to help individuals within the nation?" The difference is that a government should be serving its own people – not those of other lands. This means foreign aid is also an inappropriate use of taxpayers' money. A person who uses this line of reasoning is presuming it is a proper function of government to give aid to anyone. I do not believe that is a role government should have. I discuss this more thoroughly in the discussion of the religious left (Chapters 16) and the one on morality (Chapter 5).

It is hubris in the extreme for one nation – no matter how militarily strong or wealthy – to think it can resolve all the disputes in the world. When we look at how deeply in debt the United States is, and how costly one war is, we have to ask just how many of these military actions we can sustain.

After the removal of a corrupt political system has been accomplished, we often get involved in a rebuilding effort, attempt to establish a democratic form of government, and/or assist in maintaining stability in the conquered country. These activities and their associated costs often go on for a considerable amount of time. More than fifty years after the Korean War, we still have troops in that country.

The cost of our military is considerably higher than it need be due to our trying to manage the world. It is difficult to get an accurate count of the number of bases we maintain overseas or how many troops are stationed outside of the United States. Some estimates indicate we have over 1,000 military installations in foreign countries. By closing them and bringing the men and women home, we could actually defend our country better at less cost.

Although the idea of using the military to police the world is wrong in and of itself, what the United States has been doing is worse, because it has been done at the behest of those who have other agendas. Primarily, such people have promoted the idea that it is the concern of one country or group of nations how another country conducts its affairs. This rationale sets a precedent for international efforts to interfere with a nation's business. The goal of such interference is ultimately a global authority to police the world.

The United States pretty much followed a non-interventionist foreign policy until the Spanish American War. Key founders and early leaders strongly advised against getting tied up with the affairs of other nations. Washington, in his farewell address, warned against entangling alliances. Jefferson expressed similar thoughts, and John Quincy Adams said of the United States: "She goes not abroad, in search of monsters to destroy. She is the well-wisher to the freedom and independence of all. She is the champion and vindicator only of her own."[1]

The response to 9/11 has been such a controversial issue in recent years. And the war with Iraq is really a case study in how not to carry out foreign policy. I will deal with these issues extensively in the next section and also in the chapter on civil liberties (10).

There is little good that has come from a country meddling in the affairs of other countries. This is undoubtedly why wise founders, such as George Washington and Thomas Jefferson, counseled our fledgling country against such activities. I believe the fact that we followed that advice for the first 150 years of our existence contributed greatly to our

1 John Quincy Adams, Speech in U.S. House of Representatives, July 4th, 1821

success as a nation. We have enough problems; we don't need to go out looking for trouble as John Quincy Adams said.

Another reason it is dangerous to be at war unless necessary is that the populace will accept abridgment of their freedoms during a conflict which they otherwise would not tolerate. I will also deal with that more in Chapter 10 on civil liberties.

Foreign Aid

It is not only that the United States is sending troops all over the globe to assert our influence; we are also giving massive amounts of money to other nations in foreign aid. Nothing in the Constitution permits us to be helping other countries. Yet, this is something America has been doing for decades. Some think we should do this to buy influence and friendships. One problem with that is we give to virtually all the nations in the world – including those who are enemies of one another. So, any goodwill we get from a given country is largely neutralized when we also give to its opponents.

Some of the aid is humanitarian. But funds funneled through governments often do not get to those in need. It is merely misused by corrupt government officials; or, if it does reach the intended recipients, it is disbursed in such a manner that the nation's government gets credit for it. It is simply wrong to give taxpayers' money, not to help our country, but for other nations. And given the fact we are trillions of dollars in debt, it is grossly irresponsible to be giving away funds we don't really have. Almost no one would suggest it would be wise for a person who is deep in debt to borrow more money so he could give it away. This would not be considered generosity, but gross irresponsibility. It makes no more sense for governments to do this, as ours has done for some time.

We seem to use little discernment in the countries to which we give aid. We have given assistance to Egypt for years. Yet, when their government was recently overthrown, we continued to send funds to the successor government, although it gives every indication it is controlled by radical Muslims.

Some aid gets spent through relief organizations – including Christian ministries. While those funds are in most cases used more effectively than those given to governments, it is still wrong to spend taxpayer money in this way and to do so when we are so deeply in hock.

Should We Draft People for the Military Services?

The fighting men who have to engage in battle will experience the deprivations of war and potential injury, disablement, or death. To send them into battle to police the world is particularly unjust if a nation has a draft. To force a person to serve and then send him to fight – not to defend his own country, but for another country, often to satisfy those with other agendas – is unconscionable. Even when military service is voluntary, it is wrong since likely many, if not most, recruits do not sign up to engage in nation-building.

In the past, whether our nation should have a system of conscription was a rare issue upon which I had not adopted a position. I could see merit in both the pro and con arguments. In defense of a draft, military personnel resources are a requirement for a country in the same way a certain amount of funds are needed. So, one could look at serving in the military as meeting an obligation to the country just like paying taxes.

On the other hand, if we had a war that truly imperiled us, it seems there would be no shortage of volunteers. If not enough signed up to meet such a need, our country would be in such a sad state, we would not likely survive anyway.

What really got me off the fence on this issue was the escalating number of police actions we became involved in around the world. I realized how wrong it was to force our young men and women to fight other nations' battles, particularly when we got immersed in these conflicts due to our leaders having their own ideological agendas. It is bad enough to ask volunteers who have signed up to defend the United States to participate in such gambits. But it is particularly unjust to use forced conscripts in such a way. I am now a strong opponent of the draft.

It also seems that having to recruit people for the armed services could be a check on our ability to carry out these ill-advised police actions. One would hope, at some point, eligible, young people would quit volunteering and leave us unable to conduct nation-building activities. If that should happen, we could expect to see a very strong push from some powerful forces to reinstate a draft. I believe that should be vigorously opposed.

The Power to Make War

In recent years, many conservatives have unfortunately gotten the idea that the president can commit us to military action. Many Christians have also bought into this belief, but the Constitution is very explicit in its requirement that Congress is to declare war in Article I, Section 8 where the powers of Congress are listed including: "To declare war, grant Letters of Marque and Reprisal, and make Rules concerning Captures on Land and Water."

The president is to be commander-in-chief once a war is declared. Even then, he is limited in his powers. He can only spend money on the war that Congress appropriates. I frequently hear non-military people refer to the president as their commander-in-chief. This is incorrect. He is commander-in-chief of the armed forces – not of the nation.

What Should We Do About Iran?

Although Iran is developing nuclear weapons, they do not have the ability to deliver them to a remote target. Any such capability they may develop will likely result because of help from China and Russia. If we were to completely flatten Iran, those nations would have no problem finding another replacement client state (or states) to help develop nuclear ability. It makes a lot more sense to direct any action to restrict proliferation of nuclear weapons at China and Russia who are the primary culprits in spreading the capability to other nations.

Iran is a sovereign nation. In a world where several nations have nuclear capability and others may obtain it, does Iran not also have a right to defend itself by developing its own? What right do we, or any other nation or groups of nations, have to tell them what weapons they should have? We know their intentions may well be to use any such capability for other than defensive purposes. And we should be concerned about how they might potentially use such weapons. However, they are just one of the nations about which we need to be concerned.

Our responsibility as a nation is to be strong enough militarily that neither Iran nor any other country will dare to invade us.

Some of the nations that have nuclear weapons actually do pose a threat to the United States, China, for instance, has missiles which may be able to reach our shores. Because several countries have nuclear capabilities and others may get them, we need to build up our defenses against a nuclear attack to the point that all countries know such an invasion would be doomed to failure. It is unrealistic to think we can control which countries obtain nuclear capability. It has become a cliché, but it is very true that the nuclear genie is out of the bottle.

Concern is being expressed about Iran getting nuclear capability; but little is said about those who already have such capability. It seems it has been deemed okay for some countries to have this power but not for others to have it. Who decides? The answer appears to be the world community.

Why all this urgency about preventing Iran from getting nuclear capability when other countries already have it and pose much more of a threat to the United States and others? The reason is that this posturing about Iran isn't really ultimately about Iran any more than the Iraq War was really about Iraq. It is actually a pretext for compromising Iran's sovereignty through the concerted efforts of other countries by those who ultimately want a world authority. So an attack on their sovereignty is really an attack on all sovereignty since it helps establish the precedent for some nations to control others. If these efforts fail, it becomes a pretext for getting the United Nations involved.

Initially, action will be taken against countries behaving badly or threatening such behavior. Another criterion is that such countries must not actually be a threat, so there is a reasonable chance any sanctions can be enforced. If Iran actually were a threat, it is unlikely the discussion about having them back off would be taking place.

UN sanctions were instituted against Iraq, because they had a notorious leader, and they were a small, militarily weak nation. We never hear anyone proposing any kind of sanctions on China in spite of their military buildup and saber-rattling. It is likely they would merely laugh at any sanctions and no one would dare to try enforcing them.

Once the precedent of forcing nations to disarm (or do whatever else has been demanded of them) has been firmly established, it can be used against whatever country the world authority decides to apply it to, and nations will have effectively lost their sovereignty.

What about Israel?

This is probably the most troublesome issue for me. It is the one where I have the most difficulty reconciling a philosophy of government which I have tried to keep as consistent as possible with what, on the surface anyway, seems as though it could be considered an exception based on God's purposes for this world.

On the one hand, I am opposed to foreign aid and am a non-interventionist who believes a nation's military should only be used to protect its own citizens. But, as a Christian, I know the nation of Israel is God's chosen people. He takes care of them and has special plans for them. This issue would be easy for me if I were a believer in Replacement Theology which promotes the idea that the church has replaced Israel as God's object of special concern. If I believed that, I could follow my views on military policy and foreign aid without making any exceptions for the Jews. However, it is clear to me from the prophetic portions of Scripture that God is not done with Israel.

Being so conflicted on this issue; I considered saying nothing about it whatsoever. However, many Christians believe this to be one of the most important issues. To write a book on Christianity and politics and not mention it would leave a gaping hole. So, I will try to present thoughts on different aspects of the issue and hopefully come up with some type of resolution. In contrast to the rest of this work, where I believe I have been quite forthright and assertive in my views, it may seem like I am sort of muddling through this one. Well, anyway, here we go.

The most important point is that the United States should not do anything to positively damage Israel. This stand is not in conflict with any of my other stated views, since it is my contention that we should do no harm to any other nation unless they threaten us. I doubt any would assert that Israel has ever done that or is likely to in the future. But, doing harm, I believe, includes pressing them to make accommodations to their enemies and giving up any of their land – the land that God gave to them – to other nations. So, President Obama's proposal that they retreat to their pre-1967 boundaries is clearly unacceptable.

The sticky question relates to whether we should give them foreign aid and/or defend them militarily. We, as Christians, should be very supportive of Israel. However, is it right to give them the tax dollars of those (believers or not) who do not share our concern for that nation? Even more important, is it right to ask men and women to be ready to fight and possibly die on behalf of any nation other than our own? If such people don't attach any particular significance to Israel, is it proper to ask them to contribute their dollars and possibly their lives because we Christians believe its fate to be important? These are, I think, hard questions.

When it comes to foreign aid, related issues exist. First, is it a good idea for Israel to become dependent on aid from any other country? One of the harmful things about foreign aid is that the recipient nation has a tendency not to develop their own strength as a nation. This is analogous to the way in which welfare given to individuals promotes dependency.

Secondly, it appears we have used our giving of aid to influence them to make concessions to other nations. Concern about loss of aid may have caused them to make decisions they would not otherwise have made – decisions that may not be in their best interest.

Thirdly, while giving aid to them we have also dispensed it to many of their Arab neighbors. One could argue aid was given in some degree to buy influence on behalf of Israel. Their fear of losing such help may have restrained possible actions against Israel and made some of them at least outwardly less hostile to that nation. However, it has also helped to build up those nations, and if their government changes, they would be in a better position to threaten Israel.

I think it is instructive to note that during the tribulation, Israel will be betrayed by the Beast with whom they had an agreement, and that this leads to the invasion of their nation. So they are placed in peril by relying on the promises of another government. Contrast this with the

Six-Day War in 1967 when Israel unilaterally achieved military success and gained territory against several Arab counties.

Many of the Christians who are most concerned about our support of Israel were also supporters of the Iraqi and Afghan wars. One of the results of those two involvements is that both countries now have governments that are friendlier toward Iran (which is a threat to Israel). So our getting involved in those countries has resulted in a more dangerous situation for the Jewish nation.

Let's say I am right, in general, on the issues of foreign aid and military policy, but that an exception should be made for Israel. Let's go farther and say most Christians believe it is right to do whatever is necessary militarily and financially to help that nation and that this overrides what would be good policy in relation to any other country. It could then be said that, due to the imminence of the end times, this is the defining issue, and everything else – while it may have been important in an earlier era – just isn't important anymore.

But actually to implement such a policy would take a Congress and a presidential administration that were totally committed to Israel. This would mean no aid to any Arab countries, and no pressuring of Israel to make concessions to other nations. If this were to happen, disagreement would arise among all segments of our people over whether or not this was a good policy. It would mean a considerable amount of taxpayer money going to help Israel. It would also present the real possibility of going to war on their behalf, and soldiers who disagreed with this course would be asked to put their lives on the line for it. I just do not see how this could be justified.

Christian supporters of Israel who are soldiers may have to fight or give their lives in an effort to aid them if our government is committed to protecting them. Others may have children or grandchildren who have to serve and place their lives at risk. But it is likely a good portion of supporters of Israel will not have to make such sacrifices. When it comes to financial aid to Israel the funds given are such a small part of our huge national budget, that the amount each individual or family provides is probably almost negligible. For most Christians their support has little monetary or personal cost. As a result, it is easy for them to say the United States should support Israel, but true support for Israel should include the possibility of a real (maybe even significant) cost to believers personally.

Given that reality, what makes sense is that Christians, who know of God's concern for Israel, would voluntarily contribute monetarily to them, and those who are able would volunteer to serve in their military. In this situation, no compulsion would be used to get those to help Israel who either aren't believers or who don't think it is important to aid them. In this way, Christians could legitimately say they are supporting them. They would be making a personal commitment that actually costs them something.

When all is said and done on this issue, I must acknowledge that I could be wrong. I have and will continue to pray about this issue and what the proper approach should be.

Afghan and Iraqi Wars

Afghanistan

The initial focus on Afghanistan after the 9/11 attacks was appropriate. It became evident that those who had planned the action (Al Qaeda) were headquartered there. It was certainly proper to try to apprehend them and being them to justice.

However, instead of adopting that limited, justified goal, we chose to initiate an attempt at regime change. Rather than an invasion of the country, we should have sent in commando-style units targeted against those responsible for the attack on the United States. Since the Taliban, who were in control of the country at the time, were harboring Al Qaeda, they may not have been happy about that. Nevertheless, we should have told them we were coming in with or without their approval. By assuming we would have to conquer the country, however, it became a large-scale military operation, with troops not able to move with the speed necessary to get at the real object as soon as possible. The fact that Bin Laden was killed in May of 2011 by a commando-type operation shows such a tactic can be effective.

If we had received resistance from Taliban forces, we would have had to increase our presence accordingly. But we should have only done so to the extent of overcoming those deployed against us – not to conquer the whole nation and overthrow the government.

The result of our action was the installation of Karzai, a friend of Iran, as the head of the government. How did this help the War on Terror? The country is still so unstable in 2013 that we have thousands of troops stationed there, although it has been estimated that less than 100 Al Qaeda remain in the country.

Misadventure in Iraq

Why were we really in Iraq? The original professed reasons were the presence of "weapons of mass destruction" (WMD) and the need to enforce the UN resolution against such weapons. This action was portrayed by many as anti-United Nations because it was undertaken by individual nations – rather than by the United Nations itself. However, an action intended to enforce a UN sanction enhances the legal basis of such sanctions and the credibility of the United Nations itself.

Bush's stature among conservatives was improved by the perception that our action in Iraq was somehow anti-United Nations, but he, as a justification for the action, said several times that he wanted a strong and effective United Nations. Few conservatives I know want such a goal for the United Nations. A strong and effective United Nations means diminished sovereignty for the United States.

Debate ensued about whether weapons of mass destruction, if in fact present in Iraq, constituted a threat to the United States. However, if they actually existed, they would have been largely unusable without a delivery system – and I heard no one suggest that was available to Iraq. One could make the case that some such weapons could have been used in a terrorist attack. However, it was far more likely such an attack would originate in any number of nations besides Iraq.

The argument about WMDs devolved to the point where the administration was saying that if Iraq didn't have such weapons, they were developing them or were at least considering doing so. Developing or considering the development of WMDs hardly made Iraq an imminent threat to the United States – one of the few things that would justify initiating the invasion of a country.

The Bush Administration didn't often directly say the war was to be initiated to fight terrorists, but talked about Iraq while speaking of terrorism and 9/11 in a way that implied a connection. If, in fact, it was to combat terrorism, several other countries would have made more sense to attack than Iraq – due to their acknowledged history of nurturing and supporting terrorists.

When no WMDs were discovered, Bush asked whether it really mattered since we had gotten rid of Saddam. People on all points of the political spectrum agreed that Saddam was an evil person. However, if getting rid of him was truly the real objective, that should have been stated up front. A case could have been made for justifying such an action on that basis. However, I believe the war still would have been inadvisable. There are many oppressive regimes in the world, and one nation can't overthrow them all – nor should it. We cannot police the whole world. It is an example of extreme hubris for a country to believe it can stop all the evil in the world.

A high military official in Iraq has stated that they did have WMDs, but they were moved to Syria before they were invaded. If such weapons can be moved that easily and quickly, we could be invading countries incessantly trying to catch up with the weapons before they are moved again. Most likely, they would always be a step or so ahead of us. It would be like guessing who's got the button in a game of *Button, Button, Who's Got the Button*?

The most telling things that indicate the war had nothing to do with 9/11 relate to the activities of a neo-conservative organization called Project for a New American Century (PNAC) whose members include Dick Cheney, Donald Rumsfeld, and Paul Wolfowitz. PNAC sent a letter to Clinton while he was still the president suggesting we attack Iraq. Signers of that letter included Cheney and Wolfowitz.

PNAC positions regarding Iraq were incorporated into Bush Administration policy statements before 9/11.

Certainly neo-cons have been among the most enthusiastic cheerleaders for the Iraq war from the beginning. Neo-conservatives are not really conservatives. They are very internationalist in their perspective, and most don't have a problem with big government. As a long-time conservative, I have seen their influence among those on the right grow immensely over the years. It is particularly disconcerting to note that they have influenced many of the conservative leaders and spokespersons to whom Christians look for information and insight.

Some commentators speak of a supposed conflict between neo-cons and members of the Council on Foreign Relations in the Bush Administration. However, that is a false dichotomy since many neo-con leaders are also in the CFR – notably Dick Cheney.

Neo-cons advocate the United States being heavily involved in the affairs of the world. The CFR has, from the beginning, been one of the primary forces promoting a world government or, as they say, "a new world order." The fact that many neo-cons are in the CFR, indicates they don't see a conflict in those goals. Given the influence of neo-cons and CFR members in the Bush Administration one can be sure the real reasons for the Iraq War relate to the goals of both of those groups.

Before the invasion of Iraq, I argued that, if we did attack them, we would be bogged down for years in a quagmire. I did not say that because I am some kind of seer or because I had a lot of inside information unavailable to most others. In fact, I believe almost anyone who looked beyond the spin and propaganda being disseminated could have made the same prediction.

In 2008 I predicted that in spite of his stated opposition to the Iraq War, if Obama were to be elected, we would still be in that country (and Afghanistan) well into his administration. We finally did get out of Iraq three years into his term. Unfortunately, he drew down the presence there while he ramped it up in Afghanistan where the latest projection has us staying until 2014. When one understands that the foreign policy of virtually all administrations for some time has been controlled by the same globalist influences, it is not surprising to see there is little difference in the approach to foreign wars by the two major parties.

Conflicts existed among our currently stated goals in Iraq which were to institute democracy, provide stability to the nation, and to fight terrorism.

Most who talk about installing a democracy use the word in a way that implies it is synonymous with freedom. However, the fact that people are able to vote for their leaders in no way ensures they will enjoy liberty. Freedom is not the right to vote – freedom is the ability to conduct one's life without undue interference from government. To ensure such freedom in a nation, its government must recognize certain basic rights and must have a mechanism for protecting those rights for its citizens.

In the United States, our Constitution performs this function with its limitations on government and its checks and balances. To think we can merely export our form of government to another country is naïve. In many cultures, including Iraq, the concept of rights is quite different from ours.

There seems to be an assumption that once a country has become a stable democracy, the problem of terrorism magically goes away. In actuality, the goals of democracy and stability in Iraq potentially conflict with one another. We stayed in Iraq until an elected government was able to attain control over their situation. But we want them to be a democracy, right? So, what if they vote for those who are not able or desirous of maintaining stability? Do we then go back into Iraq?

An even greater likelihood exists that democracy will conflict with the supposed fight against terrorism. What guarantee is there that a country with the ability to elect its leaders will not elect those who will harbor or even support and encourage terrorists? Afghanistan has elected a leader who is friendly with Iran (Karzai). And the currently elected leadership in Iraq has resulted in a country that is friendlier with Iran than it was before we invaded them. Given the fact Iran is perceived as a threat, how has this contributed to the fight against terrorism?

Iran is sort of a mix of a democracy and a theocracy. So, what do we do with them when it is their turn to be invaded by us? Are they sufficiently democratic? If not, with what are we going to replace their government? Ahmadinejad is elected. Do we still depose him, even though one of our goals is to have elected governments?

We are trying to apply a military solution to problems that are virtually incapable of a military solution. Muslim societies really need to be totally transformed before they will institute governments that provide individual rights in a stable environment. No amount of troops or military equipment applied to the country will effect the needed changes. As Christians we should realize that evangelization of those cultures provides the best potential for such transformations.

Many conservatives are influenced by the fact that the hard left is so against this war, but many in the left (particularly the peace-at-any-price doves) are unrealistically against any war. The fact that they are against this particular war is not an *ipso facto* reason to be for it. In fact, if opposition by the left were a criterion for being for a war, conservatives would have to support any proposed war – no matter how unjustified or inadvisable it may be. And since those in the left are against the war, they will find many reasons to justify their opposition – including very valid ones. The fact that they cite a given reason for opposing the war does not automatically mean the reason is incorrect. As Christians, we should support or oppose policies because they are right or wrong, respectively, not based on who is promoting them or working against them.

Some on the right who have opposed the Iraqi and Afghan wars have begun referring to themselves as anti-war. I don't believe that is appropriate for a Christian since the use of such a term implies a person is against all war. Believers know that in a fallen world, at times it is necessary for a nation to go to war. For the same reason, I do not believe conservative opponents of ill-advised wars should consider themselves part of the "peace movement."

Some proponents of the war say we had to fight terrorists in Iraq or we would have to fight them over here, and cite the fact that we haven't had any major terrorist incidents here since 9/11 as proof. However, using that logic, we will have to keep fighting Muslims somewhere in the world indefinitely to prevent another attack. No one really knows why there have been no additional major attacks in the United States, but certainly nothing prevented them from perpetrating one just because we were fighting in Iraq.

There might actually be a perverse reason why the Iraq conflict prevented attacks in the United States. Just possibly, the terrorists might have realized our being there was hurting us more than any attacks they could make in this country. They saw how many lives we were losing, the money we were spending, how the war was dividing our people, and how it was being used to curtail our liberties. They may actually believe that if they had attacked somewhere in this country, we might have had second thoughts about our effort in Iraq or that the people of this country might have started demanding that we bring our troops home, tighten our borders, and focus on fighting terrorists in this country.

It is argued that not fighting Islam is some sort of appeasement. When appeasement is discussed, the example of Chamberlain's weakness at Munich is often brought up. Some are saying that not attacking Islam is parallel to the appeasement of Hitler. Certainly, when it comes to using racism and inflammatory rhetoric, similarities between radical Muslims and Hitler are apparent. However, the threat posed by those Muslims is not parallel to Hitler at all. His was a military threat in Europe with two distinct fronts. The threat of Muslim terrorism is virtually worldwide; the front is potentially everywhere.

A major reason many conservatives were defending the war when George W. Bush was president was the mistaken idea that he is a conservative and that we must, therefore, support the war for his sake. But those who have followed the career of Bush and his father know that neither has ever been a conservative. Bush threw out some bones of rhetoric occasionally to try to pacify conservatives, but his actions yielded nothing of substance toward our objectives.

Ironically, some reason in the other direction, saying that Bush is a conservative because he was prosecuting this so-called "War on Terrorism" – arguing that this is a conservative position. Certainly, conservatives have disagreed about how activist our foreign policy ought to be. However, the preponderance of conservative beliefs prior to the intrusion of neo-con influence favored a non-interventionist policy.

Some believers supported the war because Bush is a professed Christian. But professing Christianity should not preclude a politician's actions from being scrutinized. Many political figures claim to be Christians. One such person is Jimmy Carter. Yet it is hard to find a person who is more politically misguided than he. His political positions are primarily those many Christians oppose.

Among the most serious ramifications of this war are the various ways it has harmed the conservative movement and the Republican Party. Many in this country may not call themselves conservatives but share our views on numerous issues. An example is the large percentage of Americans who oppose illegal immigration. Many of these people aren't into labels, but when they hear people, who call themselves conservatives, supporting a war which their common sense tells them is inadvisable at best, that is the image they get of conservatives. As a result, they tune out the rest of our messages – many, if not most, with which they may agree.

Another detrimental effect of the war was all the time, money, and effort spent justifying the war and defending it and Bush. Wasted resources could have been used to address things like opposing abortion, the out-of-control deficit, the increasing control by the federal government over education, and the loss of personal freedom – to name just a few.

The huge amount of money used to prosecute these two wars has made it very difficult for conservatives to speak against excess government spending and the immense debt, because when they do, those on the left point to the large expenditures for the wars.

The war has also had a negative effect on the image of Christianity. Most Americans do not believe in the pacifistic views of the far left. They believe war to protect American interests is justifiable. This is also what most Christians believe. Believers supporting a necessary war do not reflect adversely on Christianity. However, when such a high percentage of Christians support a war that is perceived as wrong, it cannot help but harm the opinion of non-believers about Christianity.

There has been much said by conservatives about the good things that happened in Iraq that didn't get reported. One example I heard was a soldier telling of how he and his buddies were helping some Iraqis with their crops and to get fresh water. That is a good thing, but such activities were hardly reasons to stay in Iraq. Nor were they justifications for going there initially. If they are, we ought to find some more countries we can invade so we can help them too!

Some people said we shouldn't leave Iraq regardless of whether we should have gone there initially since it was then the front line in the war on terror. Of course it was the front line since that's the country we invaded! If we had invaded Algeria, Algeria would have been the front line. That would be true of almost any Muslim country we would have attacked. Front line only means there is much terrorist activity directed at our troops. In reality terrorists have made attacks in many places around the world, and could easily do so almost anywhere. Even speaking of a front line really doesn't have much meaning when we are not fighting a conventional war.

The bottom line is no matter which of the stated or implied goals of the Iraq war a person subscribes to, there was no reason to remain in the country so long. If the reason was to destroy weapons of mass destruction, none were found. If it was to enforce the UN resolution, that had been done. If it was to depose Saddam, he had died. If it was to establish a democracy, the limited version of having them vote for their leaders had been accomplished, and the establishment of a true American-style government is virtually impossible without being preceded by major societal change. If it was to fight terrorism – well this whole chapter is filled with reasons why this method of doing so is illogical, unrealistic, and ineffective.

So, what do we do? We can't fight terrorists everywhere in the world, but we can identify, expose, and disable them in this country. This is discussed further in the chapter on civil liberties.

We should certainly not turn to the strategy of the left. Many on that side would turn to the United Nations since they advocate a stronger world order. They talk of negotiating settlements; but, given their mindset, negotiating with radical Muslims will never get us anywhere.

CHAPTER 10

Civil Liberties

I do not know how the term "civil liberties" came to be used to designate certain rights and freedoms. Disagreements arise as to what should be included in the term. I use it here to apply generally to the freedoms detailed as being guaranteed in our Bill of Rights, although that is not a comprehensive list.

"Civil liberties" is really an oxymoron. If liberty is – as I contend – a natural right, then all liberties are innate and require no action from civil authority as implied in the name. This applies also to civil rights – which I cover more thoroughly in Chapter 4. I really question whether either "civil liberties" or "civil rights" are even valid terms since by using the modifier "civil" they imply a category of rights or liberties exist that are somehow different from others.

Some items contained in the Bill of Rights are not really natural rights, but, rather, relate to procedures the government agrees to follow in legal cases such as a guarantee of a trial by jury, prevention of double jeopardy, and a requirement for search warrants. They are important safeguards that government should abide by to ensure government doesn't act arbitrarily toward its citizens. They are often referred to as rights or liberties, and they do help protect rights and liberty, but aren't in and of themselves truly rights.

It is unfortunate that the first ten amendments have become known as the Bill of Rights. That label tends to reinforce the improper impression that these are rights given to us by the Constitution, when it actually prevents the federal government from infringing the rights we already have naturally. As such, they should be called something like "Bill of Restrictions" or "Bill of Prohibitions" so the use of "rights" and "liberties" can be consistently reserved for our natural occurring abilities to make free actions.

It is likely that the term "civil liberties" will continue to be used for these protections from government, so I have used the term in the title of this chapter since it as a convenient label for grouping some issues that generally are thought to fall in the civil liberty category. But the chapter is far from a complete treatment of all issues considered to be in that classification.

When hearing "civil liberties" one tends to think of issues championed by the left. We often do not think of things such as the right to keep and bear arms, about which those of a liberal bent tend not to be too concerned (or generally don't even consider a valid right). Unfortunately, many of the freedoms that do come to mind when we hear "civil liberties" are ones conservatives have a rather poor record of defending.

This is an area where it is likely that at least a fair number of Christians will disagree with what I have to say. But I think my beliefs on such topics are consistent with a philosophy of limited government and with a Christian worldview. Several reasons exist for why many conservatives have adopted views in this area which I believe are inconsistent with their other beliefs. One is that, in addition to protecting individuals from the actions of others, they have come to believe government should protect us from the dangerous ideas of others. But that is problematic since this means the government will be defining which ideas are dangerous. When those in authority are given such discretion, they tend, over time, to squelch ideas that threaten their positions and power.

Some conservatives also believe government should be the guardian of morality. I primarily deal with that in Chapter 5, although I do discuss it somewhat in this chapter. Conservatives also tend not to be concerned about protecting certain freedoms because many on the left are working to do so because they have distorted many issues surrounding these so-called "civil liberties." In those cases, conservatives should disagree with them. But in an attempt to be consistent in defending freedom, the left has also adopted positions that truly support rights in a proper manner. However, most conservatives do not wish to be in league with groups such as the ACLU and automatically dismiss any position they adopt. We should never be for or against anything based on who is supporting or opposing it, but rather should base our view on the merits of the issue itself.

It is quite paradoxical for those on the left to advocate so much freedom in what has become known as "civil liberties" since they are for strong government control in most other areas. They claim to be concerned about government using its power to stifle dissent. Yet, they wish to give that same government almost complete control over things like healthcare, the nation's economy, and the use of firearms. Any government with such authority will also have all the tools needed to control what its citizens say and write.

When the government effectively can decide whether you get healthcare or whether you have anything to eat, it has life and death power over you. Merely the threat of withholding these essentials is often enough to keep most of the populace in line. We have already seen in the United States the impact of government control of income and healthcare for seniors. In order to garner votes, candidates and parties routinely instill fear in seniors, suggesting that their opponents will make changes to Medicare and Social Security that will negatively impact them. Are people who vote on such a basis really free?

In this chapter, I will discuss freedom of expression which is generally considered a civil liberty. I also talk about the War on Terror. That topic isn't, in itself, a civil liberties issue; however, since so many of the measures employed in this so-called "war" present concerns about threats to freedom, I think it is appropriate to address it here.

Freedom of Expression

Freedom of expression is one of the very most important rights for believers. It impacts our rights to worship, proselytize, to speak out on issues from a Christian perspective, and communicate in various ways to further God's kingdom.

The First Amendment of the Constitution prevents Congress from abridging the freedom of speech. This is certainly a very important right

– but one which is often misinterpreted. Both liberals and conservatives claim to be very concerned about retaining this liberty. Unfortunately, they don't really agree on what the right entails.

One misinterpretation is that it prevents any level of government from interfering with free speech. In actuality, since it specifically says "Congress shall make no law …," it is a prohibition against the federal government doing so. This right must be protected, but the issue often should be handled at the state level. However, federal courts have been improperly intruding themselves into freedom of expression issues that shouldn't involve Washington.

Basically, freedom of speech gives a person or group the right to say what they please when they are doing so in their own venue, and paying any costs related to the expression of their ideas. No one should expect that others are required to provide a platform from which they can say what they wish. If a person is speaking on someone else's property and saying what the owner does not wish to have expressed, they have every right to ask them to desist or leave.

Expression in Schools

Much discussion has surrounded the topic of freedom of speech in schools. But schools are entities that can and really must have rules. Those rules will encompass what is allowed to be said. By doing so, the institution is not denying anyone's freedom of speech, only restricting what can be said within its confines. That is true for both public and private schools.

But both the left and the right have tried to assert a right to free expression in educational institutions. Believers have been upset because administrations have prevented students from wearing clothing with Christian messages. In some cases, they have filed suits to rectify such situations. This is something that needs to be dealt with in the local school – not in the courts. Certainly, administrators should be consistent and have rules that apply equitably to various political and religious viewpoints. If they are not and appeals to them go nowhere, the situation should be taken to the school board. If they don't act, Christians need to work to replace board members who are not supportive of fair standards. In Chapter 7, I deal more thoroughly with the idea of local control of education.

Another free expression issue that comes up with schools is the supposed censorship that takes place when a library elects not to carry a given book. A school library can only stock so many books. Decisions must be made as to which ones it will procure. In some cases, a school may decide to drop a book that had been in its library. Due to limited space, libraries often remove titles from their shelves to make room for others deemed more worthy. They may take away titles not being checked out very frequently. The criteria used to remove books for other reasons may vary from school to school. It certainly is proper to take away books that are in poor taste, offensive, or not considered appropriate for students. This process is not censorship.

Undoubtedly, books have been pulled merely because someone didn't like their political perspectives. Given the general bias of educators, it is likely more conservative books have been removed than liberal ones, but complaints about so-called censorship in school libraries are mostly made by the left. It is unlikely the ACLU et al. often object to a right-oriented or Christian book being removed from a library. The bottom line is that what is in a given public school library should reflect the values of the community in which it is located.

Choosing which books are to be available in a certain library (either in a school or a community library) is not censorship any more than a bookstore deciding what books it will sell. However, a bookstore is a private business. Community and school libraries are tax-supported, and, as such, citizens have every right to express their opinions as to what books they wish to have on the shelves. If parents and/or taxpayers don't like the books in the libraries of their schools, the answer is to pursue the issue through school administration and school boards. Remember, the people in these positions work for you.

Others also assert that teachers have a right to teach what they wish and that students have rights to learn certain things in schools. Such people actually believe any attempt by a school administration or board to restrict curriculum is a violation of First Amendment rights. However, educators are employees who have been hired to carry out the mandates of a school board which represents parents and taxpayers. As such, they are subject to the same type of authority as are any employees. No public relations writer would be so brash as to insist that he has the First Amendment right to extol the virtues of a competitor's product or to write promotional material in Latin. Neither does an educator have any right to teach anything against the wishes of their employers and/or that violates the values of a great portion of those who pay their salaries.

The public relations writer mentioned above could not legitimately protest that it was censorship for her employer to restrict what she writes. Nor is it censorship when schools give strict guideless to teachers about what should be taught and how it should be taught.

None of these controversies regarding schools would be problems if we would get government out of the education business. That is the ultimate answer, but this is not likely to happen for some time. Until it does, this is an issue that should be addressed by parents and school officials at a local level.

Hate Crimes Legislation

Currently, the two greatest threats to our freedom of expression are through hate crimes legislation and so-called campaign finance reform. The primary portion of hate crimes legislation where we can expect a big push is in questions related to homosexuality. Experiences in other countries show us what impact hate crime legislation will likely have on free speech.

Pastors in Sweden and Canada have been fined and/or jailed for speaking against homosexual activity. Common sense would dictate that no matter what one's views of homosexuality are, he ought to have the right to express them. That is certainly what we would expect to be allowed in a nation noted for its freedom of speech. But there are people in this country who no longer believe in permitting speech they don't approve of, and some of those are the same people who almost idolize the First Amendment.

In any issue beyond the First Amendment, the left is very hypocritical in their purported concern about violating the Constitution.

They express grave concern over a person's constitutional rights being denied (even though in many cases they have misinterpreted the First Amendment). Yet, they show no concern whatever that the courts have ignored and failed to apply the Tenth Amendment, which prevents the federal government from getting involved with any matters where they have not been given specific powers by the Constitution.

They do not care in the least whether legislation abrogates the right to keep and bear arms as stated in the Second Amendment. In fact, many liberals talk as though the First Amendment is the whole Constitution.

Campaign "Reform" Legislation

Current campaign reform legislation would prevent issue-oriented corporations from sponsoring, within sixty days of an election, issue ads that mention a candidate and ads that "express advocacy" at any time. "Express advocacy" is very ambiguously defined. Part of this law has, fortunately, been struck down as unconstitutional. However, I will nevertheless consider various aspects of the law as passed to evaluate the appropriateness of such legislation.

Such a ban would likely cause even more focus on building up the images of candidates – rather than on discussions of their stances on public policies. The worst part of the bill is its utter disregard for our freedoms. Much issue campaigning is directed at incumbents whose positions are illustrated by their voting record. Many current office-holders like such restrictive legislation since it allows them to vote as they wish with minimal accountability to the voters.

Incumbents are part of the government. To limit discussion of their records is to restrict criticism of the government – one of the primary hallmarks of a totalitarian regime. This is the United States of America – not Cuba or China! The free and unrestricted right to criticize our government is a big part of what the United States is about as a nation.

Such legislation will not solve the problems it purports to, since it is directed at symptoms rather than root causes. There are reasons why so many interests spend large amounts of money on campaigns, and why such funds are often so effective in electing candidates.

The scope of government has become so pervasive that hardly any constituency does not have vested interests in the outcomes of elections. With all the subsidies being given, it creates many parties vying to be showered with the largesse. With a large government, there exist a large number of contracts for which to compete. With so much regulation, many wish to receive exceptions for their situations. The bottom line is that many parties are impacted by government and, therefore, find it worth their while to spend money to impact elections. Too much government is the problem; the huge amounts spent in campaigns are merely symptoms of that problem.

Another problem leading to massive expenditures is that campaign personnel know expensive media campaigns which build name IDs and images, and obscure the true philosophies of candidates, will be effective because few voters know much about candidates. No number of billions of campaign dollars would cause me to vote for a Bill Clinton, Al Gore, or Barack Obama, because I simply know too much about them. However, for many voters, most of what they hear about candidates is from the campaigns. This is partially due to their own lack of interest and motivation, but also to the limited information available through the media. Here again, the spending of massive amounts of funds is merely a symptom; voter ignorance is the problem.

Another reason for large campaign expenditures is that conservatives simply have to spend a lot to get information out about their candidates and the liberal opponents to overcome the bias of media reporting and editorializing that goes on three hundred and sixty five days a year. This legislation further expands the media control by restricting those who would present alternative information and opinions.

Those who use money or information to influence elections or legislation are often pejoratively referred to as "special interests." In our representative form of government, all people should be interested in who gets elected and in working to influence officeholders to support laws they favor. Why should not those with common interests have a right to organize without the implication that they are doing something illegitimate? What makes one interest "special" as opposed to those whose interest in government is merely regular or normal? If we give government the power to silence "special interests," they will soon have the power to silence any interest whose opposition it finds threatening or annoying.

One example of those who are often designated "special interests" is those opposing gun-control laws, but they are truly working to preserve the gun rights of all Americans – even though some may choose not to exercise those rights. More importantly, they are really helping to maintain the liberty of all of our countrymen since guns are such an important check upon political tyranny.

Congress often seeks to pass regulations so excessive as to threaten the very existence of some businesses. Should those businesses not at least be able to fight back by supporting the election of those who still believe in our free enterprise system? They should not have to fight with one – if not both – hands tied behind their backs.

This campaign finance legislation placed restrictions on expenditures by corporations. When they hear the word "corporation" people tend to think of large business enterprises. And such organizations do spend a lot in elections, but due to tax laws, most organizations that deal with issues are incorporated and would have their ability to inform voters curtailed by such laws. These are composed of citizens who have organized to educate the citizenry about candidates and their records and positions. Without their efforts, voters would often get no substantive information about important issues which should help them determine for whom to vote. As far as commercial entities are concerned, it is dangerous to start taking away rights from any group. Once that is done, it is that much easier to take that right away from others and ultimately all.

We don't need campaign finance reform – we need reform that restores the federal government to its originally intended, limited role. Such a restoration would severely reduce the incentive for spending huge sums to elect candidates.

Campaign finance reform will not reduce the impact of outside influence on candidates and office-holders; it will merely result in a power-shift. The media, political parties, and professional politicians who already have so much political power will gain even more influence.

The individual citizens who voluntarily come together to organize to promote their causes will lose even more control over the government "of the people, by the people, and for the people."

Obsession with Sexual Expression

It is interesting that liberals aren't often concerned about the loss of the freedom of expression when it pertains to being critical of incumbent politicians in elections or when it involves speech codes on campuses. This needs to be qualified since there are some sincere civil libertarians on the left who stand up for everyone's right to speak.

But what really raises the hackles of most liberals is any attempt to restrict anything relating to sex. They seem to be more concerned about freedom to express ideas about sexual topics than that of political thoughts – even though the right to present ideas about government was what the founders had in mind when they added the First Amendment. They will often accuse conservatives of being obsessed with sex due to efforts by some on the right to restrict such material. However, since they have elevated the status of such material above that of political speech, one could say those on the left are really the ones who are obsessed with sex.

I believe, as Christians, we should primarily be concerned about the public display of sexually offensive material, and that should be accomplished with local government ordinances. But any attempt to prevent publication or distribution of printed material or of presenting anything on the Internet sets up a censorship authority that empowers government and puts it in the position of making them the arbiters of what should be expressed. This power can very easily be misused to prevent communication of what they deem inappropriate – like Christian and conservative ideas.

War on Terror

This issue will be discussed in relation to the situation in the world in 2013 when the main terrorist threat is from Islamic radicals.

The whole term "War on Terror" is very presumptuous since it implies we can eliminate all terrorists. This is an example of the hubris of those hyping this pseudo war. Maybe some of them know all terrorism cannot be eliminated and that, therefore, the war will go indefinitely – which will be very useful for promoting their agenda of a world order and a controlled society in our country (shades of "1984" where perpetual war was one of the tools used to control the populace). A war should be conducted against specific countries. Declaring a war on terror is leaving open-ended both the identity of the enemy and the conditions by which the action is to be terminated.

The Muslim Threat

I do not intend to minimize the terrorist threat from the Muslim world. Nor do I deny that much within the religion of Islam itself is inherently militaristic. However, it is wrong for us to assume all Muslims support terrorism. Most particularly, we Christians should treat those of that religion with personal respect. But if they live in this country, they should expect to abide by our laws and not be able to institute their own rules in areas where they are numerically dominant.

Noting the differences between our country and Muslim nations (with their Sharia Law), it is obvious laws are based on religious assumptions. Ours have been created with the Christian view that we are created by God in His image and, thus, should be able to exercise the freedom He has given us. Muslims, however, believe the government should be controlled by them with the ability to use harsh measures to force conformance with their religion.

Actually, the fact that radical Muslims are so numerous and widespread worldwide, and the religion of Islam is itself so warlike, makes the idea that we can stop terrorism by invading any country or any number of countries totally unrealistic. Muslims constitute the majority in a large number of nations. All of them have radicals and potential terrorists. Most likely, they all have actual terrorists. Of course, those countries vary in how much support they give to terrorists within their boundaries, but that can change rather rapidly.

To effectively wipe out terrorism, we would have to conquer every Muslim country in the world. But subduing those countries wouldn't ensure we have taken care of all terrorists even if we maintained a military presence indefinitely in all of them. We could not possibly muster enough troops to take over all Muslim nations and maintain adequate personnel in each. Certainly, our experience in Iraq attests to the fact that defeating a country does not get rid of all the terrorists there. We can't even secure our own borders. Who knows how many terrorists have infiltrated the United States through the Mexican border? So, how are we going to get rid of all the terrorists in every Muslim country?

Even if we were somehow able to do that, we still haven't eliminated the problem. Virtually every nation in the world has Muslims – some have large populations. The likelihood that all countries have radical Islamists and potential and actual terrorists is great. France is a good example of a country where large numbers of Muslims have already caused problems. Is there any doubt that among the rioting mobs in that country there would be some – possibly many – who could be (or already have been) recruited for terrorist activity?

It is unquestionably true that those who planned and carried out the attack on the World Trade Center are responsible for their actions. Those who have stirred up Muslims and those who have created the terrorist organizations also bear much culpability. It is not true that we as a country in some way bear responsibility for those attacks as some imply or plainly state.

It is also true that many Muslims do not like the United States because we have so many Christians, because many in this country sympathize with Israel, because we are materialistic, hedonistic, etc. However, all that having been said, it is also true that we have exacerbated the anti-American sentiment among Muslims by a foreign policy that has intruded itself into many conflicts throughout the world. It is also true that our involvement in Iraq has contributed to radicalizing more Muslims.

How Will We Keep Terrorists Off of Planes?

The War on Terror has considerably increased the size and scope of the federal government. It has led directly to very intrusive practices to try to secure safety on air flights. The logical way to handle this potential threat is to leave flight security with individual airline companies, as

Ron Paul said. They are the ones who are legally liable for their passengers and stand to lose crew and planes if incidents occur. They also need to serve and please their customers, who want assurance of safety, but also want to be treated with dignity. If these companies were to handle their own security, they would likely come up with procedures balanced between security and due respect for the privacy of fliers. Plus, the competition between airlines would work toward solutions that meet all needs. Government has no need to get involved in flight security. All it does is further empower them in a way they can use against people they see as their enemies.

I am not certain how effective the federal government's current screening efforts really are. I had an assignment a number of years ago where every week I commuted by air to a job site out of town. I had started carrying a small jackknife in my pocket prior to that time since situations often arise where it is helpful to have something with which to cut. The first Monday morning of my assignment, I placed all the items I normally carry with me into my pockets. Without thinking about my upcoming flight, that included my knife. When I was about to empty my pockets before going through the screener, I realized I had it with me. It was a cheap knife, and I would not have cared had it been confiscated. However, I made a split-second decision to wrap it in my handkerchief and go through with it still in my pocket. I'm not sure why. Maybe I just didn't want to explain why I was carrying it, and I didn't have much time to think about it. Anyway, I went through the scanner without it being detected.

A couple of months later – ironically just after telling someone about this incident at church on Sunday – I put the knife in my pocket again on a Monday morning. This time I didn't realize it was there until I had gone through the metal detector and saw the dish coming out of the viewer on the conveyor with my knife right on top of my other possessions in full view – yet unnoticed by the security people.

One thing I think is ridiculous is the rule prohibiting any humor while going through security. Does anyone really think a person who was carrying an item they intended to use to commandeer or blow up a plane would call attention to themselves by making a joke? Perhaps allowing people to say something funny would lighten things up a little. This rule was likely made by some grim, humorless bureaucrats.

Effects on Other Policies

Conservatives have also focused so much attention on the War on Terror that they do not spend as much time reading and informing themselves about other issues and concerns. A good example is the severe threat to our sovereignty posed by the proposed North American Union (also called the Security and Prosperity Partnership) which is hardly a blip on the radar screens of most conservatives. The current administration is also working on similar agreements with Pacific nations (the Trans-Pacific Partnership – TPP) and with the European Union (Transatlantic Trade and Investment Partnership – TTIP) – both of which are additional threats to our sovereignty.

Many conservatives have become willing to compromise their beliefs on limited government and support things like the Patriot Act which gives considerable power to government, because they falsely believe terrorism is the greatest threat to our nation. Never has the adage that "those who sacrifice liberty for temporary security deserve neither liberty nor security"[2] been as applicable to our country as it is currently.

Some of the more egregious parts of the Patriot Act include: allowing the FBI to write its own search warrants, permitting the searching of a party's premises without their knowledge, and penalizing those who have been victimized by such procedures if they tell anyone about it. The law clearly contravenes the Fourth Amendment that states: "The right of the people to be secure in their persons, houses, papers, and effects, against unreasonable searches and seizures, shall not be violated, and no Warrants shall issue, but upon probable cause, supported by Oath or affirmation, and particularly describing the place to be searched, and the persons or things to be seized."

The measures followed under the Patriot Act are the hallmark of a police state. They are rationalized as necessary due to what is described as the extreme threat of terrorism. Even if that is as bad as some say, the response should be, "So what?" All infringements on liberties are

2 Paraphrase of quote by Benjamin Franklin – see footnote in Chapter 17.

justified by those who would restrict rights as required to meet some threat – whether real or fabricated. And if we should end up with a totally authoritarian government, does anyone think we will be safer? Were Germans more secure after Hitler took over as a dictator?

It is baffling (and I will have to be honest, quite troubling) that so many who call themselves conservatives and are concerned about the threat of giving more power to government – including some who are otherwise consistent about adhering to the Constitution – believe that such an outrageous law is good for our nation. Christians particularly, who realize the fallen nature of humanity, should, more than anyone, recognize the danger of giving these types of powers to a centralized authority.

Unfortunately, the original bill was rushed through Congress so fast that most legislators did not read it. No lawmaker should ever vote for a bill without knowing its full contents. But some who did so could have said they voted for it because they were misled about its provisions. However, various pieces of the legislation have been extended since its initial passage. When those extensions have been considered, no one can use that excuse, since the full text is now known. Yet, most of those (including conservatives) who voted for the original law continue to support its extensions.

Some conservatives have told me that they are not concerned about the powers government has with the Patriot Act or by performing roving wiretaps, etc., because they are law-abiding and don't intend to do anything wrong. Unfortunately, it is the same government that is using these tactics that will define what "wrong" means. Once the precedence is set for exercising such powers, future occupants of government offices can easily redefine the enemies against whom they choose to deploy them. I believe the reason we have come to trust government so much is that we have had so much freedom for so long that we truly do not believe totalitarianism can happen here. But it is when a majority of the residents of a country naively have that attitude that they are the most vulnerable to losing their liberty.

If conservatives think these powers will only be used against legitimate terrorists and/or leftists, they should consider the memos sent out by Janet Napolitano, the head of the Department of Homeland Security, in 2009, asking state police to be on the alert for those she considered potential right-wing terrorists. She said such people could be identified by support for limited government, state sovereignty, pro-life, stricter immigration laws, and Second Amendment rights. Also mentioned were those opposing the policies of the Obama Administration. She even mentioned that returning military veterans could be targeted for recruitment by terrorist groups. Does anyone think that an administration who considers people in these categories (likely a majority of those reading this book) as enemies to be watched would have any compunction about using the powers of laws like the Patriot Act against them?

We do need to track the activities of terrorist groups and individuals, but we need to do so in ways more focused on them and not the average American. If we lose our individual freedom and our Constitutional rights, then our enemies have won a major battle against us.

The so-called "War on Terror" has also caused other changes in policies including the adoption of the use of torture and holding prisoners without charging them – violating the *habeas corpus* protection that has been followed in the English system of laws for centuries. It seems we are retreating from being a civilized society to being more barbaric. It is almost scandalous that Christians have been in the forefront of those who defend such practices that bypass legal protections. When I, as a believer, have been asked about Christians who have supported such policies, I frankly have no answer because I, personally, do not understand at all how Christ-followers can justify such actions. Surely, this is a case of trying to excuse the ends with very horrible means.

The War on Terror has also been further contributing to the weakening of the separation of powers of our national government. It has provided one more incidence of engaging in hostilities without a declaration of war. This has tipped the balance by increasing the power of the presidency at the expense of the Congress. And in spite of this being an undeclared war, Bush claimed all sorts of powers and privileges due to his being commander-in-chief. A good example is his signing statements along with new laws stating why he wasn't bound by the legislation.

A major impact of the war was the effect on the 2006 and 2008 elections. Because of this, a crew came into power in Washington with little regard for our freedoms or our tax money. One of the reasons issues related to the War on Terror did not appear to have as much of an impact on the 2010 election is that many more citizens had come to the realization that no real difference exists between Obama's policies in this area and that of his predecessor. And due to the massive bailouts and the passage of Obamacare, people were more concerned and focused on domestic issues.

In 2008, conservatives were considering supporting potential presidential candidates whom they disagreed with on most issues simply because they believed that person would do a good job of conducting the so-called "War on Terror." The mistaken belief that terrorism is our most serious problem is causing it to trump all other issues.

Conservatives have long recognized that the moral cancer eating away at our society and big government are the most severe threats to our nation. Many now seem to believe that terrorism is a greater threat. The 9/11 attacks caused the death of over three-thousand people. But using that event to justify means that may take away freedom of all Americans is inexcusable. We could probably live in a fairly secure, limited-crime society by stationing a soldier with a machine gun on every street corner, but who would want to live in such a world? Terrorism is a concern and needs to be addressed. However, it will never bring down our country, but moral decline and all-powerful government are increasingly destroying all that made this nation great. In fact, many issues should be of greater concern than terrorism.

CHAPTER 11

What About Faith-Based Initiatives?

Faith-based initiatives is a term used today to describe a situation where an organization based on religious faith is tasked with carrying out a social-welfare function of government. They wouldn't have to be affiliated with Christianity, but it is those I will address here. I will deal with this question as it relates to the federal government, since the discussion has centered on programs there. But most of the points made would pertain to any level of government.

It Seems Like a Good Idea on the Surface

Such faith-based initiatives have garnered much discussion in recent years. Its supporters proclaim that Christian organizations often do a better job in meeting needs than government and will cite examples to prove their point. Many people believe that to be true; I certainly do. But it does not necessarily follow that they should be funded with tax dollars. One of the reasons many Christian ministries have been successful is likely the lack of government involvement. It is possible that some of their programs would lose much of their effectiveness were they to be subsidized.

The initial response by Christians to proposals for such programs has often been favorable. However, most who offer that response have not thought through the ramifications of moving in this direction. The liberals argue against these policies, because they believe it would be an unconstitutional intrusion of church into government. Certainly, that argument is as spurious as it is in other issues where they improperly cite the First Amendment as preventing any Christian influence in government.

Christians, quite naturally, get defensive against such a position and tend to think, therefore, that these proposals must be good ideas. However, the fact that some opponents are against an idea for the wrong reason does not mean it is good. Nor is a program worthy just because it may pass constitutional muster. While using faith organizations to administer them should not be considered unconstitutional, most of the federal programs are, in and of themselves, unconstitutional regardless of who runs them and/or are spending their funds. They are involved in activities not covered by the enumeration of powers in the Constitution.

The Danger of Government Control

Programs calling for cooperation between the government and faith-based organizations are not in the best long-term interest of either those organizations or the country, and they are particularly fraught with danger to the mission of the church. When any person or organization enters into a partnership with government, the government ultimately becomes the senior partner.

What the government funds it controls. When the topic of federal aid to education was originally being debated, advocates gave assurances that the federal government would only give financial assistance and had no interest in dictating policy to local schools. Such a statement is laughable today. We now have a huge educational bureaucracy in Washington which is continually growing larger. And while they provide a small percentage of the funds expended, they require compliance with an ever-increasing number of mandates.

It is generally accepted that funds must not go to programs where proselytizing occurs. So, if a Christian organization has been evangelizing and starts getting government funds, they would have to separate the part of their organization that administers the government programs. That would probably mean actually either setting up a separate entity or acquiescing to hiring non-believers, including homosexuals, for their main organization since anyone involved with the government will surely have to comply with non-discrimination rules. Such ministries should not rely on any current exceptions since the laws could well be changed or the protections could be thrown out in court. Plus, evangelization should be part and parcel of any service a Christian organization performs. The last thing many ministries want to do is separate proselytizing from serving. Christian ministries are often staffed by those who raise support rather than being paid a salary by the organization. Will Christians contribute support to those who they know will be hamstrung in efforts to provide a true witness? This, again, would point to the need to have separate organizations if the ministry wishes to provide a witness.

But the Christian witness – both for individuals and for ministries – should be an integral part of our service. To separate the two goes against the idea that our ministry is just an extension of who we are in Christ and that our witness really flows from our serving.

The publicly funded side of an organization would probably have to have salaried employees. They would likely come under employment guidelines preventing discrimination – meaning non-Christians will have to be hired. If there are two separate organizations, would those seeking help who may have some choice be more likely to go to the one where there may be some accountability, and where they are required to listen to a Gospel presentation, or to the one where they simply get the help with no strings attached?

How much time and attention will the leaders of such Christian organizations have to give to the portion of their organization that is administering tax monies? This will be time and attention diverted from the witnessing part of the ministry where there is a much greater likelihood of producing fruit for the kingdom.

This will be particularly true of effort required to comply with government rules. Extensive record-keeping is always a part of involvement with any level of government.

Ministries that enter into such an arrangement could find it is much easier to accept the subsidies instead of raising the funds from voluntary contributions. The temptation would be to focus on the part of their ministry where they get the "free" money (the non-witnessing portion). Receiving such funds tends to have a narcotic effect, and many ministries may find themselves hooked.

Would Christian Ministries Keep Their Focus?

Gradually, the focuses of such organizations are likely to change to one of good works without any Christian message. This is what happened to mainline Protestant denominations as they moved from preaching the true Gospel to the social gospel. This presents the danger that ministries will become dependent on government funds, possibly not giving the attention they had in the past to maintaining other funding sources.

In the book *The Tragedy of American Compassion,* [3] Marvin Olasky talks of the many outstanding Christian ministries in this country in the nineteenth century. They gave aid with Christian love in accordance with biblical principles, and they required accountability as they worked to change lives – not merely fill stomachs. Christians recognize that often the way to help someone is by assisting them to change destructive lifestyles. As the government took an increasing role in welfare, most of those programs were supplanted.

However, biblical guidelines require that recipients of aid meet some criteria and/or are held accountable for their behavior. I fear that many Christian ministries are not following those guidelines even now, but many organizations would likely be forced to drop their accountability rules if they were in partnership with the government.

Christians and the government often do not agree on the source of a given social problem. Let's say that the official government position is that alcoholism is a disease. A Christian ministry believes the root cause is sin. Obviously, the way it would approach a solution would be different than the government's tactic. How can two entities partner to solve a problem when they do not agree on a diagnosis?

Will Christian Organizations Become Lobbyists?

When ministries receive government funds, they have a vested interest in the continuation of the welfare state that has been so destructive of

3 Marvin Olasky, *The Tragedy of American Compassion* (Washington, D.C. Regnery Publishing, Inc.; 1992).

responsibility, character, and family life. They would be less likely to lobby against reductions in welfare programs and could find themselves self-interestedly actually campaigning for their expansion.

This has actually happened with foreign aid. A few years ago, some Christian organizations that were receiving foreign aid funds for relief work, were arguing against a proposed cut in foreign aid – realizing that their piece of the pie would be reduced if such a cut materialized. One of the groups was World Vision. There is no reason to believe they were not spending the funds they received in an effective manner. However, a lot of funds distributed through foreign aid programs are questionable; and the Christian organizations found themselves in a position where they felt they needed to defend such funding to protect their own self-interest. If such use of faith-based funds were to be greatly expanded, the incidences of Christian groups lobbying on behalf of government programs could well increase.

Some organizations could find they are expending more effort lobbying for the continuation and expansion of government aid programs than actually giving assistance themselves. This is what has happened to liberal religious groups whose actual charitable work for the disadvantaged has been substantially replaced by pleading for more and expanded government programs to help them – and sometimes giving aid to people in applying for such programs. Believers should have a real problem when funds that have been contributed for helping people are diverted to a lobbying effort.

I wonder if one of the reasons faith-based initiatives are being proposed is to get Christians to buy into the welfare state – particularly since so many of us have been skeptical of many existing programs.

We must remember that charity is equated with love in the Bible. Historically the idea of Christians helping people either individually or through the church has been one of voluntarily giving of money and time as an offering to the Lord. Administering funds extracted from taxpayers completely cuts the tie to any sense of Christian motivation. We should be concerned that non-believers will increasingly view Christians merely in the same manner as they do other dispensers of good works, rather than as people whose lives have been totally transformed by the power of Jesus Christ.

It is said that no Christian organization will have to accept government funds. However, the availability of such money will likely prove to be a seductive lure. As time goes on, many organizations who initially resist that lure could ultimately give in to the temptation presented by "easy money" – particularly if they find themselves in a situation where fundraising has become difficult.

It is even possible that, at some point in time, such programs will predominate to the point that there will be an effort to apply the rules that government-funded programs follow to all charitable organizations. This would amount to a *de facto* government takeover of charity. While this may not happen for some time, there is no question that when government enters an area it often ends up completely in control.

A couple of incidences that have happened in the past point to potential problems with government funding of faith-based ministries. In one case, then-Senator Jesse Helms indicated he would support a substantial increase in foreign aid funding if a commitment would be made to have a certain percentage of the additional monies administered by faith-based ministries.

Whatever one's views about foreign aid are, it raises the question of whether it is a good idea to be using money for ministries as a carrot to entice votes for programs. When it can cause such a formerly implacable foe of foreign aid as Jesse Helms to support it, it is an indication such enticements could be quite powerful. I believe votes on programs should be based on the merits of the program itself – not because interests one supports may benefit from them. While we know this is often the way politics is played in Washington, do we really want Christian ministries to become pawns in such political brokering?

The other situation involved someone accusing Samaritan's Purse of using public funds they had received for relief efforts in some disaster to proselytize for Christianity. It turned out the funds in question had not yet even been expended. However, as the use of ministries to administer government programs becomes more widespread these types of challenges to the actions of Christian ministries will undoubtedly increase dramatically.

If Christian organizations are merely going to be conduits for tax monies, using non-Christians as they administer programs where they cannot provide a witness and cannot apply scriptural principles, how would such involvement contribute to advancing God's kingdom?

Meeting Government Criteria

The questions for Christians should not only be those of constitutionality, but whether the criteria are ones that will allow ministries to function in a way that preserves their Christian uniqueness and does not compromise their missions.

It is said that the effectiveness of faith-based programs will be ensured by outcome-based testing. Use of that term certainly raises some questions and red flags, given the fact that this is the same language used in government educational mandates that attempted to substitute politically correct social engineering for proficiency in basic, traditional subject matter.

Even if outcome is being used in a generic sense, it is more than possible that the outcomes the government desires may be different from those of a Christian ministry. Once the precedent is set for such testing, what will prevent changing the outcomes?

It is true that a ministry could opt out at a point where it believes its desired outcomes are incompatible with those of the government. However, once any ministry has begun receiving funds, the pressure to rationalize modifications to their programs will be great. While those adjustments may be small or seem subtle, the cumulative effect of multiple changes over time could have the effect of completely compromising their original mission.

The goal of dismantling some of the failed programs of the Great Society is laudable. However, subsidies to fund faith-based ministries are more likely to perpetuate government involvement, since the participation of Christian groups in programs could lessen opposition to them. It has been said that government increased its role in charity, because the churches failed to provide for needs. While there may be some truth to that, I believe a more accurate assessment would be that churches reduced their efforts, because government became more heavily involved in social service.

There seems to be an attitude on the part of some people, both Christians and non-Christians, that there is no need for them to be involved in charitable efforts, either as participants or monetary contributors, since, "the government is taking care of that." An increased awareness that ministries are receiving government funds will likely cause even more people to believe there is no need for their donations.

Government should have sovereignty in preserving order in society and adjudicating differences between its citizens. Churches and private institutions should have sovereignty in funding and administering charitable enterprises. Government support for faith-based ministries violates this sovereignty by attempting to mix the roles of government and charitable organizations.

If we were to observe strict "sphere sovereignty," we would not have any government involvement whatsoever in social service endeavors. That was a situation we were close to in this country for a good part of our history.

Can We Trust the Government?

It seems that most of the Christians who support the concept of government funding of faith-based ministries have some reservations, but believe it is a matter of whether the legislation is being crafted carefully and the programs are being managed properly. This assumes all those promoting the idea are people of good will and sincerely concerned only with the well-being of the country's needy and the viability of Christian ministries.

However, we have seen extreme hostility exhibited towards Christians in recent years both by those within and outside of government. Can we assume those who have frontally attacked Christians would not resort to more subtle methods to destroy our effectiveness? In almost every area there have been those who have used the existence of problems as an excuse to increase the size and scope of government rather than actually to improve the situation.

I believe the one aspect of the Christian worldview that should have the greatest bearing on issues relating to politics is our view of the fallibility of man. It was this view that prompted our founding fathers to establish a government with checks and balances and to adopt a constitution that severely constrained the role of the federal government.

References abounded in the writing of the founders that indicated men were not to be trusted with power. The Christian worldview was so prevalent at that time that even Thomas Jefferson, who was probably not a believer, recognized they should "put no confidence in men" and that it was necessary to "bind them down with the chains of a constitution."[4]

We have taken for granted the amount of freedom we have in this country. We have forgotten that this freedom is very fragile and indeed has been very rare in the history of man. Truly, the fact that we have enjoyed such liberty is largely the result of the founders' efforts at controlling the scope of government.

Today, even we Christians who should understand the tendency of men to abuse power have been too ready to look to government for solutions to problems and to place trust in government entities to administer programs that address those solutions. I believe it is this misplaced faith that allows many to believe the subsidization of faith-based ministries can safely be entrusted to government if we just have the right people in charge, establish the right rules, and manage it properly.

Even if all those things were done correctly in the beginning, people in government change. What is to prevent a future administrator from sabotaging the efforts of ministries for such programs if he is antagonistic to Christianity? The initiation of such programs is allowing the camel's nose into the tent. And initial safeguards built into legislation to prevent control of participating organizations may be eliminated or modified over time.

The other thing that could easily impact the implementation of such programs is court rulings. Federal courts have ruled that small colleges who receive no direct subsidy have to abide by government guidelines merely because attendees use government-subsidized loans or veteran's educational benefits for their tuition. If courts can enforce compliance

4 Thomas Jefferson, Kentucky Resolutions, 1798

based on such tenuous connections, what will they do with ministries that receive direct subsidies?

Should Government Even Be Involved in These Activities?

It is clear from the Federalist Papers and the straightforward meaning of the Tenth Amendment that any social service activity by the federal government is unconstitutional. People may reasonably disagree as to whether it is a good idea for that activity to be carried on at the federal level. However, those who do believe so should work to get the proper amendments passed that would allow such activities to be done in a legal and proper manner.

Until that is done, those who receive monies for their ministries are helping to perpetuate unconstitutional activity. Christians should follow the rule of law in society. I believe it would be wrong for Christians to participate in something that violates our most basic law – the Constitution.

Is It Appropriate to Use Government Funds for Christian Ministries?

Christian ministries should be efforts by Christians. They should certainly be staffed by believers, and also funded primarily by Christians. It is certainly not feasible to prevent giving to Christian ministries from non-believers, so such contributions will be received by ministries. However, most givers realize a given ministry is operated by Christians. Certainly, their contributions are voluntary. However, when the state begins contributing to a ministry they use funds extracted from taxpayers who have not made a decision to contribute to that ministry. For those who are already predisposed against Christianity, this could be a further cause for resentment and, as such, would present a poor witness.

Even if there were no resentment, Christians should not accept these monies since it is just plain wrong to fund ministries with involuntary contributions. This may be a particularly high standard, but believers should always function at a much higher ethical level than non-Christian entities.

It has been demonstrated by some televangelists and investment scam artists that those who name the name of Christ are not above engaging in financial corruption. Does anyone believe that any such incidences involving a Christian ministry using taxpayer funds will not be highly publicized? The ramifications of any such cases will be greater than that of the televangelist scandals, since they would involve public funds rather than voluntary contributions. The negative impact on Christianity from only one such case could be tremendous.

Government programs often deal with problems by merely mitigating the results of some poor policy or practice. But should Christian ministries be involved with efforts that just treat symptoms and do not attempt to identify and deal with the ultimate source of problems?

There could be a number of reasons a given Christian ministry is not receiving adequate contributions. One certainly could be that they are perceived by potential contributors as being ineffective or as squandering too much money on administration. The necessity of relying on voluntary contributions serves in this manner as a natural method of accountability. If ministries are funded by government, it is the government that will make the decision as to who deserves to be funded. Given government's dismal record in wasting taxpayers' money, this should not be looked at positively. How many unworthy organizations will receive funding? How many ineffective or even corrupt entities will be rescued from a well-deserved death by government revenues? It can be expected that some of the organizations that have had the most difficulty in raising support will likely be the first to line up at the federal trough. This group will include some that have trouble getting contributions for good reason.

It may be that faith-based groups initially will be able to administer public funds without some of the pitfalls I have mentioned. But, over time, they will likely lose their distinctiveness as Christian organizations, and will come to be perceived more as just an agency doing its job, rather than a group of individuals selflessly serving others in the cause of Jesus Christ.

Chapter 12

Is Globalism Good?

Till the war-drum throbb'd no longer, and the battle-flags were furl'd. In the Parliament of man, the Federation of the world. There the common sense of most shall hold a fretful realm in awe, And the kindly earth shall slumber, lapt in universal law. – Alfred Tennyson, *Locksley Hall*

Due to enhanced communication and travel capabilities, it is understandable and almost inevitable that greatly expanded commerce would take place at a worldwide level, and that companies would organize to market globally. As information about events on various parts of the earth becomes more widely available, people recognize many commonalities between the problems and issues facing nations in various areas on the globe. Nothing is inherently wrong with that. However, with efforts to make laws that apply worldwide, the potential for loss of freedom is immense.

Globalism in Biblical Prophecy

Revelation 13 speaks of a period near the end of the age when the beast will be worshipped by all unbelievers and have authority over the whole world. Many Christians believe we are drawing close to that time – the time when Jesus will return. They base that belief on developments that appear to be signs of the end times mentioned in the Bible.

If we truly are approaching the end, we should not be surprised to see evidence of the beginning development of such a world government.

That is, in fact, what we have been observing in recent decades. Such indications are likely a sign that we are nearing the last days.

Efforts Toward a World Government

The first real effort to establish a framework for world government was the League of Nations set up after World War I. However, it was short-lived due to the US Senate's rejection of our participation in it.

The United Nations was established after the Second World War and most nations have joined it. It is not a world government at this time, but since it has a structure already in place, it is quite possible it will become the world authority mentioned in Revelation. The European Union is of particular interest to Christians due to the prophecies in Daniel and Revelation that many believe speak of a revived Roman Empire that has a major role in the end times.

Some who do not want the United Nations to gain more power believe it has some value as a forum for discussing world problems. It is important that leaders do talk over some issues. However, those discussions should be between the nations directly involved in various situations that arise. Having them brought before a worldwide body implies that a global authority should adjudicate affairs among individual countries. This thinking will likely lead to efforts to have world organizations enforce solutions.

The United Nations was putatively set up to promote peace in the world and to resolve conflicts. However, many of its member states are the greatest disturbers of peace in the world. Most communist states have been members, although their stated goal is world domination. Including such members in an organization designed to promote peace makes as much sense as forming a crime-prevention committee and inviting all the criminals to join.

Some claim the problem with the United Nation is that it is merely a debating society – that it doesn't have adequate authority to act. The intention from its inception is that it would have complete authority over the world. That has not been realized due to opposition from various quarters. We, as Christians, should not desire or work for the United Nations to have more power, since it is likely the framework for the world system to come at the end of this current age on earth. If so, investing it with more authority would hasten the enthronement of the world government we know to be evil and opposed to God.

The only way the United Nations (or any similar body) could really enforce peace is by becoming all-powerful. If that were to happen, those who gained control of it could impose their will over the whole earth. Freedom would become extinct everywhere. There are those who criticize the United Nations because they believe it to be so ineffective. However, a more effective United Nations would be a much greater threat to liberty and the sovereignty of nations. Due to such threats, Christians in the United States should work to have our country leave the United Nations and ask it to remove its headquarters from our shores.

It appears likely that the beast from Revelation will come out of a restored Roman Empire comprised of several nations. But it will also, at some point, wield global authority. How that will work is not entirely clear, but we should keep an eye on both the European Union and efforts at globalization.

Many members of the Council on Foreign Relations (CFR) were signers of the UN Charter. Since the Council on Foreign Relations has been working for world government since its inception, it is likely that organization sees the United Nations as the vehicle to bring that about. Various conventions and treaties have been established under UN auspices. The United States has declined to sign on to many of these. Due to our pre-eminent position in the world, our failure to participate in these agreements has prevented the United Nations from gaining the power it sought through them.

The populations of many of the nations of the world are not too keen on the idea of a world government. This is particularly true of Americans. As a result, efforts to establish smaller organizations have been made in which participating nations relinquish some of their sovereignty in a given functional area. Often these are organized in a given geographical area of the globe.

One example is the North Atlantic Treaty Organization (NATO) which was set up ostensibly to counter potential aggression by the Soviet Union and its client states. With the supposed "fall" of communism, one would have thought NATO would have been disbanded. However, it actually has been expanded and used to justify joint military efforts in places such as Iraq.

Trade Agreements

Many other regional organizations are centered on trade agreements – such as NAFTA (North American Free Trade Agreement). The most developed organization of such arrangements is the European Union. It began as a trade agreement to regulate prices on coal and steel, but has morphed from this very limited function to where it now has a parliament with ever-increasing powers.

Agreements like NAFTA have been sold as free-trade pacts. They are anything but that. It has set up about 300 agencies to regulate trade activities. Many conservatives have been supporting NAFTA and other such agreements because they believe in free trade. I believe the issue of free trade is one on which conservatives can legitimately disagree. Since the beginning of our republic, conflict has existed over whether we should have protective tariffs. I generally believe in free trade, but this issue becomes more complex when US companies export products to other nations that interfere in ways that protect the goods they market.

I am not going to discuss those issues here. What I am addressing is the trade agreements that establish international bureaucracies. As Ron Paul said in debating CAFTA (Central America Free Trade Agreement – a version of the same type of a pact as NAFTA, but with Central American countries), "I believe in free trade, but this is not free trade. This is regulated, managed trade for the benefit of special interests".[5]

I have a novel idea. Why don't we free trade up in this country from all the suffocating regulations manufacturers and merchants labor under? We are worrying about free trade between nations when we don't even have it within the United States!

Ironically, many on the left oppose these trade pacts. However, in most cases they are not concerned about the loss of sovereignty. They actually want a more powerful organization with more authority for trade organizations to monitor labor, environmental and other policies

5 1 Ron Paul, Floor of the U.S. House of Representatives

in member nations. Such authority would lead to a greater surrender of sovereignty.

Regulations that come out of the trade organizations take precedence over our laws and take power from our elected members of Congress. They, in effect, override our Constitution and the protections it has against overbearing government. Globalists have admitted that such trade organizations are steps toward world government.

The next step as far as trade in the Western Hemisphere is the Free Trade Area of the Americas (FTAA) which basically intended to expand NAFTA to all the countries of Central and South America. Due to resistance from many in the United States, the effort to ratify FTAA seems to have been put on the back burner for now.

There has also been an effort to expand NAFTA vertically. George Bush met with Vincente Fox of Mexico and Paul Martin of Canada in 2005 and signed the Security and Prosperity Partnership (SPP) statement. The pretext for this agreement is the purported need for the three countries to work together for security and jobs. The goal is to erase the boundaries between nations. This effort is also known as the North American Union (NAU). One of its chief activities is promoting the building of a number of superhighways from Mexico to Canada, supposedly to facilitate trade.

Advocates of a New World Order have admitted the EU is an example of the type of polity they are really working for in the Western Hemisphere, and that the NAU is its precursor. Meanwhile, efforts have begun to enmesh our trade policies with other parts of the world. A Trans-Pacific partnership (TPP) would link us with Pacific nations and a Transatlantic Trade and Investment Partnership (TTIP) would entwine us with the European Union. Both would bring restrictions on our national sovereignty.

One World Religion

Many indications point to ties between the United Nations and the push to build a world government, and efforts to promote a one world, unified religion. At the UN's Millennium Peace Summit of Religious and Spiritual Leaders in 2000, discussion of how to usher in the peace of the New World Order through religious universalism arose. The head of the meeting was Bawa Jain who was, at the time, Secretary-General of Millennium Peace Summit.

Jain was also involved with the United Religious Initiative (URI). The URI was originally proposed by Dr. Robert Muller in the 1990s at the centenary meeting held to commemorate the first Parliament of World Religions held in Chicago in 1893. Muller was a co-founder of UNESCO and has held the number two post in the United Nations as an assistant Secretary-General. He also was co-chair of both the World Commission for Global Consciousness and Spirituality and the World Wisdom Council (sharing that position with Mikhail Gorbachev).

In a tribute to Muller, his wife, Barbara Gaughen Muller, indicated their pantheistic, inclusivist religion as follows: "Just decide to be... every dream you ever dreamt create a Bench of Dreams and your wish shall be sent straight to God, Buddha or a tree. You see God is everywhere inside you and me. So, quit wasting time and thinking you can't and don't blame anyone who says you can't. It's your choice now to decide to be...like Robert Muller."[6] The United Religious Initiative claims that over 1,000 religious groups have endorsed its charter. Anglican bishop William Swing has said that the URI is intended to be to religion as the United Nations has become to global politics, unifying the world's religions as the United Nations is unifying the world's nations.

These efforts at globalizing religion are also tied to environmental efforts as the URI charter states: "The root of this ecological crisis is a spiritual crisis. Just as the religions and spiritual traditions of the world teach respectful interaction with a sacred whole, so must spiritual values and moral imperatives help humanity to rediscover a reverence for all life and respect for the sacredness of the whole of Planet Earth. Therefore, we call for interfaith cooperation in furthering this vision for love and protection of the Earth, reverence for life, and harmony with all living beings".[7]

---

6 THE SECOND FIVE HUNDRED IDEAS OF TWO THOUSAND IDEAS FOR A BETTER WORLD - http://www.robertmuller.org/voladnl/v2adnl.htm

7 THE GREEN AGENDA – http://green-agenda.com/unitedfaith.html

Due to biblical prophecy about the role of world government, Christians should be opposed to efforts at establishing global authority, both political and religious. But these efforts can often be subtle. It is not enough to work against direct efforts to create a world order. We must also educate ourselves on the more indirect methods, inform others, and work against the implementation of legislation that contributes in any way toward global government.

If there were no indication of a global end-time entity that would be used by Satan, believers should still question things that compromise the sovereignty of nations. It appears from the Bible that God intends there to be individual nations. He confounded the languages at the Tower of Babel. It was inevitable that the people who spoke different languages would establish separate nations. God also references nations many times in Scripture.

In the millennium, Jesus Christ will rule over the whole earth. Now that's the kind of globalist government all believers can heartily endorse! It seems nations will still exist during His reign since Gog and Magog are mentioned as attacking Jerusalem when Satan is released at the end of the 1,000 years (Revelation 20:7-9). So, the preservation of the idea of nationhood seems to be a worthy cause for believers.

There is a sense in which we Christians can rejoice as we see the signs of the development of world government herald the time when "our redemption draweth nigh." But that does not mean we should desire the establishment of a world government or do anything to hasten its arrival. It will be the vehicle Satan uses to oppress the world and attempt to impose his will. So, it is evil, and something we should oppose.

CHAPTER 13

Are There Conspiracies?

For our struggle is not against flesh and blood, but against the rulers, against the powers, against the world forces of this darkness, against the spiritual forces of wickedness in the heavenly places. (Ephesians 6:12)

The Idea of Conspiracy

A suggestion of a conspiracy orchestrating any of the events of the past several decades is often met with scorn. Even many, if not most, conservatives (including Christians) will look askance at such a possibility. In fact, some groups and leaders on the right make a special point of declaring that none of what is taking place in politics is the result of conspiratorial actions. It is quite foolish to make such statements since it is difficult, if not impossible, to prove something doesn't exist.

The mere mention of conspiracy is met with such a Pavlovian response that it seems like the populace has been conditioned to react that way. The power of the media, particularly in the United States, is immense. They have definitely molded the values of Americans by the way they present the news. The fact that they have used their position to belittle anyone suggesting a conspiracy raises the possibility that they have deliberately tried to create a negative gut reaction to the word.

If the idea of men and women conspiring to achieve their desired political results is so inconceivable or unlikely, why have so many found it necessary to go to such lengths to discredit it? If it is such an absurd idea, why not just ignore it and let it die on its own? The major effort to dismiss the idea of conspiracy should actually cause people to raise their eyebrows and wonder if there may just be something to it.

An Unexamined Possibility

Most people who deny the reality of conspiracies acting behind world events have never examined the evidence suggesting their existence. A lot of well-documented sources point to people working behind the scenes to effect certain political objectives. A conspiracy generally involves people working in secret, so one would not expect the reality of one to be apparent. It definitely takes some digging to come to such a conclusion. Of course, one is not likely to investigate sources that point to a conspiracy unless he has reasons to believe it is feasible.

I would submit that the movement within the past several decades toward increasingly centralized political control at the national and international level is so strong that ample reason exists to suspect it is being promoted by clandestine operators. There is a natural tendency for government authority to increase and become more pervasive over time. However, this movement has been so inexorable it seems unlikely to have happened completely by accident. Events that have occurred present enough possibility of a conspiracy that one should be inclined to at least look at evidence pointing to one.

Christian View of Conspiracy

Christians seem as likely as others to disbelieve any conspiracy exists. This is surprising. Most evangelical Christians believe Satan is active in this world and that he is working to topple God from His throne. We also believe he uses people to promote his schemes. Scripture tells us that, at the end of the age, a world system will be in place controlled by a person Revelation calls "the Beast" who has been given power by the Serpent who represents Satan.

I have heard Christians indicate they don't believe any human conspiracies lie behind the events of our time. They say we should rather attribute these happenings to the work of Satan. But it doesn't seem likely to be an either/or situation where either Satan or scheming people are behind what's going on.

It does seem likely Satan would have been involved in working for the establishment of a world authority. He does much of his work by enlisting men and women whom he can induce to do his bidding. Satan is able to delude people into doing things that contribute to his designs. He could have influenced a considerable number of people to be involved as individuals in promoting a world system. But it certainly seems likely he would also use his influence to get people to join together to work toward that end. We cannot say any identifiable conspiracy is definitely a tool of Satan, but given what the Bible says about his role in the end-times world system, it certainly seems likely he could be behind many efforts at establishing a global government. That does not mean everyone who participates in such a conspiracy realizes he is a tool of Satan. In fact, most probably don't recognize that. Many are personally power-hungry; some may even believe they are working for the good of mankind.

Believers who know Satan's methods and his goals should not discount the possibility of a conspiracy and should be open to examining evidence pointing to the existence of one – particularly when we see world events exhibiting signs of the end times with its movement toward world government and religion. In fact, for the Christian who observes events moving toward the situation described in biblical end-time prophecies, it should rather be difficult to believe no conspiracies are involved in moving Satan's plans forward. Because of prophecy, a Christian should believe the possibility of a conspiracy exists even if there were no evidence of one at all.

Reasons People Are Reluctant to Believe in Conspiracy

In this work, I do not intend to prove the existence of any conspiracy. Others have already done that, and I will refer to their works in the bibliography. It is my objective, rather, to present conspiracy as a plausible possibility, to address many of the misconceptions about it, and the invalid reasons for which many people dismiss the possibility of conspiracies.

As one looks over the past several decades, it is apparent there has been a steady march toward larger and more concentrated government in the U.S. There has also been a very strong push for more global government. Some have ascribed this trend to the fact that it is being promoted by a conspiracy. Such people and groups have been derisively accused of believing in "conspiracy theories." Such disdain seems to come as often from others on the right as from those on the left.

Individuals have pointed out people and organizations who have worked in secret to promote world government. They have used documentation from those people and organizations to make the case that they are in fact working for such globalist goals. I would say this is really exposing conspiracy – not fabricating "conspiracy theories."

A couple of the organizations which have been most frequently mentioned as working for world government, or as some say, a "New World Order," are the Council on Foreign Relations (CFR) and the Trilateral Commission. They do produce public materials. For example, the CFR publishes a quarterly journal called *Foreign Affairs*. One could make the case that they are not conspiratorial since their views are out there for the public to see. This is a little misleading. Such a publication as *Foreign Affairs* is hardly a mass-market periodical. In fact, the CFR and the Trilateral Commission rarely get mentioned in the type of publications that the general public reads. It is certainly quite likely the leaders of these organizations count on the fact that a small percentage of those who might disagree with their globalist intentions will actually read their material. There are those who acknowledge the role of organizations like the CFR and Trilateral Commission in promoting world government, but do not see them as being part of a conspiracy since they are at least somewhat public.

A misunderstanding also exists about how the conspiracy to create a world government actually works. Those who believe in the possibility of such a conspiracy are represented as thinking that every Tom, Dick and Harry (and Sue and Mary) who promote globalism or who are working for a leftist agenda are knowing participants in the conspiracy. Some who snub the idea of conspiracy will say all these people would have to be in on the secret for it to work. In either of these scenarios, it is then said that with all of these people involved, some or many, would surely have spilled the beans. It is also often said that it would be impossible to recruit the number of people required to pull this off without having some who decline the invitation to join in exposing it.

There may be some who believe the conspiracy works that way. However, that is not what many exposers of conspiracy have been saying. The evidence shows the conspiracy is a series of concentric circles – with those in each circle closer to the center having increasingly greater knowledge of its goals and methods.

Only those in the most central circles should probably be termed conspirators. Those in a given circle are influenced by those in the one just interior to their own – who are in turn influenced by the one inside theirs. People in the outer circles are often politically ambitious and learn what they need to believe, say, and do to be accepted by those farther inside the conspiracy. Within a given organization, leaders are often more deeply aware of its plans and activities than the general membership.

It is apparent that neither the CFR nor the Trilateral Commission is at the center of the conspiracy. It appears that up-and-coming individuals in politics, the media, business, and academia are often invited into CFR membership. It should not be assumed they are conspirators. Those invited to join are not always those we would think of as being on the left. For instance, CFR member Dick Cheney had a fairly conservative voting record while in the House of Representatives.

Most of those who join the CFR do not become leaders, and may never really rise in the ranks of the conspiracy. Many may be very sincere in believing the organization is working for worthy ends. They may think world government is a good thing. However, I believe, over time, most come to a realization of what one in the organization is expected to promote, and that it is not considered acceptable to deviate too far from such views if one wishes to be accepted and well-regarded in the "right" circles and/or move forward in fields like politics, education, big business or the media. And most increasingly adopt a globalist perspective. But those who remain at the lower rungs of the organization probably do not believe they are part of a conspiracy. Some may, in fact, have the same disdain for the idea of a conspiracy as do other deniers in the political sphere.

There is another reason why belief in conspiracies is discredited. There seems to be a certain mindset prone to believing in conspiracies. People with such tendencies are susceptible to believing in them without much substantiation and they are fascinated with such ideas. So, they will latch on to legitimate evidence demonstrating conspiratorial organizations and events, but will also embellish those ideas with a lot of additional more bizarre information that lacks credible evidence.

And many disbelievers in conspiracies see all of these ideas as one piece – they do not differentiate between unsubstantiated and well-documented information. They dismiss the whole idea of conspiracy out-of-hand. The fact that some people spew out a bunch of far-out ideas makes it easier to discredit all such thoughts by associating them with those saying some very improbable things. But the fact that some who speak of conspiratorial matters are off base and some of their information is questionable in no way should cause anyone to dismiss the idea of conspiracies or not to listen to those who present credible, substantive evidence of the existence of one.

Does it Matter if One Believes in Conspiracy?

Is it really important whether one believes in a conspiracy or not? Can't we just oppose the ideas and principles of those who are trying to implement plans we believe to be wrong without caring whether they are part of a conspiracy? Of course, that can be done – many, in fact, are doing so. But what I have found, after years of study and observation, is that knowing there are organizations working furtively to promote centralized government in this country, and for a world government, is an immense help in understanding what has been and is going on in the political realm. If I were not aware of the influence of groups like the CFR, I would be quite befuddled about many of the events that have occurred in recent decades. Frankly, without that understanding, they would make no sense at all.

I have also noticed that people who do not recognize the conspiratorial aspects of politics can be quite naïve in whom they support as candidates for public office. They will support those who have CFR connections and who are asked to write articles for Foreign Affairs –

the CRF quarterly publication. Writing in that publication is likely a signal that the insiders believe that person is someone they can at least manipulate, if not control. For example, most of the leading contenders for the Republican endorsement for president wrote such articles during the 2008 campaign. Yet, some of these men garnered considerable support from conservatives.

And, of course, many conservatives continued to be supportive of George Bush and believe he was sincere in spite of his loading his administration with CFR members – as have all presidents since the mid-fifties.

CHAPTER 14

What Should the Role of the Courts Be?

The powers delegated by the proposed Constitution to the federal government, are few and defined. Those which are to remain in the State Governments are numerous and indefinite. – James Madison, "Federalist Papers No 45"

Legislating from the Bench

Many of the problems with the current political situation in this country are not the result of the actions of a legislative body, but are rather due to court rulings that have, in effect, created laws. Federal courts have largely done this by ignoring the original intent of the US Constitution which clearly placed stringent restrictions on what our nation's government could do. It lays out a very small, defined set of functions. Particularly the Supreme Court has allowed the federal government to take on a multiplicity of roles beyond those described in the Constitution.

Those favoring such expansions of federal power have justified them by saying we have a "living constitution" that has a lot of flexibility built into it to allow the functions of government to change as society progresses and develops new needs. But the only flexibility in it is the ability for it to be amended. That is the correct or constitutional method for dealing with items that may come up where a change seems appropriate. Other than that, the Constitution is very specific and extremely rigid.

One of the reasons cited for the need for flexible interpretations is the fact that values change, and society has new ways of looking at things in modern life. Some say humans are evolving, and law must change accordingly. However, we, as Christians, should not be buying such reasoning since we know human nature does not change – an improved race of men and women is not emerging. We should not believe changes in our society and culture are necessarily good or that they should be incorporated into law by judicial fiat. There may be some cases where changes do call for Constitutional modification. But that's where the amendment process should come into play.

Amending the Constitution is a very cumbersome process by design. The founders determined to ensure hasty changes would not be made that would alter the character of the government, and that a preponderance of states is in agreement with any change before it is implemented.

If, however, five men and women can – by constituting a majority on a court decision – make significant changes to our government and increase its powers without any justification from the original language and intent of the Constitution (as they have been doing for decades), we don't have a flexible constitution – we don't really have a constitution at all. And we then have a government of men – rather than one of laws.

An Outrageous Decision

A well-known case where the Court negated laws for the whole country was the *Roe versus Wade* decision that mandated a right to abortion. This ruling was problematic for a couple of reasons. The first was that it intervened in an area where the federal government had no jurisdiction, and in which legislation should have been left to the states. Secondly, the Court members used specious reasoning and tortuous logic to find a general right to privacy in the Constitution. The Fourth Amendment that prohibits the federal government from entering premises without a search warrant obtained for justifiable reasons specifically involves preserving our privacy. Neither it, nor anything else in the Constitution, says a crime that may have been committed is justified because it occurred in private. It merely deals with how the solving of a crime can be dealt with by government.

If one says there is a general right to privacy, the obvious question is "privacy to do what?" Privacy just deals with the setting where an action takes place. It says nothing about the legality of the act itself. If the mere fact that abortion is done in private makes it legal, one would have to say that it is also lawful to beat your husband or wife as long as you do it in the privacy of your home.

The Constitution Is the Ultimate Precedent

Finding such a right to privacy and applying it to abortion was a major break in precedent. However, those who favor this ruling hypocritically now accuse those who wish to re-address this decision of not following precedent. When a major new precedent is set that they agree with, they are fine with breaking the old ones. But if a ruling goes in a direction they do not like, they will appeal to a previous precedent and cry foul.

One thing that is lost in all this discussion is that the original intent of the Constitution is the ultimate precedent.

If there has been a case where the Constitution's meaning has been violated, it is always appropriate to override it and return to the original understanding. To continue to build upon a bad precedent is akin to getting off on the wrong path and continuing on it rather than retracing one's steps to the correct one.

In a country like Great Britain, which doesn't have a written constitution, a court precedent does become a rule or guide for future cases. Even then, if a ruling deviates too much from a long history of previous cases, it should be appropriate for it to be overthrown by subsequent judgments, based on its not being consistent with an established body of precedent. But in our case, where we have an actual document that contains the basis for law, it should always trump any previous precedent-breaking rulings.

Other Problems with Court Rulings

There have been situations in recent years where some Supreme Court justices have not cited the Constitution, or even previous cases, but rather laws of other countries, to justify their votes. This is predicated on the idea that the world is changing and this country needs to keep up with what is happening elsewhere. In many cases, it also promotes the attitude that there are no permanent values, but that what is right shifts with the times based on popular opinion, etc. Laws or rulings from foreign countries are absolutely irrelevant to any cases before the Supreme Court. Citing them is *prima facie* evidence that a justice is not following his or her oath to abide by the Constitution and should be grounds for impeachment.

The most glaring error in Supreme Court cases in recent decades is the complete ignoring of the Tenth Amendment – which explicitly states that powers not delegated to the federal government are reserved to the states and the people. "Reserved" is the word used since all powers originated with the states. Only certain ones were given to the central government. So, by default, all others remained with the individual states.

The Tenth Amendment is really redundant since it should have been obvious any power not given to the federal government remained with the states. On the surface, it seems like it was unneeded, and that was the view of some of the founders. However, others who were concerned that, without it, the central government would take on powers not delegated to it, insisted on its inclusion. History has shown just how prescient these men were, since even with the specific prohibition of the Tenth Amendment, the federal government has violated our founding document to the point where most of what it does is well beyond its constitutional purview. But only rarely has a federal court ruled such actions as unconstitutional.

States are a Big Part of the Remedy

One would hardly expect that the Supreme Court, which is part of the federal government, would often make a decision that goes against that level of government. This is why the states should not rely on federal courts to keep the central government in check. The way for states to rein in Washington's powers is to refuse to implement and/or obey law that calls for the Feds to exercise functions clearly outside their jurisdiction, because it involves powers not granted to them by the Constitution. This has been done in the past through a process that has come to be called nullification.

Much is said about the checks and balances built into our system by having three branches of government. These are very important, but a potentially greater check on the growth of the federal government is available to state governments. They can keep Washington within the confines of the Constitution by not participating in extra-Constitutional legislation. There are 50 separate governments that can oppose such power grabs.

One thing that mitigates states' power to check runaway government is that much of the revenue available to the national government comes directly from citizens. If it came via the states, they could withhold monies being used by the federal government to implement unconstitutional programs. This would give them more clout in their opposition to such power grabs. The states should never have ratified the 16th Amendment that allows this type of collection for income taxes. However, they could pass legislation that directs individuals and businesses to send their federal taxes to state governments which would pass on only monies being used for constitutional purposes.

In recent years, the question has been raised more frequently as to whether a state could leave the union. It is very encouraging that this question is seriously being asked. The answer is that, of course, they could secede if they wish. Our general government was a compact formed by sovereign states to grant a few of their powers to a union for very limited purposes. They kept all other powers for themselves. When the federal government violates that compact by self-aggrandizement and seizes powers which it has not been given, it has broken the agreement that formed the union. That agreement is no longer binding on those states that wish to remain true to the original compact.

It is not likely any state would actually leave the Union. However, the threat that one or more were seriously considering such a course of action could help bring the federal government back in line or prevent it from further overstepping its boundaries.

A Constitutional Check on the Courts

There needs to be an effort to rein in the Supreme Court. The best way is for Congress to use the power given it in Article III, Section 2 which states: "In all the other Cases before mentioned, the Supreme Court shall have appellate Jurisdiction, both as to Law and Fact, with such Exceptions, and under such Regulations as the Congress shall make." Laws should be passed that remove from federal court jurisdiction those areas where judges have seriously misconstrued the Constitution in their rulings. This would be exercising a much needed check on the courts. Examples of issues that should be removed from the court's purview are education and abortion.

If the courts ignore the Constitution and use their positions to implement laws, and there is no control on their power, they become virtual dictators. The ultimate check must come from the legislators which are chosen by the people – rather than from unelected judges. Using Article III, Section 2 is a good way to bring some accountability to an out-of-control judiciary.

Judicial Advocacy

Sometimes judges or candidates for the bench will say they want to use the position to be an advocate for some group or a pet issue. Sometimes what they want to promote is a good thing. I have heard a judge say she would like to be an advocate for children. That could be admirable if what she specifically proposed had merit. However, a judge is not to be an advocate – they are to apply the law. It raises a real concern when one who is inclined to be an advocate for any class of people or cause will not be able to give unbiased judgments. If they wish to help certain groups or promote certain issues, they should rather run for a legislative position where it is appropriate to work for changes in the law.

Christians and conservatives should be just as much against court rulings that seek to implement policies favored by the right as those who have done this on the left. We need to promote legislation to remedy situations we think need changing – not try to accomplish our objectives through court rulings. In fact, this does not often happen since those on the right who believe in limited, constitutional government usually want the various branches of government to stay within their proper limits. Those on the left who wish to grow government aren't often as concerned about the concentration of power, so they don't care as much whether judges respect constitutional boundaries.

Christians should realize that due to the fallen nature of humans, concentrating power in a small group of individuals is never a good idea. We should recognize that allowing courts to make laws is giving them more power than men and women should have. Believers should also not buy into the idea that evolving values should cause reinterpretation of the constitutional text. It is certainly true that values do change – but that is usually for the worse. Whether a new value is good or bad it shouldn't be enshrined in the Constitution without an amendment. We know God laid out timeless standards in His Word. So, too, the document that is the basis of our government should not be modified by the personal preferences of judges.

Chapter 15

How Should Christians Relate to the Environment?

For they exchanged the truth of God for a lie, and worshiped and served the creature rather than the Creator, who is blessed forever. Amen. (Romans 1:25)

Caring for the Planet

Although much difference of opinion exists among believers about how to approach issues concerning the environment, most likely think we should be good stewards of the natural resources God has placed on earth for our use. Recently, some Christians – particularly evangelicals – have been referring to believers' involvement with the environment as "creation care." That actually is an apt name since it acknowledges our natural world is God's creation, and that, like all gifts from Him, humans should take care of it. This response of believers could well be considered part of the directive God gave to Adam and Eve to till the Garden of Eden. Unfortunately, most evangelicals who express the need for care of creation have largely uncritically accepted most of the assumptions and proposals of the secular environmental movement.

The commands given to Adam and Eve would seem to imply they were to do things to promote the better growth of plants. This would likely include things like pruning trees. A view of many environmentalists is that stewardship is just letting areas grow wild with absolutely no interference from men and women at all. This could hardly be considered "care" at all. If God wants us humans to nurture the earth, then believers should certainly not include abandonment of nature as "creation care," although it may be appropriate to leave some areas in their pristine state.

When it comes to stewardship, Christians believe God owns all the resources He has created. However, he has placed the control and use of those resources in the hands of human beings. The question then becomes which humans will determine how such resources will be used and maintained. Although there are variations, the two basic possibilities are essentially either: individuals (and groups of individuals) or governments.

Individual Christians should be good stewards of resources directly under their control. They should not waste them or use more than necessary. Since the use of resources is often tied to a cost, stewardship of them can be related to the wise use of financial assets. If a believer uses more of an item than necessary, the money expended for that excess involves funds that may have otherwise been used more profitably. Any money saved by the frugal use of resources then becomes available for other items – including funding kingdom work. Using less of a given resource means its reserves will not be used up as soon. The collective effort of many people following such a wise usage policy can be substantial.

Since conservation efforts can involve financial costs, individuals who consider beginning any such practice should weigh the amount of expenditure likely needed against the possible benefits. Christians particularly should do that, since money required for such efforts involves funds that could otherwise be used for other purposes – such as contributing to a Christian ministry.

Believers should do the same type of evaluation to compare the amount of time required for a given conservation effort vis-à-vis other ways they could spend that time. They need to ask themselves if that time might be better spent to promote some other kingdom work or in some more critical project. We are stewards of our time and financial resources as well as of nature, and there are usually trade-offs in our use of these items. Exercising stewardship in one area may require not doing as much in another area. Balance needs to be employed when making such decisions.

When believers join together to engage in some ministry, they should also use resources wisely in those efforts. Such organizations also have to make decisions on how to balance the use of time and funds with the conservation of natural resources.

An attitude of pride and sanctimoniousness exists on the part of some who engage in wise use of resources, recycling, etc. They often look down their noses on those who don't follow such practices as being unenlightened. It is admirable for a Christian to engage in such stewardship activities, and to try to encourage others to do so. But I do not believe it is proper for a Christian to adopt a superior attitude because he or she is being a good steward. This demonstrates pride which is frequently proscribed in Scripture. One doesn't always know all the circumstances of another's life. Perhaps a person who is believed to be wasteful in their use of resources and/or is not recycling like they should is spending a considerable amount of time caring for a sick friend or relative and literally cannot find the time to practice good stewardship of physical items. Making activities like these priorities could constitute very good stewardship of their time.

Preserving Natural Resources

Let's consider a larger question regarding preservation of resources: should stewardship policies be enforced by governments? Governments should use resources wisely in carrying out their functions, but should they dictate the stewardship practices of their constituents? Many believe they should. Such beliefs are often predicated on the putative need to prevent the exhaustion of the supply of a given resource.

One problem with that thinking is that most resources are dispersed throughout the world, so the actions of a particular government cannot by themselves control the total supply of a given resource. It is unlikely enough countries would voluntarily agree to submit to such an authority. Nations that control a substantial portion of the supply of a certain resource would tend to believe any quotas on their use of the resource would be unfair.

Possibly, such an effort could be effective if it becomes part of an international organization like the United Nations, but it is unwise to give that type of authority to a world body. Stewardship involves control. A person designated to be a steward of some asset is usually given almost complete authority over how it is used and/or managed. If we make any level of government a steward of anything, we have effectively ceded control of it to that body. That is the very great threat to freedom inherent in government enforcement of private stewardship.

Considerable concern has been expressed that we are running out of energy sources. Such concerns usually look only at reserves of resources currently being used to produce energy. Throughout history, new sources of energy have been developed. Not too many decades ago, nuclear material was totally unknown as a source of energy. Today, it has huge potential, and it is being used to supply a good portion of Europe's electrical power.

Well over two hundred years ago, Thomas Malthus speculated that earth could not sustain much of an increase in its population. In fact, the number of people on the earth has increased dramatically since his time, driven by a large increase in available energy resources and technology that has allowed for the production of more food. In spite of his being proven so wrong, the neo-Malthusian pessimists of today still project an approaching doomsday where the earth runs out of the energy needed to serve current and future population levels.

In Philippians 4:19, Paul wrote, *And my God will supply all your needs according to His riches in glory in Jesus Chris*t. The perspective of a Christian should be that, just as God provides for our needs as individuals, He will provide the resources to meet the needs of our earth for as long as He has ordained it to last.

Stewardship means wise use – but it does mean use. Some environmentalists want to preserve resources just for the sake of saving them, not to conserve them for future use. This seems to be the same attitude as a miser who holds tight to his or her money – admiring it and even gloating over it in an idolatrous manner. Not to use resources can fall into the same category as the error made by the unfaithful servant who buried his masters' money rather than invest it (Matthew 25:14-30).

While glorying over money has no profitable results, there is value in admiring the beauty with which God has endowed our world. It certainly seems appropriate to leave some natural wonders as God has created them. Observing them can be an act of worship for believers as long as we make sure it is God, and not His created things, we revere. The natural things God has created are part of His revelation, which are intended to provide a witness (Romans 1:19, 20). Destroying all of them would certainly not be right, but the question that should be asked is whether it is necessary to lock up millions of acres of pristine areas such as has been done in Alaska and some of our western states. To prevent the accessing of needed resources like oil in a preserve like ANWR, when it involves such a small portion of the area, seems almost silly.

When considering portions of creation being a testament to God, we should not think only of those things we consider natural wonders. What we call man-made objects like skyscrapers and suspension bridges can be things of beauty also. They also point us to God since only the physical laws He has built into the universe allow such things to be constructed.

Natural wonders can also be used to worship in ways inappropriate for Christians. They would include the worship of nature itself – rather than the God who created it. It goes without saying that such worship would be wrong for Christians. The environmental movement contains an element whose motivation is the promotion of pantheistic ideals, which Christians should reject as idolatrous. One common way this is done is by deifying nature through what could only be considered worship. For example, Gaia the Greek goddess of the earth is often mentioned in certain circles of environmentalists.

Another question that should be addressed is whether it is appropriate for government to acquire and hold natural preserves. When government funding is provided, taxpayer dollars are being used for something not all agree is important. Environmental groups spend very large sums of money lobbying to promote their agenda and force it on everyone. Why should they not use those funds to privately purchase and maintain land where they preserve nature? One environmental group, The Nature Conservancy, actually does that.

Preserving Species

This voluntary approach could also be used to preserve plant and animal varieties threatened with extinction. Where a habitat has been identified as critical to the continued existence of a given species, organizations could buy up land containing the particular life form and maintain it in a nurturing way. This approach could replace legislation that currently seeks to preserve endangered species. The problem with such laws is that they mandate public participation in an effort not everyone believes is essential.

It would be worthwhile for Christians who value species preservation to contribute to such efforts. Because of the worship and witness value of such species, I believe it would also be a legitimate ministry to start organizations and raise funds to preserve them, but contributions should all be given voluntarily.

Many environmentalists will say that such an approach will not work well for all species since some have migratory patterns that range over hundreds of miles. But animals are often very adaptable and many could well change their travel habits. However, if some don't and are adversely affected, we must ask whether it is appropriate to curtail human freedom for the sake of animals. That seems to give their welfare a higher priority than that of humans – which is not what God intended.

When it comes to the preservation of species, some environmentalists support their views on the basis of the organism's having rights. God said His creation is good, so all life has value to Him, but it is clear from the Bible that many plants and animals were intended for the use of humans as beasts of burden, food, etc. At least some of their value to God is that they are provisions for man. One could almost hear the screams of anguish if God were still requiring animal sacrifices!

Having value is not the same as having rights. God gave man the capability of rational thought. One of the real intriguing things about God's creation is the way animals "think" compared to the way we think. It's obvious animals do make decisions, and they do remember things. It is also very obvious their mental powers are vastly inferior to those of men and women.

The only possible way one could properly use the term "animal rights" is in reference to a policy that lets them run totally wild and not attempt any control of them, since rights involve making decisions. If we are talking about human action to preserve and/or help them, then it is really men and women who are exercising decisions on behalf of animals – so it is not proper to refer to such efforts as involving their rights. Did anyone ask any of them whether these efforts were what they wished? In effect, people who use "rights" in reference to non-human organisms are misusing the term. In their lexicon, rights are not related to freedom of speech and action, but entitlements to things like food, well-being, etc. Christians should realize rights are tied to our ability to think, speak, and act, using the minds God gave us, and that such capabilities are a large part of our bearing His image. As such, they apply only to humans – not to animals.

Plants and Animals in the World to Come

It should not be surprising that Christians, on average, may be less enthusiastic about preserving all species than others. We believe there is a limited existence for this earth as we know it. If the last of a species expires, it is only lost for the time the earth is to remain. Those who believe the world will continue indefinitely will see the given plant or animal as lost forever.

It is not really clear what plants will be in the new heaven and earth, and we aren't told whether there will be animals at that point. But if God wants that world to be populated with the same selection of animals currently on earth, it will certainly not be a problem for Him to recreate any that may have become extinct during human history. It could also be that He will fill the new earth with completely different plants and animals than those currently here. This is hinted at in Revelation where it speaks of *the tree of life, bearing twelve kinds of fruit, yielding its fruit every month; and the leaves of the tree were for the healing of the nations.* (Revelation 22:1-3).

We are not told the earth will be renewed or that the supply of natural resources will be replenished prior to the millennial period. If not, and Christ just takes over the earth as He physically finds it on

His return, we, as believers, can be assured adequate supplies of what is needed to sustain life for 1,000 years will be available. Since we do get a hint that life during that time will be generally good, we would not expect serious shortages of anything required for abundant living. If the earth is actually restored at the beginning of the 1000-year period, then we just need a supply of resources adequate to keep life going until Christ's return. Most Christians believe signs point to that occurrence not being too far into the future. Such believers will not be as concerned as secular people about the need to have reserves of necessary materials that will last hundreds or thousands of years. Of course, if the earth is not replenished for the millennium, that fact would provide a reason to preserve plant and animal species before that time, since it would give them the possibility of being around for up to another 1,000 years.

It is understandable that non-believers, who for the most part think that life on earth will go on forever, would be much more concerned about conservation – thinking that we could actually run out of resources.

As technology has advanced, cleaner methods have been developed to create energy and produce goods. This has resulted in less pollution. When we do not use cleaner sources of energy, such as nuclear, we are rejecting a tool God has given us to provide for our needs with less damage to the environment.

Of course, in the case of nuclear energy, one of the reasons for not using it is the putative risks. However, energy production is creating the ability to do work. That cannot be done on a massive scale without some risk.

The potential for harm exists in all energy production. In comparing different methods, one has to consider not only the actual production of energy, but also the obtaining of the fuel. The amount of activity required for hydrocarbon-based energy production is considerably more than that needed for nuclear power. A lot more drilling, mining, storage, and transporting has to be done to obtain fuel for such power plants. All of those activities involve risks and potential for disasters which are multiplied by the large amount of fuel required.

Many people, including Christians, think first of preservation and wise use of physical resources when they use the term "stewardship." But when the term is used in the Bible, it usually refers to using our talents and personal resources to serve God and grow His kingdom – not to taking care of the environment.

What About Global Warming?

One of the main environmental issues of the day is the purported warming of Earth, the contributions of humans to that condition, and the alleged resulting negative effects on life. This issue had been referred to as "global warming" and is increasingly being called "climate change."

I do not intend to discuss in detail all the pros and cons of this debate. There are really more than two sides to this multi-faceted issue, but the question ultimately gets down to whether there should be governmental action to stop alleged warming. That is despite the fact that various groups and individuals differ as to the existence and extent of warming, the causes of any temperature increases, and the amount of harm that has or could potentially result. Certainly much information is available about the scientific components of the controversy, but I want to present thoughts on how Christians should look at this issue.

The issue of global warming really involves several questions – the first is, not surprisingly, whether the earth truly is warming. Certain considerations need to be addressed to determine if that is the case. The first is what time period is to be used. If one uses the past hundred years, we can say there has been a slight rise. Differences in opinion exist about the past 10 to 15 years, depending on whether satellite temperatures or surface measurements are used. Some think there has been an increase, some, little change, and others a slight decrease. In the late seventies, using data from the previous 20-25 years, many determined we had a global cooling problem. Those years are now encompassed in a hundred year-plus range where a global warming trend is alleged. In reality, whether one wished to state either that there is, or was, a period of warming or of cooling, at many times, he could truthfully do so, just by picking the length of his period.

There is also the related question of what time period is significant. For instance, is it more of a concern that temperatures increase over a hundred years or decrease in 20 years (or decrease in 100 years, but increase over 25 years)? It would seem that to determine what time period is most significant, it is necessary to look at long-term historical trends, to see what the impacts were of decreases or increases of various lengths.

Many who dispute the threat of global warming assert that there have been long and short periods of both warming and cooling throughout recorded time. If they are correct, are temperature changes over any period of time anything to be concerned about?

Another consideration in determining if there has been warming is the consistency of temperature tracking from year to year. Have the same precise locations been used to gather temperature data? Of those that are the same, have local conditions surrounding the weather station remained constant, or have they changed? Temperatures at a station located in an area that has become more urbanized would likely increase, due to things like heavier traffic, the amount of concrete, etc. The question of whether the same instruments have been used to measure temperatures is another factor, or a more direct question in this regard would be: is it possible that increased precision of improved equipment has skewed the variations in temperature? Also, are the points where temperatures are being recorded ones dispersed properly to provide an accurate estimate of changes over the whole globe? Are some of the stations in areas subject to environmental factors that often result in wide temperature fluctuations? That too would tend to distort overall numbers. Given the variation of climatic factors over the face of the globe, I wonder whether it is even possible to get an accurate measure of the earth's temperature.

If it could definitely be established that temperatures have been and are continuing to significantly increase, the next question to be answered is whether they have or are likely to cause deleterious effects to man or the planet. There have been many projections of scenarios that could occur if temperatures continue to increase for longer periods of time. But in speaking of things that have global impact, such as a rise in ocean levels, they are very hard to predict. With all the factors that affect the earth, can anyone really know what might happen as a result of a temperature surge? The best way to determine possible effects is to look at what has happened during past periods of warmer temperatures.

Those who have studied such history report there have been times with higher temperatures when the earth and its inhabitants have experienced considerable prosperity and well-being. At one point, Greenland was ice-free. It was during this period when it was largely settled by people who grew crops – which is why it was called "Greenland."

If it appears likely that increased temperatures will adversely affect life on Earth, the next question to be asked is what role humans play in contributing to the warming. It is not just whether the activities of man cause a rise in temperature – but, whether the warming they contribute is significant compared to that added by natural phenomena.

If, in fact, mankind is responsible for a substantial portion of the warming, it has to be determined if anything can actually be done to reduce it to the point where the negative effects will be mitigated enough to make a difference. If, in fact, carbon dioxide is the culprit, there would have to be a mandated effort to reduce such emissions. Since the United States is the most industrialized nation in the world, possibly a severe reduction would have an impact. But what good would that do if other large nations who are rapidly industrializing their economies are putting more carbon dioxide into the atmosphere while we are reducing ours? Only a world authority that forces all nations to decrease their carbon dioxide levels would have any hope of making an impact. Establishing such a world authority has several other negative results – including a loss of freedom and national sovereignty.

If we could know that a massive government effort would result in a carbon dioxide decrease that would forestall the most serious effects of warming, we would still need to weigh the resultant benefits against the costs which would not just be monetary, but would also involve a reduced standard of living, loss of freedom, etc. If we assume we can accurately measure global temperatures, that we can definitely say they are rising, that such a rise will cause substantial negative effects, and that a given effort could reduce emissions and prevent the negative consequences, it does not necessarily mean we should make that effort.

All the questions to this point have been objective ones; however, the question of benefits compared to costs is very subjective. How great a reduction in our level of living are we willing to trade to solve the problem? Is the problem great enough to warrant returning to 19th century lifestyles? Do we want to live in a regimented, Soviet-style society so we can enjoy a more perfect physical environment? These are all value questions. Unfortunately, most who want to restrict human activity to achieve lower temperatures never even consider such questions. People will answer these in different ways. Some place a higher value on freedom – others on a better physical environment for themselves and other humans. Those who propose legislative efforts to solve the perceived problem of global warming wish to make such decisions for everyone – in effect imposing their values on all, as statists always do.

A Christian Response

How should a Christian look at this issue? Before taking a position, we have a responsibility to make certain we are getting good and accurate information. We should ascertain that global warming is actually taking place. Before advocating steps to try to stop the increase, we should be definitely convinced the warming will have serious negative effects on life on earth, that a significant portion of the warming is due to human activity, and that it is feasible to make changes that would substantially lessen the threat.

In attempting to get answers to these questions, Christians need to be aware of the way the media controls the information disseminated and the agenda on this issue. Believers should seek out sources that present the other side of the global warming issue – and there are many. We have a responsibility to evaluate arguments on both sides before making a decision on our positions.

We should definitely not buy into the idea that this is a settled issue where the debate is over, and there is no serious opposition to the idea that global warming is a threat. There is no scientific consensus on this issue. In fact, 31,000 US scientists, including 9,000 with doctorates in atmospheric science, climatology, environment, and related fields, signed a petition disputing the contentions of global warming advocates. Those who claim no serious debates remain on this issue are being disingenuous at best.

Those who believe warming is a problem claim that most who question that fact are supported by various industries that have a vested interest in minimizing any human role in impacting temperatures. However, most of the information I have seen refuting the standard global warming claims has been presented by those with positions at universities. What may be much more significant is the number of those warning about global warming who are getting government grants to study the issue. Does anyone really believe a person or group that is skeptical of any of the claims of those hyping global warming would have much of a chance to get a government subsidy for a study?

The Christian leaders who signed the *Climate Change: An Evangelical Call to Action* statement which called for curbing carbon dioxide emissions appear to have bought into the idea that it is a settled issue that global warming is a problem. Signers included Rick Warren, World Vision President Rich Stearns, and National Association of Evangelicals Chairman Leith Anderson. They are unaware of, or have ignored the fact, that the left controls the information on this issue that gets to the general public. They also do not seem to realize there are those who have an agenda that goes far beyond merely reducing carbon emissions – an agenda which has a lot more to do with expanding the role of government and controlling people. Anderson claimed to be speaking for himself on this issue, but when high-profile people who are Christians take positions, they carry a lot of weight. So, they have a great responsibility to make certain they base their views and statements on accurate information and that corrective actions will not have severe secondary consequences.

Those believers who have jumped on the anti-global warming bandwagon have stated that it is important for believers to be involved in creation care. So far, so good. But that doesn't mean we should join every campaign that claims to preserve our environment.

Carbon Reduction Legislation's Impact on Freedom

Christians should bring a more important value to the debate on climate change. Any steps to curtail carbon emissions will inevitably involve restrictions on freedom. Initial proposals in the United States are primarily geared towards companies, but controls on businesses always impact people. Since much of what a person does adds carbon dioxide to the air – from breathing to raising cattle, to building a campfire, etc.– it seems almost certain that eventually attempts to control activities at a personal level will be introduced.

Restrictions on carbon creation really involve tradeoffs with freedom. If the dire predictions of the global warming true believers were to materialize, it would involve physical consequences for at least parts of the earth and impact some portion of its inhabitants. Legislation to attempt to forestall those events will definitely severely restrict the freedom of most of the residents of the jurisdiction where it is passed.

This is really a conflict between stewardship involving our physical environment and the stewardship that cares for the gift of volition given to humans by God. Christians should always value freedom higher than mere physical impacts to the earth or to its people. Our freedom is related to our decision-making processes. It involves cognitive powers that distinguish us from animals. Those powers are a large part of what stamps us with the image of God. The extent to which we maintain our freedom is the extent to which we are able to be obedient to God.

To give up freedom is to make us less human. It is not surprising that humanists frequently value liberty less. They are most often materialists who believe men and women have evolved totally through natural processes, rather than having been created in the image of God. It makes sense they would value the physical world more highly. In fact, a strict materialist doesn't believe anything other than the physical even exists. Logically, if they are honest, they must be determinists and not even believe humans have free wills – much less value them. It makes sense that some of the most ardent proponents of limiting carbon emissions are humanists.

It seems many on the left believe as long as people are well-fed, get adequate healthcare and plenty of unrestricted sex they should be happy.

Ironically, though, efforts on cutting carbon emissions will reduce the standard of living for many and make even meeting their basic material needs more difficult.

The bottom line is that based on our valuing of freedom, Christians should be against governmental measures to cut carbon dioxide – even if we are convinced the worst of the predicted scenarios of those pushing for such legislation would play out. It is an imperfect world and believers have, and will have to, live in situations where their freedom is severely restricted. However, when we have options, we should never be willing to trade our freedom for mere material well-being.

However delicate one may believe our physical environment to be, the history of the world shows clearly that human freedom is much more fragile. Those times and places where humans have been able to reasonably freely exercise the rights God has given them have been rare. For the most part, governments have run roughshod over the liberty of men and women.

Those who believe global warming to be a problem will often recommend we adopt measures to control carbon output even if it is uncertain whether it is contributing to the problem. They see it as playing it safe. If it turns out there is not and will not be a problem, they say the conservation undertaken to achieve the reduction is a good thing in itself.

This argument would only be valid if no other consequences resulted from the proposed mandates. In fact, there would be considerable impact on society. The funds required for implementation, monitoring, etc. would be taken out of the economy where it could have been used to provide jobs. This likely would have the most effect on the marginally employed at the bottom of the economic ladder – those about whom liberals purport to be the most concerned.

It certainly would severely reduce freedom. When we start talking about reducing carbon footprints, we are talking about controlling people. A Christian should value freedom more than a mere maintenance of physical life.

If there is any chance certain legislation may reduce our ability to make individual choices, we certainly should not advocate it. Even if one could say with absolute certainty that global warming will, in the future, cause major problems, we should not sell our freedom by implementing policies that empower government to enslave us. The history of the world shows liberty is a scarce commodity and we should never take its preservation lightly. A Christian should consider the use of our minds as a value that it is of far greater magnitude than physical considerations, since that is what makes us human and allows us to exercise the image of God in our lives.

If Christians, in spite of the threat to freedom, still wish for laws to restrict carbon emissions, they should certainly refrain from referring to such activities as being part of a green effort. Carbon dioxide is required for plant life. Having more of it in the air provides more floras and makes our world a greener place. Restricting it makes things less green. Yet, those working to reduce carbon dioxide insist on referring to such actions as green. This shows how foolish and lacking in common sense people become when they latch on to some of these causes. So, please, Mr. and Mrs. Environmentalist, if you wish to reduce carbon dioxide, admit that it will result in a less green environment. This certainly applies to Christians who should be honest in all they do and say.

Most secularists, when considering an issue like this, focus only on the purported physical considerations with no concern or even regard whatsoever for the spiritual impact, thereby treating people in an almost animalistic way.

I am not a scientist. Neither, I suspect, are most of those reading this. I cannot say definitely whether or not a significant warming exists, whether any such warming could be harmful, or whether human activity is contributing substantially to the warming. However, when advocates of any position try to convince people an issue is decided (as has been done with global warning and evolution) rather than engage in an honest debate with those with other views, I become skeptical. Those with the truth on their side do not need to overpower their opposition by maintaining the argument is settled. I do know human freedom is valuable and that it has been severely restricted by most governments. I am not willing that we in the United States, who have been able to exercise our liberties more than any other peoples in history, would trade that ability for a system that severely controls us to avoid a calamity that may or may not ever happen.

Reducing Pollution

Another main concern of environmentalists is the reduction of pollution. Certainly harmful substances in our air and water affect human, animal, and plant life. When one party pollutes, it affects others. So, it is proper for government to be involved in preventing such parties from injuring others. In fact, protecting people from the pollution created by others is the one aspect of environmental concerns in which government has the most legitimate role.

But pollution is a byproduct of the creation of energy and manufacturing – processes required to maintain life. It can be reduced, but will never be eliminated on this earth. It is another negative result of the fall. God will be the direct source of all we need in the new heaven and earth. It is unlikely a need for those processes that create pollution in this life will exist. So, a Christian perspective should be that efforts at reducing pollution be realistic – since some level will have to be endured. Some environmentalists have proposed reductions in the level of pollution that either can't be achieved or where the costs would create hardships. Christians should reject such unrealistic policies.

What level of a given pollutant is acceptable? At what point does a toxic substance become a great enough problem that it shouldn't be tolerated? There aren't always easy answers to such questions, and there will inevitably be differences of opinion as to proper solutions. Christians should always try to balance the need to restrict pollution with such considerations as jobs, costs, and loss of freedom. I believe there should be restrictions primarily when substantial harm has been proven.

However, some things like excessive noises and smells that do not necessarily cause harm are legitimate to control. But this is not an easy issue since various individuals have considerably different tolerance levels for such things.

The issues surrounding pollution are, I believe, some of the most difficult to address. Many other issues deal with whether some activity should be legal or illegal. Often it involves the question of whether some function should be controlled by government. In many cases, it can be addressed with an either/or answer. Such issues can be addressed objectively. But with pollution, once it is determined that it is legitimate for government to be involved, it raises the question of what is the proper level. That question has to be answered for each substance being controlled. People are not going to agree on what is an acceptable amount of pollution from a given source. So, this is a highly subjective issue.

The difficulty of dealing with this issue is greatly increased due to the fact that there are those who wish to use environmental problems as an excuse to give more power to government. This makes it all the more important to work for balance and make sure government is not given any more authority than absolutely necessary to deal with real concerns only.

Whenever possible, efforts at reducing pollution should be at lower levels of government. The Constitution gives the federal government no authorization for such activities. It is possible that some environmental problems should be dealt with at a national level since air flows and rivers do not respect state boundaries. The founders likely did not foresee industrialization would create noxious byproducts – at least not to the extent that it has. That's one of the reasons they provided for an amendment process – to address unforeseen needs.

But the federal government has taken on the whole pollution control function just by arrogating to themselves the power to do so. If this is truly a need, then we should amend the Constitution to grant the legitimate jurisdiction. History tells us such an amendment should be very explicit to prevent the assumption of blanket authority.

CHAPTER 16

The Religious Left

The "religious left" could refer to those with a wide variety of Christian beliefs. Over many decades, a large body of thought has risen among mainline Protestant denominations with a left-oriented focus. The term could also include the thinking of those with various non-Christian religious backgrounds.

What I will primarily be dealing with here is those with a left-of-center orientation among evangelical Christians. There has been a definite growth in their numbers in recent years – due in great part to the influence of such people as Jim Wallis, Tony Campolo, Ron Sider, and movements like the Emergent Church. Since my message in this book is directed toward evangelicals, I believe it is particularly important to evaluate the beliefs of those at least claiming to be in that movement. This discourse is not intended, however, to be a point-by-point response to what has been said by specific people on the evangelical left. Rather, it counters the general philosophies and ideas espoused by that movement.

Who Should Help the Poor?

The one area leftist evangelicals most often focus on is aiding the needy. They cite Bible verses regarding helping the poor as a justification for their views. Those verses tend to be either from the Old Testament or those relating Jesus' words from the New Testament.

A number of passages in the Old Testament contain directions for dealing with the poor – some of which were to be carried out by Israel's government. But the government at that time was essentially a theocracy

– God was ruling it directly. The state and the church were the same (although the church as such had not yet been created).

Although we don't really know, it may be that in the millennium when Christ will reign, church and state will again be united as one entity. At that time, it could be that aid to the needy will be carried out by government. But that will be a very different situation than we have today where church and state clearly should be separate.

Some evangelicals refer to themselves as red-letter Christians, since they focus on the words of Jesus, which in some Bibles are highlighted in red. Jesus said many things in the gospels, but self-styled, red-letter Christians seem to attach more importance to what He said about helping others than they do His other teachings.

The command He left with His followers just before leaving this earth was the Great Commission. And immediately prior to ascending to heaven, He left a directive for them to be His witnesses throughout the world (Acts 1:8). Neither of these instructions is explicitly about helping the poor, although that would be part of being Christ's witness. If assisting the needy was something Christ wished to be a major initiative for the church, it does seem like He would have specifically mentioned it during his final times with His followers before departing earth.

Jesus did issue commands to help the poor. These were directed toward his disciples and/or crowds that were gathered to hear His teaching. It was the people in these audiences that Jesus intended should carry out His commands. When He discussed helping the needy with individuals, it was regarding their personal obligation to the less fortunate. This was true, for example, of His dealings with the rich, young ruler to whom He asked to sell his possessions and give the proceeds to the poor (Matthew 19:16-23). And He told the story of a rich man's personal punishment for his failure to help Lazarus (Luke 16:19-25).

Jesus' words do not indicate or even imply that government should be helping the poor. Nor did he ever ask His audience to lobby for the creation or expansion of aid programs for the poor. Of course, Israel was ruled by Rome at the time, and it is unlikely its rulers would pay any attention to what Jesus or His followers said. Nor was it likely that anyone hearing His words would be in a position to appeal to that government.

Nevertheless, based on the context in which Christ was teaching, it seems obvious that He was telling individuals to help the poor. Once the church was established after His resurrection, we see it doing such work. In Acts, individual believers were selling items, and the church was using the proceeds for aiding those in need. These examples from the New Testament church appear to constitute a model for how people are to be helped, and it had nothing to do with government assistance.

One has to look at the context of the whole Bible, and particularly the New Testament, to get a better idea of what helping the poor should really look like. Often, when the command is more specific, widows and orphans are mentioned. It certainly doesn't appear that the biblical model is to help anyone who asks for it. Nor should Christians expect to be entitled to such help for themselves.

It is instructive to look at I Timothy 5 where Paul discusses the church giving aid to widows. It is apparent that just being a widow was not a sufficient qualification for receiving help. In verses nine through eleven he said that those who are to get aid must be at least sixty years of age, have a reputation for good works, and show hospitality. Typically, government programs do not have such qualifications. If there is to be quite a narrow requirement for those who are to be helped by the church, it seems that should also be true of government aid. I don't believe the singling out of widows and orphans necessarily means it is an exclusive list of those categories of people who should be helped. But it does point to the principle that it is those who are particularly vulnerable who should be aided.

Believers may differ on what role we think government should have regarding aid to the needy, and if a Christian is sincerely convinced government programs for the poor are a good thing, he or she can work for laws that implement or extend such aid. However, such a person should not promote government relief as a command from Scripture as some of the evangelical left do. To do so takes a responsibility Jesus gave to Christians and transfers it onto the public at large. It is effectively forcing even non-believers to carry out the mandates of the Bible – using the immense power of government as a club.

The whole welfare system in this country has engendered multi-generational dependency. This, in turn, has led to a severe values deficit, broken families, crime, drug use, etc. It seems very unlikely that Jesus would look on this situation and say "You're doing a great job, brothers and sisters – keep it up."

The typical conservative position on the question of whether government should be involved in helping people in need has been that the state has a role, but it should be limited to those who are not able to help themselves. The problem with that thinking is that we started out in the United States some time ago pretty much following that concept, and we now have this huge entitlement bureaucracy. Knowing of the flawed nature of humans, Christians should not be surprised that we have fallen so far down the slippery slope once the coffers of government were opened for aid.

Some on the Christian left will acknowledge that churches, ministries, and voluntary giving (by both Christians and others) are an important part of helping the needy. They may even state that the bulk of the need should be met from those sources. Then they say private funds are inadequate, and the government must be involved. But if government programs had not created such a culture of dependence, the need would likely not be as great and could well be met through voluntary contributions. If such great sums were not being extracted from the economy in taxes, more would be available for such contributions.

Advocating that the government help people in need can be a cop-out. For many individuals it can be an excuse that absolves them from personally doing anything to aid people.

Another problem arises with such thinking, because what such people are really saying is that, if we can't get enough from voluntary giving, we should force people to contribute. It is really the same rationale as a thief who says he believes it is okay for him to steal if he can't earn enough money to meet his needs. In both situations, it is a case of the ends justifying the means.

One of the biggest complaints from the left about Christian involvement in conservative politics is that such participants will try to enforce rules from the Bible on everyone. Some even mention they see the danger of Christians establishing a theocracy. For liberal Christians to use the Bible as a justification for government programs to help the poor actually mandates biblical values for all of society – which of course includes non-believers. It is really such believers on the left who are trying to impose Christian values on others through government.

But one doesn't hear complaints from the secular left against those who use biblical passages to promote social welfare, since such programs are consistent with their views. They are being quite disingenuous in their complaints about Christian political involvement. They don't seem to have a problem with those like Jim Wallis who advocate that Christians work for government aid programs. It seems it isn't Christianity in politics they are really against, but just Christianity that works for ideas with which they don't agree.

What about Economic/Social Justice?

I see real problems with the way liberals – including those on the religious left – use the term "justice." Before getting into that discussion, I will briefly address the use of that word in the Bible. It is used a considerable number of times in the Old Testament in various contexts – some of which relate to helping the poor. It would involve a considerable study to examine all such uses, which is beyond the scope of this work.

There isn't universal agreement that the Hebrew word often rendered "justice" is most appropriately translated in that way. Some commentators believe "righteousness" would be more accurate. Whether that is true, it seems unlikely the concept of justice from Old Testament times is the same as that of the twenty-first century, where we associate the word with specific sets of individuals receiving what they deserve or is due them. The Old Testament references were made in a theocratically-run society, and most deal with general concepts rather than commands to help specific people.

When looking at the idea of helping the needy from the context of the whole Bible, we need to consider that the New Testament contains some more specific guidelines about who should get aid – and in what circumstances. It gives no indication that getting assistance involves any sense of entitlement, which contemporary people think of when they hear the word "justice." So, it is quite misleading to import the term "justice" from a society very different from ours into today's world. These are some thoughts to consider as I talk about the use of "justice" by the left.

Those on the evangelical left (and others on the port side of the spectrum) quite often say they believe Christians should promote and work for economic or social justice. But justice involves a person getting something that is their due or that they have earned. Leftist notions of justice in economics imply all people are entitled to such things as food, shelter, healthcare, etc., whether they have made any contribution to its cost or not. Individuals, including believers, will differ in how far they believe government should go in providing such things, but such aid should never be considered a right. And it should not be called economic justice. Rather, the meeting of these needs, whether by the government, Christians, or others, is a matter of mercy, compassion, and grace – not justice.

Christians presuming upon God and not being concerned about their behavior because they believe He will forgive them anyway has been referred to as "cheap grace." Likewise, I believe a presumption that people are entitled to certain benefits in society without any effort on their part could be termed "cheap justice." This is too often the "justice" those on the left advocate dispensing.

Christians, however, should not use the term "justice" in this manner. The system of justice God set up for this world for meeting our physical needs involves labor as stated in Genesis 3:19, where God told Adam, *By the sweat of your face you will eat bread.* It is reiterated by Paul in II Thessalonians 3:10, where he said, *If anyone is not willing to work, then he is not to eat, either.*

There are people in society who are either physically or mentally unable to meet their basic needs. Others have been the victims of misfortunes beyond their personal control. These people should be helped. Whether that help comes from government or private sources is open to question. Whatever its source, it should not be called "justice" just because it is considered the right thing to do.

Christians know we, as well as everyone else in the world, deserve to be eternally separated from God due to our sins. However, He provided for Jesus' death on the cross to pay for those sins. This He did out of His mercy and because of His love. It was not from a sense of justice, since we did nothing to merit the forgiveness He gives. It was certainly not an entitlement or anything we had coming. The end result for those who accept this payment for their sins is that God does justify them – they are made right or just before Him.

God set the standard by mercifully granting us forgiveness at a great cost. But God's sending of His Son was not undertaken to meet any injustice. In fact, it was the opposite of justice, since the just thing would have been to punish us for our infractions against His law. This is because God declares us to be just based only on what Christ did – not due to anything we did to deserve justice.

Even solid Christian organizations that do a very good job of serving the poor and needy refer to their ministries as dispensing economic or social justice. If it is proper to consider aiding the needy by Christians as justice that does not mean it should be a matter of justice for government to dispense such aid. However, the problem is that once we use the word "justice" people tend to think of entitlement by government.

In places in the New Testament where giving to the poor is discussed, there is no indication of it being a matter of justice. And when considering the restrictions placed on providing for widows as previously mentioned, it doesn't seem to support considering helping the poor as an entitlement or dispensing justice. When it is used today, one almost always thinks of it in a legal sense (e.g. references to our justice system when speaking of administering our set of laws). So, even when justice is used to describe giving by a Christian ministry giving non-governmental funds, it implies the idea of entitlement. It seems that what justice is coming to mean in our society is anything given to someone that they or another thinks they should have. The idea of justice has been completely divorced from the idea of merit or receiving one's due.

When the term "justice" is used, it quite often has a quantitative aspect to it. It is also usually applied to a specific person or members of a specific group. In its most basic use, a particular person is owed or due a given amount of something. Money or items with value that can at least be estimated may have been stolen from him or destroyed. In cases where a loss can't be assigned a certain monetary amount, there is often an attempt to arrive at the worth of the loss. For example, if a person has been injured by another party's actions or negligence and lost the ability to work, he might be granted an amount equal to what he likely would have earned had he been able to continue working. So justice -- in a legal sense at least -- often involves named individuals gaining compensation based on a loss of an actual or derived amount. Even in a class-action suit, specific individuals are involved, although their number could be quite large. The amounts awarded by a court will be proportional to their share of the total loss.

Exceptions exist, such as a settlement where the payment is due to culpability in a person's death, since it is impossible to place a value on a human life. Also, many civil lawsuits involve punitive amounts that make the total settlement considerably larger than any actual or estimated loss. I question whether the additional amount should be considered satisfaction of justice since it is intended to punish the perpetrator rather than reimburse a loss.

Other situations arise such as an action taken by an Indian tribe to receive some consideration for land taken when the government broke a treaty. It is hard to determine what they should be owed since there would be many ways in which the land could have been used in the intervening years that – if known – could determine the lost value. Some would say there is a similar situation pertaining to proposals to give reparations to blacks due to losses they suffered as a result of having been slaves. However, no one currently living suffered a direct loss from slavery. Also, the situations of individual blacks vary so considerably it would be difficult to determine how much a given person should receive. In the case of the Indians, many still have operational tribal governments that have some continuity back to the time the treaties were signed.

The point of the preceding discussion is that justice usually has a tie to specific people and at least approximated values. But when the left speaks of economic or social justice they are often referring to general government programs that will provide benefits to whole classes of people. While a given program will have criteria for qualifying, most often recipients do not receive help tied to a value of some loss. Whatever one believes about the merits of such programs, it would be hard for them to say that a given person is being a given a certain amount, since they had it coming. The benefit they receive may be based on a determined need, but need does not equate to justice.

If we move from the realm of government to consider the idea of private giving being a matter of justice, we still have some problems. First, we are faced with two major questions: to whom do we give and how much should we give them? We certainly cannot give to all who ask since most of us would quickly run out of funds if we did that. If we look at criteria in the New Testament for giving it would seem we would need to qualify to whom we give. If we determine someone is worthy, how do we decide what they should be given? Even if we know their need and/or what they rightly should receive, we may not know of other contributions they are getting to help meet the amount.

Some might say that due to these dilemmas, we should just give to organizations ministering to the needy, and let them determine how to allocate the funds. But those ministries will be faced with the same difficulties in determining how to dispense funds. These questions are ones that individuals and organizations – both government and private – do, in fact, face and with which they struggle. Since what is given to a certain person may not be based on what they rightly are due, how can it be considered justice? And if giving is a matter of justice, how does a party know if they have been just when no amount is tied to a claim or loss?

For many who receive help, it is actually a case of injustice, since based on the lack of merit, they should justly suffer the consequences of their actions. Yes, we should pity such people, and, in some cases, help them if we can do so without enabling the behavior that caused their situation. But we certainly shouldn't label it justice. It is mercy – which often goes far beyond justice.

Just because many persons who are very needy may be in that position due to their own actions or lack of effort, does not mean Christians, either individually or collectively in ministries, should not help them. But we should never give it in a way that the recipients come to expect it as something to which they are entitled. We should use wisdom in making certain our aid is not enabling behavior such as indolence, alcoholism, etc.

Many in our society have gotten so used to thinking government will – in fact is obligated to – meet their needs that they do not receive help with the gratitude and thankfulness one would expect of the recipients of a gift. This attitude often carries over to help received from non-governmental sources. This hampers the work of the gospel when those getting aid from Christians do not regard it as something flowing from the love of God and His people – but rather as something to which they have a right.

Can Government Guarantee Anything?

Many who promote government supplying the needs of everyone believe this should be guaranteed. The impossibility of ensuring all have a minimal living can be seen more clearly by looking at a hypothetical, prehistoric example. Let's say we have a community populated by only three cave people. One person has the responsibility of hunting, fishing, and gathering fruits and vegetables. Another collects firewood and keeps the fire. The third cooks the food.

They decide to form a very rudimentary government and make a pact guaranteeing hot food for all. But if the hunter decides he will stop bringing in anything because his food is guaranteed, all three will starve unless one or both of the others takes on his responsibilities. The problem is that the second person has stopped taking care of the fire since her food is now guaranteed. She refuses to get involved in filling in for the hunter for the same reason. The third person now would have to take on the tasks of the other two, as well as his own, to be able to eat hot meals. He could, if he is willing to do the hunter's job and not the other's, eat raw food. If he is unwilling to do so, the whole system would break down and the three would starve. The guarantee of hot meals would not be realized. Their law wouldn't be worth the paper (oops, I don't think they had that) it was written (guess they weren't doing that either) on. The only way the three will meet their needs is if they realize there are no guarantees and that each must accept responsibility to do his job.

One could say this would never happen in reality since all three of the people in our hypothetical community would easily see that each has to bear his or her responsibility for them to eat as they wish. Nevertheless, it illustrates the fact that something requiring the labor of others can never be guaranteed, since it depends on someone else providing it. The problem is that those who are expected to provide what is guaranteed are themselves assured the same provisions without any necessity of labor.

Any guarantee has to have guarantors. When they are the same people as those receiving the guarantees, it creates a problem. When a government claims to guarantee something, it is really the residents of its jurisdiction who are expected to pay for the guarantee with their taxes. These are also the same people to whom the guarantee is given. So, it is really a logical impossibility for government to guarantee anything. When it purports to do so, it is really making the same kind of promise made by an operator of a Ponzi scheme.

In a larger society, the failure of one person to contribute will not cause the whole economic system to collapse. However, with any guarantee in place, some members will realize it is not necessary for them to do anything because their needs will be met regardless. That means a larger burden will be placed on those who are productive. Over time, more and more individuals will tire of carrying the load for others and will become idle themselves. This, in turn, causes yet more people to go from being producers to being consumers only. Eventually not enough is being produced and the amount being guaranteed cannot be sustained; the law has become worthless.

This should not come as a surprise to Christians since we realize that, due to their fallen nature, men and women have a propensity to shirk their responsibility to care for themselves and to take advantage of any situation that allows them to do so. This is essentially what happened when the Pilgrims started their colony in Plymouth. They initially held all property and cropland in common. So many people, believing they would eat regardless of the amount of work they did, contributed little or nothing to the common effort. The colony almost starved before instituting a system of private croplands. Any government guarantee assumes some people will be working and providing needs. Christians, being aware of the flawed character of man, should particularly realize that people are prone to get by in life with as little effort as possible and to take advantage of a system where they can live off the labor of others.

Eliminating Poverty

Examples of helping the poor in Scripture usually involve aiding individual people. We do see the church in Acts organizing a ministry for helping widows and the selling of assets to distribute aid to the poor. When parachurch organizations start ministries to help the poor, they are acting on behalf of a segment of the church. Their mission is consistent with biblical mandates. Such ministries have historically also worked with individuals – although a given ministry may focus on a certain geographic area, ethnic group, social problem, or other segment of the population.

In contrast, those on the left have spoken of ways to end poverty for all people. The first thing that can be said of such an ambitious idea is that it is not realistic. At least a certain amount of poverty is the result of sin. We know in the imperfect world, on this side of heaven, sin will not be eradicated. As a result, we should not expect situations caused by it will totally go away either.

Although the Bible speaks of helping individual poor people and doesn't really mention ending poverty, there is nothing specifically wrong with making such an attempt. However, most evangelical Christian social welfare ministries have sought to provide a witness to Jesus Christ along with the amelioration of social problems. In moving beyond that, to actually trying to end poverty, the left seems to have made improving social welfare a larger goal than winning souls for God's kingdom.

Those on the Christian left usually seek to address poverty by trying to fix systemic problems they see as causing or contributing to the plight of the poor. This usually means governmental action. Certainly, if we, as believers, see policies that cause problems for any portion of society, we should point them out and try to have them changed. One example is the government subsidization of ethanol which has caused an increase in the price of corn – both for that used for ethanol and for food. This impacts the poor the most (in places like Mexico). In many cases, when public policy is contributing to poverty, it is because of something government is doing – not due to its failing to act.

Any success in helping people by changing policies will depend on accurately assessing how current policies are causing a problem, and how they should be modified to affect a better outcome. Unfortunately, the analysis of the sources of societal problems provided by the Christian left is pretty much the same as those of secular liberals. And their proposed solutions also usually involve more government programs and large amounts of taxpayer funds.

Christians who recognize the fallen nature of man should realize that such methods are doomed to failure. When benefits are provided for free, the tendency for flawed humans is to take advantage of them. Liberals can always find anecdotes that relate how some individuals were helped by a particular program. But if we look at the whole effort to eliminate poverty through government in America, it has been a colossal failure. The War on Poverty has been going on for forty-some years. If it has been so effective, why is there still such a need? And why is the left proposing new and larger programs for ending poverty?

An old proverb says "Give a man a fish; you have fed him for a day. Teach a man to fish, and you have fed him for a lifetime." I think many on both the left and the right recognize the wisdom of this saying. But, in addition to helping a person learn how to provide for themselves, it is also important to work for a societal environment where roadblocks to doing that are minimized. This would include not having too many rules about how, where, and when he can fish. It would also not place a lot of rules on how he could trade his fish to obtain the products of the labor of others. Teaching one to fish offers limited value if laws are in place which make it difficult for a fisherman to feed his family and use excess fish to meet other needs.

The closest this world has come to eliminating poverty is in this country. This happened without an effort to end it. Our founders just established a system that allowed maximum freedom. The result was unprecedented prosperity and an economy where the poorest have lived better than the average person in many other countries. Poverty will never totally end. But if we truly seek to minimize it, we should promote free enterprise in other countries and seek to remove all the shackles placed on it in the United States.

So, Christians, in addition to ministering to the needy, can help them by promoting these ideas. This is not what the Christian left is doing. Rather, they are working for solutions that throw public funds at social problems in a way that has actually exacerbated them. They are also advocating policies that will further hamstring what has been a very productive economic system and make it closer to those that have failed in other countries. If they truly believe in ending poverty, the very best thing they could do would be to promote the free enterprise system.

Christians should realize better than others that, due to human imperfection, a free market system where people are forced to take responsibility for their own lives and the consequences of their actions, will lead to a better, more prosperous society – which will mean less poor people. We should understand also that, for the same reason, when government, in effect, provides a cover for irresponsibility and unrighteousness, the result will be lack of productivity – and more poor people. The policies promoted by the Christian left are those that have, and will, create more poverty. What is worse, they will cause more people to become irresponsible.

To put more emphasis on meeting the earthly needs of the poor than on saving souls is very short-sighted. No matter how much help is given to meet a person's material needs, he will eventually die and either end up in heaven or hell. How comfortable a life he had on earth will have had no impact on his eternal destiny. Such help may have added to his well-being and/or health and even may have extended his life, but it will have been of little use if he ends up in hell. The time one spends on earth is infinitesimal compared to eternity. Should not a priority be given to a person's eternal well-being over meeting his needs for a short time?

Some on the Christian left talk about the inequality between classes of people. While the Bible says we are to help people in need and not take advantage of those less fortunate, it also says clearly that we are not to discriminate in favor of either poor or richer people. Nowhere does it say there should be efforts to equalize peoples' situations. In fact, the assumption is there will always be people with varying amounts of this world's goods. It is inevitable in a world where people have freedom of action that some will make good choices and prosper as a result. Others will make poor choices and their lives will not thrive. Attempts by government to equalize their situations in life will cause those on the receiving end to have little incentive to produce and those on the giving end to have less to invest and create wealth. The end result is a poorer society with less for all. It is those on the lower end that are hurt the most. In a fallen world, inequality is absolutely essential.

What About Materialism?

Those on the left (including Christians) rail against materialism and imply, or directly state, it is caused by the capitalist system (their term – not mine). Since the free enterprise system promotes greater prosperity, it does result in more material goods in society. Due to our flawed natures, those who have more purchasing power often spend a lot on unnecessary items. Believers with a greater amount of wealth often spend more on gratifying themselves than they should and less to advance the kingdom of God than they should. However, it is not the economic system that is at fault. It merely enables wealth to be created. Individuals are responsible for how they use what God has allowed them to have – whether that be a lot or little. People are greedy and/or spend excessive amounts for selfish wants, not because of an economic system, but because they are fallen human beings. At least the free market economy provides a choice for many. In collectivist systems, fewer people even have the financial means to significantly contribute to help grow God's kingdom.

We need to acknowledge that much funding for domestic and foreign Christian missions has been contributed by those in this country due to our great prosperity resulting from economic freedom. Certainly, the potential for giving is way beyond what has actually been contributed. But one can't blame the free enterprise system for that. Does it make sense to hamstring our economy so less wealth is created just because the percentage of what is produced isn't distributed as some think it should be? How many believers in the Soviet Union ever had enough income that they even had the option of giving much (or even anything) to Christian ministries?

One thing that happens in prosperous societies is that people tend not to use items for as long and trade more often for newer and/or better replacements, often while the original possession is in almost perfect working condition. From the standpoint of the person discarding the item, this can often be considered wasteful. However, their actions actually are a boon for poorer people. Used items are then available to them that are often in very good shape. They show up at places like garage sales and thrift shops, often at very low prices. And because many people trade automobiles frequently, people who might otherwise not be able to afford to drive can get used vehicles that provide reasonable transportation at a much lower cost.

It is possible that Christians on the right could become so focused on restoring our nation that they also would lose interest in saving souls. All Christians should be involved with such evangelism. However, that isn't as likely for conservatives since we are primarily working to provide a framework whereby the gospel can be freely proclaimed. Ultimately, the objective is still to add souls to God's kingdom. However, the left wants to use government to provide material needs such that this, rather than individual salvation itself, becomes the goal.

The Christian Left on Other Issues

Initially, many in the evangelical left were pro-life and recognized the need to stop abortions. They also acknowledged a scriptural condemnation of homosexuality and opposed same-sex marriages and the homosexual agenda. Recently, many of their leaders have backed away from those positions or at least downplayed them. Also, as they have increasingly focused on the poor and efforts to alleviate physical suffering, they have become less concerned about winning souls. Some, particularly those in the Emergent Church, have softened their theology to the point where one could question whether they should still be considered evangelicals.

It is understandable that many who have been influenced by the Emergent Church teaching would be more receptive to leftist political ideas. Those in that movement have downplayed sin and the need for salvation. Without a strong belief in the fallen nature of man, they will not see how improbable such solutions are that don't require accountability on the part of those being helped. Also, since they emphasize love and the solving of temporal problems over eternal ones, they are more apt to promote the social gospel.

Some positions the evangelical left has taken have been admirable. One is their opposition to the Iraq War. I make a case against that conflict in Chapter 9. The problem is that they go beyond opposing a war that we shouldn't have been in to advocate the positions of the so-called peace movement. They have the attitude that wars can be eliminated by merely talking to an enemy – even when their intent is conquest.

Are All Political Positions Equally Valid for Christians?

Christians who may personally be either conservative or liberal (or neither) have commented that the church shouldn't take a stand on issues because believers disagree on them. They often say this in a way that implies or directly states that the opposing positions are equally valid. We certainly need to acknowledge all believers' right to form their positions on political ideas. However, it is not true all of those positions are equally right. Based on a proper view of the nature of the world and man there is a correct view on most issues. By that, I don't mean it is right to spend two percent of a budget on some item rather than three. When it comes to issues where stands are based on philosophical differences, there is one that is better. None of us flawed humans will ever figure out what is best in each situation. However, God knows that taking a particular position will result in the best outcome.

Even more than with individual issues, a particular philosophy of government is more in tune with the real world God created than others. I have fairly consistently asserted throughout this book that limited-government beliefs are more compatible with a Christian worldview, so I naturally believe that is correct. Some believers think just the opposite is true, but we cannot both be right. To say all views of government by Christians are equally valid is like the postmodernist lie that you can have your truth, and I can have mine.

What Might Be Some Motivations for Those on the Christian Left? One wonders why evangelicals would adopt the positions of the left. I believe there are a number of reasons. Some who have such views are very sincere. They may have great compassion for needy people and believe that whatever can be done to help them should be done, including government programs. I think some of those are not very discerning in that they don't realize the harm that can actually come by doing for people what they should be doing for themselves. Others have just allowed their views to be shaped by the culture around them. I think all believers have been influenced by the world – more than we realize. That includes those who make a concerted effort not to let such ideas impact them. The lure of humanistic thinking is very subtle, and it can often be difficult to detect the fact that one has let it shape one's thoughts.

Some Christians try to find common ground with unbelievers. They view it as a positive thing to work with non-Christians for some worthy cause. They believe that when others see them helping to solve some of the world's problems, it will reflect positively on Christianity. This probably motivates some who have joined the push to curtail the supposed global warming problem, for instance. Undoubtedly, many who get involved in such activities are sincere. There is nothing wrong with wanting to work with unbelievers for a common goal. However, believers need to be more astute in judging whether the basis for a given cause is legitimate and in detecting when those promoting them have other agendas that might not be consistent with a Christian worldview. Any activity engaged in by a Christian should not contribute to results detrimental to the cause of Christ or to our nation and our freedom.

Another thing that draws some to certain issues is a desire to be well thought of by the right people. This particularly affects Christians who are academics. The views in many disciplines are so skewed to the left that a person opposing them is noticed. Anyone who challenges the "correct" viewpoint may well be looked down on by their peers and colleagues. They may even be thought of as un-academic (horrors!). This is likely why Christian scientists too often adopt at least some part of the theory of evolution. It is also a reason why a believer with a scientific background may buy into the global warming scare.

In some situations, those who dominate in the academic world try to shut out any opposition by claiming a strong consensus exists which agrees with their position. That certainly applies with both evolution and global warming. Then, rather than debate the issue, they engage in what can only be called academic thuggery to discount and even ridicule anyone who dares to disagree. This is, of course, the direct opposite of what academics should do – allow open and free discussion of all viewpoints. The pressure to conform may not be as strong for political views, but it nevertheless exists in many academic environments.

It takes a person with strong convictions and intellectual courage to resist the browbeating of such tactics. However, Christians, of all people, should be willing and able to stand up for what they believe to be the truth. It should matter to us more that we do what is right than whether we are considered academic or thought of well by the supposed experts. It is often pride which causes people (even Christians) to unquestioningly go along with prevailing viewpoints rather than risk being labeled in an unflattering manner – possibly even being called ignorant.

CHAPTER 17

The Christian Right

Because this book is being addressed to them, I will focus almost exclusively on evangelical Christians in this discussion. It is we who are normally thought of when references are made to "the religious right" or "the Christian right." No appreciable blocs of organized political conservatives exist within non-Christian or mainline Protestant religious bodies.

A large body of Catholics are positioned on the right on life issues, and many of them go beyond these issues and are consistently conservative in their other political views. Substantial numbers of mainline Protestants are also political conservatives. However, neither they nor the Catholics have organizations or leaders that deal with conservative politics as evangelical Christians do – although they may partner with us as individuals.

One key reality that has to be considered when evaluating the religious right is that the media has greatly distorted our beliefs and our methods. They have created a caricature that only applies to very fringe elements. Nevertheless, it is true some leading evangelical conservative leaders and organizations have said and done things that have made them easier targets for criticism.

A Narrow Focus

One way conservatives have left themselves open to attack is by focusing on such a narrow range of issues. Most evangelicals on the right are concerned about much more than what have been dubbed moral issues. However, in discussions about legislation, they often provide lists of concerns that only contain items like abortion, homosexual issues, pornography, etc. When rating legislators or developing questionnaires for candidates, the items used are often mostly the typical "moral issues" – with possibly one or two thrown in regarding something like taxes. Often, mention of issues other than the moral ones appears to be little more than an afterthought.

When education is mentioned, the concerns raised are usually in relation to the anti-Christian bias or opposition to the pro-gay agenda in the classroom. Of course, we should be very concerned about those problems. However, not enough emphasis is placed on what really allows such things to take place: for instance, the fact that parents have lost control of what is taught to their children because of increasing state and federal mandates which have overridden the authority of local school boards that represent parents and taxpayers.

The focus of the efforts should be returning control over education to our communities. Here we will find many allies among people who recognize the danger and/or folly of centralizing educational decisions. They may not all be comfortable in working for prayer in school, but agree that the federal government should get out of education.

The Christian right has also made major issues of items that aren't all that important. One is using marijuana for medicinal purposes. Since it is mind-altering, it is not wise for Christians to use pot – even if it met a medical need and were legal. Some believers may disagree. However, the political issue is not whether it is advisable for Christians to use such a treatment, but whether it should be allowed in our society. I have dealt more extensively with the issue of drugs in general in chapter 5.

I believe there may be arguments on either side of the issue, but the main point is that this affects only a small number of people and should not be considered a big issue. Our debt is skyrocketing, our whole economy is crashing, secularists are trying to impose their views through the educational system, millions of babies have been aborted, and we are losing our freedoms in so many ways, and yet we are worrying about whether a few people can use marijuana as medicine. It doesn't make sense. Yet, it often appears on candidate questionnaires conservative groups use.

Another issue that has been overemphasized is whether it is legal to burn the US Flag as a protest. As a very patriotic American, I certainly do not like to see the emblem of our freedom being desecrated. However, whether such a practice should be a crime is another question. One can make various points as to whether it should be classified as freedom of expression or not. Those calling themselves conservatives could conceivably take opposite positions on this issue, and it really isn't actually done that much. When it is done, there really is no significant impact on our society. To treat this on par with issues that concern the very survival of our nation and, indeed, our very civilization, makes conservatives appear shortsighted.

An example of an issue not that important in the scheme of things was the opposition to the building of a mosque near ground zero of the 9/11 terrorist attack. It may well be considered insensitive for Muslims to construct a religious center in such a location. It may even be that they purposely chose the site to make a statement. However, if they acquired the land legitimately, on what legal basis could they be prevented from using it for their building? Yet, many conservative organizations spent much time and print opposing its construction. The American Center for Law and Justice (ACLJ) devoted a considerable amount of time on its radio program "Jay Sekulow Live" to this issue over what seemed like weeks. ACLJ has done much good, but what a waste of air time that could have been used to inform Christians about issues where they could have made a greater impact.

How We Present Our Ideas

I believe the primary concern of Christians in politics should be preserving our ability to proclaim the gospel freely. Although some exceptions exist, most believers do not favor laws to outlaw unrighteous behavior – at least that is not a priority. However, many non-believers have gotten the impression Christians are trying to impose their religion by mandating the behavior called for in the Bible. One reason is that the media twists our message, but there are other contributing factors.

One is the way the religious right has referred to "moral issues." This has caused others to believe Christians in politics are only interested in this type of issue and that we want to impose morality through law. As discussed in chapter 5, an aspect of morality exists in most laws; however, the reason we should support or oppose certain legislation is not because of its morality, but because it involves a questions of rights. I believe we should never use the term "moral issue."

We need to make it clear we are just as interested in protecting the freedom of those who may use it in ways we don't approve of as we are in maintaining our liberty to practice our religion. If it is apparent that we only care about our own freedom as believers and no one else's, we cannot expect much sympathy for our cause.

One thing we will still have to deal with is the confusion over the concept of rights. For example, we should not try to attempt to legislate against fornication. People should be free to do things like that as long as they are willing to suffer the consequences of their disobedience to God. One of the consequences may be that some rental housing may not be available to them, since apartment owners should be completely free to deny rental to unmarried couples. Forcing someone to rent to people living in sin would be enabling a lifestyle they believe to be wrong.

Such rights should be available to anyone – not just a person who makes this decision for religious reasons. Too often, Christians have sought exceptions for themselves when they should have been working to get rid of the non-discrimination laws that take away people's right to choose. When we ask for an exception, it is rightly perceived by many as a privilege – rather than a right. There is then resentment toward the Christians who want this special treatment.

Some would protest that allowing anyone to deny someone housing would be taking away their rights or freedom, but nothing could be further from the truth. Their right to practice sin (or any activity for that matter) does not extend to an obligation on the part of anyone to provide them a place to do it. That many believe such a refusal to rent to be a violation of rights is due to the misguided ideas that have been promoted about the right to discriminate.

A similar issue involves the right of a printer to decide not to print wedding invitations for homosexual couples. Anyone – Christian or not – should be able to choose with whom they will do business.

How We Label Ourselves

Another way some individual Christians and ministries create misconceptions is in how they describe their mission. They may speak of "capturing (or recapturing) the culture" or "reclaiming America for Christ." Use of such language cannot help but cause people to think Christians are trying to take over the country. They frighten off even some (perhaps many) who should be our allies. We do want more influence in the culture and in the political world. Such influence has, in the past, worked to the benefit of our society for all our citizens, and it would do so again in the future. But that is quite different than statements from some in the Christian right that seem to imply we are interested in controlling the nation and its residents.

We should be seeking to influence society by first bringing people into a relationship with Jesus Christ. One of the ways of doing that is through ministries that help others in various ways. Also, the way we live our lives should be a positive witness to others. As I have been advocating in this book, we can work to preserve and restore our nation to its former principles, and in the process promote more freedom – not just for ourselves, but for all people. This will be a witness to many. But if we use our influence to promote laws that proscribe certain behaviors, we will just alienate people.

Also, a problem is the number of Christian conservative organizations that use the term "family" in their name. Right off the top of my head I can think of "Focus on the Family," "American Family Association," and "Family Research Council" among the larger, better-known, and more influential ones. In my state, we have the "Minnesota Family Council."

As believers, we know the family is one of the most important foundations of any nation. We also know it is under attack from many quarters in our society – not the least of which include existing and proposed government policies. Many who are not Christians would agree with those assessments. However, the use of the term in the names of so many of the organizations many associate with the Christian right, gives the impression that the scope of their concerns is quite narrow. In actuality, that is not true. The organizations mentioned, as well as others, have done a lot to alert believers to many threats to our society. They have dealt with many items beyond ones that would be considered strictly family issues. Of course, much of what government does directly or indirectly affects families, but most would not consider them family issues. Why not use words like liberty, freedom, etc., more in the names of our organizations?

Perceptions are important. And perceptions are often formed to a great extent by terms and names used by a group. Many will never get beyond the names of organizations and statements quoted in the media to see that what Christians are working for is not anything that threatens them – that, in fact, many will likely agree with much of our agenda. Our enemies will use our names and anything we say to distort our message and objectives.

Criticism from Other Evangelicals

There has been a fair amount of criticism of the religious right from solid evangelicals. Some of them do not believe Christians should be involved in politics at all. Others think it is okay for individual believers to participate, but don't think the church itself should get involved and/or have problems with past efforts by Christians in the political sphere.

One common theme of both of these types of critics is their contention that efforts to change society through political means are doomed to failure, that such change will only occur when lives are changed through the transforming power of the gospel of Jesus Christ. They are absolutely correct! However, the effort of Christians in politics should not be directed toward using the power of government to change people, but rather to preserve the environment that allows the gospel to be proclaimed. I believe this is where much of the focus of the religious right has been.

Take the example of homosexual issues. I have heard almost no believer express an opinion that we should start enforcing sodomy laws to prevent homosexual behavior. Efforts in this area have mostly been confined to stopping "gay" activists from pushing their agenda through venues like the public schools and preventing the forced acceptance of their lifestyles, which results when government places its imprimatur on them by allowing them to marry.

Critics also point out many cases where religious right leaders have employed methods that are much like the world's, and have, thus, tarnished the image of Christ. You will note that throughout this chapter I, too, have directed criticisms at methods used by Christian conservatives. But it is a *non sequitur* to say that because an effort has not always been done properly, it should, therefore, not be done at all.

To the extent that the religious right's efforts are directed toward trying to modify the behavior of individuals or society, their critics are right. In actuality, the effort to maintain and restore our freedom and to stop government from forcing secularism on us should go on – by continuing to work for these things, learning from past mistakes and trying not to repeat them.

Ed Dobson and Cal Thomas in their book *Blinded by Might*[1] make much of the fact that, after years of effort and millions of dollars spent, there has been no success in improving the moral climate in the country. Again, the political effort should be to reestablish freedom. That could be accomplished and America could remain as pagan as ever, because, as they repeatedly (and correctly) point out, improved behavior results from heart change – not political enforcement. It also must be admitted that there has not been much progress in stopping the loss of freedom either. However, the question for a Christian regarding any action should be whether it is the right thing to do – not whether it has brought success in the past. If it is right for Christians to work to restore our freedoms, we should continue to do so – whether we are seeing progress or not. The ultimate result is really in God's hands. It is very possible that without the efforts of Christians and other conservatives, we might be much farther down the road in losing our liberties.

1 Cal Thomas, Ed Dobson, *Blinded by Might* (Grand Rapids, MI Zondervan Publishing House; 1999)

Evangelical critics are concerned political efforts that ally us with non-believers will distort or dilute the gospel message. If, in fact, such alliances are trying to use political power to enforce conduct consistent with the Bible, that is a legitimate concern, but it is less likely if the goal is to preserve freedom. This should be something both believers and non-believers should be concerned about and cooperate on as a worthy objective.

Dobson and Thomas also mention the problem of names like "Christian Coalition." If such a group lets anyone join, it will not truly be a coalition of believers. If there are no restrictions on memberships, there is a real possibility that some who aren't believers will join, and their activities, attitudes, statements, etc. will reflect badly on Christians. Even if membership or participation is restricted, these authors point out that the very name will give some the impression that the goal is to impose Christian beliefs or behavior through government, and I believe they are correct.

Another problem arises when Christian leaders who are in politics issue joint statements or sign documents with other groups or individuals with whom they are involved politically. When these documents address Christian ideas and issues, it can give the appearance that all the signers share the same evangelical beliefs, and this may not be the case. As a result, the gospel message is "watered down." It is fine for Christians to ally themselves with others who share common political objectives. But it is wrong to issue any declarations that even imply a common religious belief among all the signatories.

Recently, some Christian conservative leaders have partnered with Glenn Beck, a Mormon, in a way that implies they are working together as Christians. While I don't agree with Beck on everything, I think he has been quite helpful by informing people on various issues. It isn't wrong to work with Mormons on political concerns. However, when there are common political efforts with any who don't share our view of salvation, it needs to be made clear by evangelicals that it does not involve a religious partnership.

Some have criticized Christians who are involved in political efforts with those who are not believers since the fact they are working so closely with them for a common goal makes it more difficult to witness to them by challenging their religious beliefs (or lack thereof). Often, those we know the best can be the hardest to talk to about salvation. However, if a believer does not get involved in politics, he or she may not even meet such a person. It is particularly difficult to talk to them about religious things when you never meet them! Following this logic to the extreme, we should never try to get to know any non-believer since doing so makes it harder to talk to them about their eternal destiny.

Continuing that line of thinking, we would not even be employed in a job where we work with others (which includes most jobs), since we would then get to know people with whom it would be harder to speak to about our faith. In actuality, working with someone for a common goal actually presents one with a good opportunity for witnessing. We, as Christians, just need to be faithful and obedient and take advantage of such opportunities.

Dobson and Thomas assert that those who are called to preach should keep their focus on the gospel and not get involved in political issues. Certainly such individuals should not be so active in political affairs that it takes precedence over their work to grow the kingdom. However, that should not preclude their speaking out on important issues of the day (even in a sermon when appropriate) as long as they keep the gospel as their priority.

Some evangelicals criticize Christians on the right who claim God has a covenant with America, and/or that believers should be trying to take control of the United States and use its government to promote establishing God's kingdom. Those are valid criticisms. However, they are not reasons for Christians to stay out of politics. The fact that some believers have approached political efforts in an inappropriate manner does not mean others should not be involved in politics at all.

Some evangelical leaders say believers need not be involved in politics, since God will take care of our concerns in such things, and that if a society becomes more Christian, its government will also improve. But that doesn't happen automatically. Good government depends on the application of the right principles to the law; ones based on a Christian view of the world. Such principles are most likely to be used when the believers who know and understand them are involved in politics. Scientific advances are also made by discovering the principles God built into the world He created. But unless they are applied, they are useless. This is also the case for those principles needed for an effective government.

Christians and Power

A charge has been made from both within and outside of the evangelical community that many Christian right leaders have been seeking power. Whatever their faults may be, most in that category favor a limited government with less concentrated authority, so they don't seek government power. In some cases, they are accused of throwing their weight around within the Republican Party. An example is when a certain leader threatens to withhold support for a certain politician if he doesn't toe the line on certain issues. This is considered a power play because of the number of people who look to that leader for political direction. However, this is really more about influence than power. Even if it were considered power, it is not being asserted for their personal benefit, but, rather, for what they see as a positive direction for the country. Elected politicians of both parties have abused their power. Unfortunately, that has included Christians. Such assertions of power really demonstrate the wisdom of not investing much authority in government.

Neo-Conservative Influence on Christians

Another problem with the religious right is that so many in the movement have been influenced too much by the neo-conservatives. This has particularly played out in foreign policy views – especially as it relates to dealing with terrorists in the wake of the 9/11 attack. I have devoted a section in Chapter 9 to the Iraq and Afghan wars and another in Chapter 10 to the so-called "War on Terror," because I believe these are key issues where many Christians and conservatives (including the religious right) have gotten off track.

I have been involved in conservative politics for a long while. I have noticed a shift in emphasis among many on the right during that time. The largest concerns for conservatives in the 1950s through the 1970s were the growth in the size of government (particularly at the federal level), the loss of freedom, and the huge debt. Increasingly, the focus has changed to having our nation police the world, which is one of the main priorities for neo-cons. They also are not as concerned about government debt, abiding by the Constitution, and checks and balances, and are more supportive of social welfare policies. They are often in favor of high educational standards, but, unfortunately, are willing to impose them from higher levels of government and are less concerned about local control of teaching.

Some very specific individuals and publications were instrumental in the early neo-con movement, who, while anti-communist, would not be considered conservative at all. I will not go into their history, but a good source of information on the early neo-cons is *William F. Buckley: Pied Piper for the Establishment*[2] by John F. McManus.

At this point, those who would be considered neo-conservatives vary in how conservative they are in issues beyond foreign policy, but they virtually all support the involvement of the United States in nation-building. More significant than who is, or is not, a neo-conservative is the fact that the ideas of the early devotees of that philosophy have permeated the conservative movement to the point that many one might not call neo-cons have, nevertheless, adopted many of their positions – particularly in the foreign policy area.

One problem for Christians, as well as other conservatives, is that most of the very visible people on the right tend to either be neo-cons or have been heavily influenced by them. So, many conservatives have been drawn to their messages. I believe many, if not most, of those who have been influencing Christians to adopt neo-con positions are doing so because they have, in turn, been swayed by others. However, the possibility exists that some of the opinion molders have been deliberately promoting neo-con views to promote their agenda.

2 John F. McManus, *William F. Buckley: Pied Piper for the Establishment* (Appleton, WI; The John Birch Society; 2002)

What About George W. Bush?

A related area of misguided thinking is the support conservative Christians gave to George W. Bush. This was primarily based on his supposed handling of the War on Terror and his professed Christian faith. It is certainly true that not all conservative believers gave Bush their unqualified support and many had problems with some of his policies. However, primarily because of their belief in his efforts in the Iraq War and the War on Terror, they defended him. This has really damaged the credibility and effectiveness of the Christian right. As it has become apparent to an increasing number of Americans that the engagement in Iraq was very ill-advised, the credibility of conservatives suffered dramatically which – in large part – was what caused the defeat of many good candidates in 2006. It also had a role in the election of Barack Obama in 2008, since many people wanted a president who was as far as possible from George Bush.

It did not really impact the 2010 elections for a couple of reasons. First, due to the big bailout and the opposition to the Obama healthcare law, economic issues were much in the forefront. Also, many people had come to realize after two years of an Obama presidency that there really wasn't much difference in his and Bush's foreign policy – with both being committed to interventionism.

I believe Christian support for Bush's foreign policy has done much to harm efforts to restore our nation to its founding principles.

Christians, when evaluating a political person who claims a Christian faith, should look at his views and positions with the same critical eye they would those of any other politician. In such an evaluation, we are judging their policies, not them personally – nor their faith.

In the following paragraphs, I will discuss George W. Bush's faith. He is no longer president and, at this point, does not appear to be impacting public policy. So, one might suggest there is little benefit in such an evaluation. The reason for bringing up these points is that I believe they illustrate the kind of discernment we should use in looking at an individual's beliefs – particularly a public person. Hopefully, it will be instructive to some as they assess others' faith.

We, as Christians, shouldn't judge the salvation status of those who claim to be believers, because we don't know their hearts. However, we should not assume everyone who professes Christian faith is a true believer. This is particularly true of politicians. We can point out inconsistencies in their lives or statements they make that tend to indicate they either may not be believers or they are not walking in the right paths.

With George Bush several questions arise. He positions himself as an evangelical Christian, yet when he made it to church in Washington, he attended a mainline Episcopal church – not an evangelical one. Some defend the fact he seldom went to church while president due to the problem of finding time and the need for security. Yet both Carter and Clinton went to church quite regularly, with Carter even finding time to teach Sunday school. Bush and his wife belonged to the Methodist church while in Texas.

Bush admits in his autobiography that he was in Skull and Bones at Yale. Then he says he cannot say more about that fact since he is pledged to secrecy. Although I question whether a believer should be in secret societies, he wasn't a Christian when he joined. Not too much is known about Skull and Bones. However, based on what has leaked out there appears to be some nefarious activities that have taken place in the organization. Wouldn't a member who later became a Christian want to expose such things?

His father was an insider while holding a position as a director of the CFR and was a member of the Trilateral Commission. Both those organizations are in the forefront of the push for globalism. He openly talked about working toward a New World Order. He, as have all presidents since WWII, had a preponderance of CFR members in key appointive positions. While George W. isn't a CFR member, I have never heard him say anything that indicates he had any substantial policy disagreements with his father. The fact that he, too, stacked his administration with CFR members indicates no real deviation from his father's goals. Christians should realize the push for global government is very likely tied in to the coming of a world system as described in Revelation. As such, we should oppose all efforts toward that end and not help to enable it.

Bush's wife, Laura, who also claims to be a Christian, revealed on Larry King that she supports gay marriage and is pro-choice on abortion. This does not mean she is not a Christian, since some believers have found a way to justify such positions. However, a large majority of evangelicals are pro-life and oppose same-sex marriage. Whether she truly is a Christian, husbands and wives do sometimes disagree on such issues – even when both are believers. More often, though, they do agree on questions like this. This does raise the possibility that her stated views on these issues represent the true beliefs of the Bush family, and George's are views adopted merely for pragmatic, political reasons.

Back in 1977, George W. lost a congressional race to a candidate who defeated him by mobilizing Christians. Perhaps I'm being cynical, but one has to ask if his Christian decision was really a political ploy. One cannot discount the possibility that he, or others, have feigned Christian faith to gain support from believers. Those who are working toward a global order consider it a high-stakes endeavor. It certainly wouldn't strain credibility to believe that some would pretend to be Christians to gain support for what is a very strong passion. I certainly cannot say definitely this is the case with George Bush, but neither should it be discarded as a possibility.

Any of these considerations taken individually do not point strongly to Bush not being a Christian. Even looking at the sum of them does not prove he is not a true believer. But taken together, they do raise enough questions to cast some doubt on his stated religious beliefs. They are enough for Christians to not just accept his word that he is a believer.

Even if his faith is completely genuine, we, as believers, must evaluate the policies and views of all political personalities by the same criteria, whether they are Christians or not. We should support them only to the extent that they advocate and promote the right things politically. When seeking public office, a person should not ask for or expect support from fellow Christians just because he or she is a believer.

The Need to Be Consistent About Big Government

Another issue where the religious right has come down on the wrong side is that of human rights and civil liberties. Views on these issues have been impacted by the concern over terrorism. Many on the right have been properly concerned about the growth of big government and the consequent threat it poses to our freedoms. They have, however, been inconsistent in their concern when it comes to giving government broad and unconstitutional power to track terrorists. This has led to their support of things like warrantless searches and monitoring phone and e-mail messages. Anyone who is concerned about the power of government should see the potential for using such mechanisms against those whom authorities consider their enemies – which may include many ordinary Americans who oppose their efforts to grow government.

Many believe that because terrorism is such a threat, we have to give up some of our freedom to oppose it. I think we need to consider what Benjamin Franklin said: "Those who would give up Essential Liberty to purchase a little Temporary Safety, deserve neither Liberty nor Safety."[3] If we lose our freedom, we will be dependent on those who have taken it. There is no reason to believe they will honor or value our security any more than they did our freedom.

Some conservatives have likely been deceived into supporting things like the Patriot Act because groups like the ACLU opposed it. That organization definitely has a distorted view of rights in many cases, but that does not mean everything they support is bad or all they oppose is good. We need to look at each issue and piece of legislation with a critical eye and judge it on its own merits – not based on who else may be supporting or opposing it.

Those on the left are much more inconsistent in their views of government power. Although many of their number have had both legitimate and proper concerns about civil liberties, they have no problem giving government control over just about everything else in our lives. If they are truly so concerned about government gaining inappropriate power, they should certainly realize a government that decides who has guns and who gets health care has immense power over people, and a government that controls the economy can ultimately determine who eats and who doesn't.

---

3 Benjamin Franklin, *Memoirs of the Life and Writings of Benjamin Franklin*, 1818

Quick Fixes

Conservatives have promoted what seem to be at least some partial solution for political problems, but which turn out not to be such good ideas. One is term limits. Many believe that if people can only serve in an office for a short period, they won't get so entrenched and will remain responsive to the electorate. However, a couple of problems arise with such a system.

Very few Congressmen are genuine, limited-government, constitutionalists. There needs to be a lot more if they are to make a difference, but if the good ones are forced to leave after a few years, it will be difficult to ultimately build a majority of those who are willing to restore our nation to its founding principles. We have to keep the conservatives we have and add to their number.

The real problem is that voters don't pay enough attention to the views and records of those they elect. It is very likely they would pay even less attention to what office-holders are doing if they knew they would only be serving for a short time. Do we really want to set up a system which encourages people to be even more ignorant about their representatives?

New Right Legacy

There arose in the 1960s and 1970s a variation of the conservative movement that came to be known as "the new right." It was characterized by more emphasis on correcting social and moral problems and somewhat less on the maintenance of freedom. Its adherents tended to rely more on government to solve such problems and trusted more in legislative solutions.

As more evangelical Christians became involved in politics, many of them became associated with the new right. This contributed to a real irony. The new right with its Christian influence and recognition of man's propensity for evil should have been more distrustful of giving government additional power. Yet, the old right – which certainly included believers, but was not as closely associated with Christians – was actually less willing to accept solutions which involved giving more authority to government.

The new right essentially became the religious right of today. That appellation replaced new right as much larger numbers of evangelical Christians got involved in politics and became a substantial part of the movement. It also didn't make sense to refer to the new right when it had been in existence for over 20 years.

Unfortunately, the tendency for government solutions still persists in the conservative ranks. Even more unfortunately, this seems to be particularly prevalent among Christian conservatives – who should know better. Believers must become much more wary of solutions to problems (real or perceived) that give more authority to government.

Who We Support for Political Offices

One of the greatest failings of conservatives in recent years is a lack of discernment in their choice of candidates. This has been most evident in presidential elections.

Christians should be the most discerning of people. We need to look very closely at any ideas to see how they square with the Bible. This is to be like the Bereans of whom Paul said *Now these were more noble-minded than those in Thessalonica, for they received the Word with great eagerness, examining the Scriptures daily to see whether these things were so* in Acts 17:11. Although this passage refers to scrutinizing God's Word, I believe our experience in "rightly dividing the Word" should also cause us to be more astute in evaluating political issues and people. Too often, Christians have decided to support a person as a candidate because they claim to be a believer, or they appear to be more Christian than other options for a given office. It is not enough that a candidate be a strong believer. A person could be very solid doctrinally and be quite conscientious in living out his faith in his personal life, and still not be a good candidate. If he has made no effort to apply a Christian worldview to issues and policies or lacks a consistent political philosophy, he may be a poorer candidate than one who is not a strong Christian or even one who professes no faith in Christ.

Sometimes believers, even strong, long-time Christians who are new to political activity are not well-grounded in philosophies and issues. They often haven't done a lot of reading or studying about such things and do not have a good understanding of the ramifications of various policies.

Particularly, I believe the Republican Party too often picks and endorses people to run for office who are good candidates, but end up being poor office-holders. There is a big difference. Many have been selected because they are personable, attractive, and have had a large amount of community involvement in things like service groups, which gives them many contacts and much visibility. These are all attributes that will help them win elections and, thus, make them good candidates.

They often are generally conservative and know the right things to say to appeal to both party activists and to the public. However, they may have little or no depth of understanding of the underlying conservative ideas on government. Often their busy public life has left little time for the reading required to develop a well-thought-out, consistent political philosophy. So, when they get into office, they are tossed about by the winds of faddish ideas and current public opinion.

I think Christians also make the same mistakes in evaluating which candidates to support for office. They place too much stock in the fact that a potential candidate is a believer. That is important, but is no substitute for having a deep political understanding. Christians need to evaluate candidates based on what they believe. Then, we need to measure candidates by their firm commitment to those beliefs – not strictly on their Christianity.

It is also true that some people see human nature in a way consistent with a Christian worldview – although they are not believers. Those who honestly observe the way people act and/or are students of history should recognize how fallible humanity is. Many who have not been redeemed have been blinded from seeing this – it seems that even their perception is flawed. Despite this, some unbelievers see the truth about our fallen nature, and those who do and apply that knowledge to issues may be better candidates than Christians who may even have the right worldview – but fail to make the connection to the logical ramifications when it comes to political positions.

A good example of Christians not using discernment in candidate selection is the presidential election of 2008. Originally, many Christian conservatives were quite leery of Mitt Romney because he was a Mormon. However, as the campaign progressed, many conservatives (including Christians) moved into his camp.

While evangelicals have very substantial and serious theological differences with Mormons, many of them are solid conservatives – including some who have held political offices. I do not believe it is necessarily wrong to support a Mormon candidate – particularly when they have proven themselves to be consistent conservatives in previous offices or terms in their current position.

This was definitely not the case with Romney who had an extremely liberal record as Governor of Massachusetts. He signed bad legislation, like the bill that set up their state healthcare system – which, for conservatives, should, in itself, be a disqualification. He was also pro-abortion and in favor of so-called "gay rights." Conservative support for him in 2008 seemed to be based primarily on his claim to have reversed his position on those issues. It is naïve to believe a person who claims to have changed his views on key issues just before running for an office is sincere and not just being political and pragmatic. Christians should particularly be distrustful of such conversions. I believe one should completely discount any of a candidate's positions that were modified prior to an election. Plus, we need to look at a potential candidate's positions on a much broader range of issues. Romney became the 2012 Republican candidate for president. While not as many Christians supported him this time due to having more options, the credibility he got in his 2008 bid helped greatly to propel him into securing the nomination in 2012.

In contrast, Christians largely shunned Ron Paul's candidacy in both 2008 and 2012, although he was the logical choice for all conservatives. In over 20 years in Congress, Dr. Paul has consistently voted against anything not in the Constitution. No current federal legislator has stood up more for the limited government our founders gave us. And Paul is a born-again Christian believer. He hasn't played that up much since he believes many candidates have exploited their Christianity. That is true. However, I believe he has gone a little too far in not mentioning his Christianity – to the point that many evangelicals do not know he is among their numbers.

The main reason many didn't support him was that he didn't support the war in Iraq. Again, this points to the influence of the neo-cons within the conservative movement. It indicates that many conservatives are looking to the wrong people for direction. Some were concerned about Paul's streak of libertarianism. Friends, it is not libertarians who are escalating our debt into the stratosphere, promoting a national healthcare system, or working to have the federal government take over jurisdiction of our schools! They are not the ones who are taking away our freedoms. While most of us believers will have differences with Libertarians on some issues, they are not our enemies! In fact, for much of its history our country pretty much followed a libertarian philosophy.

We must remind ourselves that evangelical Christians are not a majority in this country and may never be. Add to that the fact that an increasing number who call themselves evangelicals are moving to the left, and it is apparent that we alone cannot control elections. There are, of course, other conservatives who share most of the views of what has been called the Christian right.

There are many other Americans who wouldn't call themselves conservatives who also agree with much of what we do, but have been put off by what they perceive that term to mean. Of course, many have been influenced by misconceptions planted by the media, but they also justifiably have real problems with our support of the Iraq War, inconsistency on issues, and support for the imperial presidency (including that of George W. Bush). The hypocrisy of those in Congress who call themselves conservatives who failed to be fiscally responsible hasn't helped either. There are also the libertarians and many who wouldn't use that appellation, but who basically hold to their views. We may not agree with them on all issues, but are much closer to them philosophically than to those who call themselves moderate Republicans. If we can convince them we are serious about promoting liberty, they may be willing to work with us.

Keeping Them Accountable

Part of the problem is in our not holding our legislators to account once they have been elected. Incumbents seem to believe they own the right to another endorsement no matter how far they stray from party principles and their own stated positions. Unfortunately, Republican delegates generally confer such endorsements as though they also believe the incumbent has a right to them.

Another part of the problem is the unwillingness of anyone in the party to challenge such incumbents by opposing them for endorsement. The case of Michele Bachmann, I believe, is an excellent example of the kind of success conservatives can have if individuals will come forward to oppose incumbents, and delegates are willing to consider replacement alternatives. Republican delegates in her district in Minnesota were quite unhappy with their long-time state senator. Nevertheless, he was expected to be endorsed again by Republicans for his position. But Michele was approached at the endorsing convention and asked to oppose the incumbent for the party nomination. In spite of not being prepared for such a possibility (and being dressed very casually), she agreed to do that. She wrested the endorsement from the incumbent, beat him in a primary and went on to be elected as a state senator. She later had an opportunity to run for Congress and is now a four-term incumbent in that body, and was a credible candidate for president in the 2012 endorsement race. Her case is a good illustration of how liberal Republican incumbents can successfully be challenged.

To "endorse," according to Webster, is to "give approval to" – to "sanction." Is it honest to confer an endorsement on those who are voting to a great degree for things of which we do not approve, and to give our stamp of approval to views we do not sanction? Endorsements should mean something – particularly to those who are looking at them for an indication of what a particular person stands for. To endorse those who do not vote even fifty percent of the time for Republican principles is to deceive voters. How can we expect to have any credibility with the electorate if we continue to give our approval to those who have strayed far from the Republican philosophy? Would Good Housekeeping continue to give its seal of approval to a product that no longer met their standards?

Why Are So Many Christians Republicans?

Christians have been criticized for associating themselves too closely with the Republicans. But the platform of that party at least indicates it is fairly consonant with the views of conservative believers, although the track record of office-holders endorsed by them in actually following that document is not that great. The Democratic Party, on the other hand, has worked for years in direct opposition to all that has made this country great and against Christian principles. The Democrats have annual events they called "Jefferson Jackson dinners." This is almost laughable. If either of those limited-government advocates came back today, they would likely say to the Democrats: "Depart from me, I never knew you." If a believer is going to be involved in partisan politics today, their only real choice is the Republican Party – as much as it falls short of its stated principles.

There is one criticism about Christian involvement with Republicans that is somewhat deserved. It is said believers have been too subservient to that party. To be effective in politics one has to ally themselves with a particular party and demonstrate some loyalty to it. However, one does not have to place allegiance to it above their political principles and philosophies – particularly when the party doesn't follow its own platform. Some Christian right leaders have been too quick to defend Republicans – even when they stray far from conservative principles. This was particularly true of the failure to criticize George W. Bush, although he did little to promote conservatism.

Republican legislators, particularly at the federal level, when in a majority, have tried to pacify conservatives with tax reductions, while doing little or nothing to cut government or its cost. The lowering of taxes is a good thing, but not nearly as important as trimming the size and scope of government. If government were reduced, taxes could also be rolled back substantially. But too often conservatives have been satisfied with tax cuts and have not insisted Republicans actually slash government.

The Smearing of Conservatives

The left and the mainstream media (is it really necessary to distinguish between the two?) have used pejorative terms to describe conservatives for years. Among those are: "far right," "radical right," "right-wing extremist," and "ultra-conservative." These epithets continue to be applied, and Christians who are conservative seem to bear the brunt of their use. You may have noticed they rarely refer to anyone as "far left," "radical left," "left-wing-extremist," or "ultra-liberal."

Much has been said in the media about the level of civility in political discourse. Due to the leftist bent of the media, the right has borne the brunt of this criticism. In reality, there have been those on both sides of the spectrum who have been guilty of this – at least at some times.

One of the worst violations is the left's characterizing of conservatives as being haters or racists. I'm sure some of all political persuasions advocate certain policies, because they believe they will harm certain segments of society, but I believe they are rare. In a lifetime of political activity, I certainly have met few such individuals – and none who have been Bible-believing Christians. But those on the left regularly attribute hate and/or racism to those who do not share their particular views on how to deal with issues surrounding race, poverty, homosexuality, etc. Such *ad hominem* attacks are surely as bad, or worse, than much of that with which conservatives are charged. I wonder if the people who engage in such name-calling ever stop to think of how hurtful it is to the objects of their words. Particularly in cases where those doing the name-calling know very well that those they are attacking are not haters and/or racists. Rarely do the media ever call anyone on the left on their use of the terms "racism" or "hate" to vilify their enemies.

Christians should be careful to counter the ideas of others without attacking them personally, but it is certainly appropriate to expose the nefarious activities and questionable connections of leftists. I also think it is appropriate to use humor to point out the follies of those holding certain views. Satire has always been part of politics, and those who are in the public eye should expect to be the target of some barbs. But we should not be mean-spirited in our humor.

I'm not certain all the terms used to smear conservatives, if properly understood, are necessarily negative. However, those who use them are counting on the general public lacking the understanding which allows them to use these labels to cast conservatives in a bad light.

Many of the people who are characterized as being far out of the mainstream have views that mirror those of our country's founders. If our beliefs are truly radical or extreme, it is because we, as a nation, have deviated so far from our original principles. Christians should never be concerned whether our beliefs are in the mainstream – we should only want to make certain they are right.

There has been some criticism to the effect that believers involved in politics are trying to build a Christian society or civilization. That might be true of some. I believe that is not a proper goal for Christians. However, we can see that the result of basing a political system on Christian principles led to a very magnificent society in the United States.

The Bible makes it quite clear that believers will be persecuted for their beliefs. We should expect this. I believe it is instructive that, in the United States, it is those Christians who are taking political stands that are being castigated by the secular left. Such people don't appear to care how many Christians there are as long as they just go to church on Sunday and make no attempt to impact society. But those who get into politics often experience the wrath of the secularists. Of course, some have angered non-believers by actions that are wrong or inappropriate. I Peter 4:15, 16 says, *Make sure that none of you suffers as a murderer, or thief, or evildoer, or a troublesome meddler; but if anyone suffers as a Christian, he is not to be ashamed, but is to glorify God in this name.* This Scripture is a good guide for the attitude and behavior of believers who are involved in politics.

CHAPTER 18

Where Should We Go From Here?

There is a tide in the affairs of men, which, taken at the flood, leads on to fortune. We must take the current when it serves, or lose our ventures. – William Shakespeare, *Julius Caesar*

Once to everyman and nation comes the moment to decide,
In the strife of Truth and Falsehood, for the good or evil side
– James Russell Lowell, *The Present Crisis*

As Christians survey the current political landscape, what should their attitudes be? I think it is useful to make an analogy from Scripture. The apostle Paul chided the Galatians with the query "Who has bewitched you?" He goes on to question why they had begun their journey as believers with faith, but were trying to perfect themselves through the flesh.

In a similar manner, one could ask present-day residents of the United States, "You foolish Americans – who has bewitched you? Why, when you have established your country based on limited government and prospered immensely as a result, are you now trying to perfect it with big-government solutions?"

Not all Americans have been so foolish. Throughout the last several decades, many have opposed the trend toward larger, more centralized government and the attempts to aggrandize it. Today, many recognize we must reverse that trend and restore the limited government conceived by our founders. However, far too many are oblivious to the threats posed by big government or are actually looking to it as the solution to our problems. Those people are certainly being foolish, but few of them can blame it on being bewitched. A future observer looking at our history might well believe we, as a nation, would have to be fools to have allowed such a unique and marvelous system to devolve into the monstrosity we have today.

If we have been bewitched, it is probably by the fruits of our success. We, as a nation, have been so absorbed with enjoying the blessings of our freedom that we have not taken time to preserve the system that has enabled us to experience these blessings from God to such a great extent. In fact, many (if not most) have not even looked for an answer to the question of why we have prospered so much in contrast to other parts of the world.

Wisdom mandates that we look to the past when seeking solutions to today's problems.

Who Is "We"?

This chapter is entitled "Where Should We Go From Here?" We, as Americans, are certainly in this thing together and we have things we need to do as a nation. I will also deal with changes I believe need to be made by various subsets of the US population. You should also ask yourself, "Where should I go from here?' depending upon in which of these groups you see yourself. Some may find themselves in more than one of the sets. The points I make are mostly brief. They are really a summary of the assertions I have made throughout the body of the book.

I will, first, define the various groups and then proceed to detail what I believe the course of action should be for each. The first group includes those who have been at least somewhat involved in political issues or have some interest in them and generally hold to the views of the Christian right – including those who may not personally be believers in Jesus Christ. Second are those evangelicals who have only a passing interest in politics, are indifferent, or who are actually antagonistic to the idea of Christian involvement in politics. Third are those evangelicals who have adopted some or all of the agenda of the Christian left. Fourth are those believers in liberty who do not claim to be Christians. Finally,

I will speak to those with a variety of political philosophies who have not come to have a personal relationship with Jesus Christ. I will then address some strategies for all those on the right.

The Christian Right

The Christian right needs to stop listening to and following the programs of the neo-cons – particularly as it pertains to foreign policy. They should support a strong national defense, but oppose the nation-building use of our military forces. They should insist that wars once more be declared by Congress – not just carried out by an out-of-control executive branch pursuant to international bodies or their own whim. Wars must once again be waged against nations – not against an activity like terrorism.

When government mandates something bad, the response should not be to countermand it by replacing it with another directive or to provide exceptions, but rather to work to repeal the mandate. Attempting to fix problems by increasing the size and scope of government should be rejected.

They should also be more consistent in their concerns about big government and its powers to control people by opposing broad grants of authority such as warrantless searches, the Patriot Act, etc.

Although all Christians may not be able to accept all of the positions of some libertarians, they should not be antagonistic to them and realize they are allies on most issues against those who would take away our freedoms.

It is important for those in the Christian right to be with other conservatives in organizations to inform fellow citizens, and influence legislation. In general, I believe local organizations are more effective than national ones, which often do little more than send out mailings and seldom have much of an action program. Some of the local tea parties are quite good at both informing people and coordinating political activity.

One national organization that is an exception is the John Birch Society, because they organize local chapters and have specific agenda items for members. In the prologue, I mentioned the extensive, vicious attack on conservatives and anti-communists by the media in the nineteen sixties.

The John Birch Society, a fledgling organization barely two years old, bore the brunt of this smear. It seems strange that a group that was largely unknown to the general public at the time would be so severely vilified. I believe this occurred for two primary reasons. The first is that the left needed a name they could use as a smear term, so they could discredit their opponents using guilt by association. If they would have used a better-known organization, most would have been aware of it and would not have believed the untruths about it. Secondly, the left had already observed in the John Birch Society the organization, leadership, and plan they realized would be very effective in opposing them. They thought it essential it be thoroughly discredited and that the threat it posed to their plans be nipped in the bud.

In the intervening years as I have observed the Society, I believe their early enemies were very much correct in considering them a threat. I have found them to be "right on" in the information they have provided and the analysis of the problems facing America. And they have effective programs and plans for opposing collectivism.

Non-Political Believers

To Christians who are not very predisposed to political involvement, I'd say that if you're still with me at this point near the end of this work, I must have piqued some interest. You should consider the points made in Chapters 1 and 2. All believers should do a reasonable job of informing yourselves on the issues at least to a level at which they can vote somewhat intelligently. You should determine if it is God's will as to whether political activities might fit into your life. Those who believe they have a calling to be more involved should then seek God's face to determine specifically how He would want them to carry out that calling.

Christian Left

Those who have adopted some of the views of the Christian left should recognize that the commands of Jesus are directed to believers and the church – not to government. If they believe in an activist government in social welfare, they should start justifying it by some other method than biblical commands. They should also open their eyes to the fact that there are forces promoting government involvement not primarily to solve some problem, but rather to enhance the power of the state.

Believers on the left should come to recognize that due to the flawed nature of humanity, there will always be those who will seize opportunities to aggrandize their personal power by growing government, and that the policies they have been advocating will ultimately lead to tyranny.

Non-Christian Libertarians

Those who recognize freedom is a human right, but don't recognize a deity as its source, need to realize such views of rights are built on shifting sands. You need not fear most Christian involvement in politics. You should acknowledge that the idea of inalienable rights proceeds from the Christian view that men are created in God's image, and that this belief is the source of most of the freedom in the world. You need to realize that although many, if not most, Christians may not carry their belief in freedom quite as far as you do, at least those who are on the right share your concern about oppressive government and will work with you to remove its burden.

I think some in this category need to realize that what is at stake is the very survival of our nation, and that this is more important than the right to live particular lifestyles. You need to realize many Christians will be offended by the foul language I have noticed in some libertarian publications and forums. They will be put off by that and, as a result, won't listen to your message and recognize the commonality of many of our concerns.

A Strategy for the Right

As a country we need to return to the limited-government principles upon which our nation was founded. We need to once again start following the Constitution as it was conceived.

Of course, saying what we should do and actually getting there are two different things. Ultimately, we need a transformation in society that will result in the election of a substantial majority of representatives in Congress who actually believe in the original ideas of the United States. It may be some time until that happens.

There is a method which can possibly reverse the course we are on as a nation in a somewhat quicker fashion. That is through state action. Representatives at that level are much closer to the people – they actually still live among their constituents. As a result, they are more responsive to those who elect them.

So many legislators in Washington have become part of its establishment and are more interested in perpetuating themselves in their offices and in pleasing their colleagues than in serving the people back home in their respective states who sent them to Congress. This includes some who went to Washington with the right ideals and motives, but, due to becoming seduced by the glory and power of their office, lost sight of their reason for wanting to go there.

Action taken at the state level is a method that may more quickly reverse the course we are on as a nation, at least partially. The Tenth Amendment to the Constitution reserves to the states and the people all power not granted to the federal government. Most of what is being done today in Washington is not authorized by the Constitution.

When the states joined to form a federation, they ratified a Constitution in which they delegated a few, very specific powers to the government being formed. All others, they reserved to themselves. The states have kept all authority and sovereignty in matters not covered by functions authorized to the national government by the Constitution.

The states need to start exercising their sovereignty by challenging the federal government in those areas where it has gone beyond its Constitutional mandate. It is okay to file suits to reclaim their powers. But the venues in which such cases would be heard are federal courts – which are a branch of the national government. It is not likely they will, in most instances, rule against the federal government of which they are a part.

So states should not rely solely on such legal actions. Rather, they should refuse to participate in unconstitutional programs foisted on them by a recklessly runaway national government. They should not enforce unconstitutional programs within their boundaries or cooperate in any way with federal agents who are doing so. Likely, if enough states do this on a given issue, the federal government will back off. This process is known as nullification. It has been used before in our country's history.

Beware a Constitutional Convention

An action is being pursued in some states of which we should beware. The Constitution has provided two ways of initiating amendments. One is through an act of the US Congress. The other, which has never been used, is by a petition of two-thirds of the states to call a constitutional convention to make changes for a particular purpose. Both require any amendment be ratified by three-fourths of the states before being inserted into the Constitution.

Attempts have been made by states for a number of years to call for a convention to address various amendments. Most notable has been one to require a balanced budget. Often the proposed amendment is intended to correct legislative abuse by the federal government and has a particular appeal for conservatives. However, such a method for changing the Constitution is fraught with danger to our liberties. There is no guarantee a convention called for a particular issue could or would be held to dealing with only that issue. Many believe such a convention could, in fact, rewrite the whole document. This is what actually happened when the last such convention we had in 1787 scrapped the Articles of Confederation and replaced them with our current Constitution.

A real possibility exists that something similar could happen again. Those who dismiss such concerns say there is little to fear in that the results of any such convention would have to be ratified by three-fourths of the states. But there is nothing to prevent such a convention from changing even the rules by which a new constitution or a greatly modified one must be ratified.

There is nothing substantially wrong with our current Constitution. The problem has been that it has not been followed. Why would we believe courts, legislators, and executives would obey a revised constitution any better than they have the one we have – even if substantial improvements are made? And why would we want to risk a runaway convention for the possibility that we will get modifications that may just be disregarded? Rather than trying to correct the Constitution, we should initiate action at the state level to insist that the federal government abide by the restrictions already in it (as mentioned above).

One thing I believe is essential to restoring our nation is to eliminate the Federal Reserve and return to a currency backed with precious metals. The Federal Reserve is an unelected, unaccountable entity that has fueled much of the growth of the spending and debt of the federal government. The return of sound currency would exert a natural check on the excesses of the federal government.

Election Procedures

I am going to spend some time talking here about what I see are some major problems with the way we in America choose our elected officials – particularly the president – and make some suggestions for changes. The first is that most citizens place too much importance on who occupies the presidency. In fact, for many, the person who gets elected to that position is the only real political action to which they pay much attention.

The president is supposed to be primarily in charge of administrating the laws Congress passes. Vetoing bills does give him, in effect, some input into legislation. That is an important function which does give him a fair amount of power. However, the executive branch which falls in his bailiwick has asserted more and more authority over the years for a number of reasons. One is the sheer number of laws passed by Congress – many of which should have been declared unconstitutional. And, then, many of those laws have given too broad authority to the executive agencies charged with enforcing them. This allows their administrators to create rules and guidelines – effectively making law. Legislators need to tighten up the authority they grant and be much more specific in what the enabling laws entail.

Another problem is the number of executive orders presidents now issue, and the fact that many of those orders give the executive branch great power. When the president oversteps his authority, Congress needs to take action to countermand his decision – rather than, in effect, ceding their legislative authority to him. What has been particularly troublesome is that Congress has effectively given the president their power to declare war. They should never let him get by with that.

If we can get Congress to scale the powers of the president back to what the framers envisioned, it would not be as important who we elected to the office. Even without such an action, he still is only one person. Americans need to pay much more attention to who they vote into all other offices – at the national, state, and local levels.

Although we have placed too much importance on whom we elect as president, there are some things I believe we should change in how we choose the person for that position. The best thing we could do would be to go back to using the Electoral College closer to how it was originally intended. The president would be voted on by electors who would be chosen in a variety of ways as determined by individual states. However, if the electors are actually chosen by the citizens of a state, only their names would appear on the ballot – not the actual presidential candidate's. The electors would actually choose the president under this system. Doing this would somewhat de-politicize the process of picking a president. It would severely reduce the huge amounts spent on campaigns and greatly cut back the influence of the media in determining nominees and ultimate winners. Inevitably, some men and women would run as electors on the basis that they would vote for a particular person for president. However, not all would. If a person wanted to vote for electors committed to a particular candidate, at least they would have to put out some effort to determine which elector supported their preference. It is also unlikely all states would choose to have electors chosen by the populace.

It would be difficult to get such a change made, because such a high percentage of Americans think voting for president is their most important function as citizens – in fact, many think this is what is the most distinctive and important feature about the United States. If this cannot be achieved politically, the next best thing we could do would be to eliminate presidential primaries and caucus preference polls. The nominees would then be chosen simply by the delegates to the national conventions as selected through the respective party processes. This would have several advantages. First, those with the greatest say in who gets nominated would be those actually involved in politics, who usually are much better informed about issues and candidates and are, therefore, more suited to making decisions on candidates. Second, there would be little reason for candidates to mount expensive media campaigns. Rather, they would have to work more closely with and rely on the support of people in the party. Third, it would be an encouragement for more people to actually get involved in the political process – rather than thinking they have done their duty by merely voting in a primary (or maybe just showing up at a caucus and voting in a preference poll and then having no further involvement). It would also greatly curtail the power of the media in the selection of party nominees.

The way the game is played today, developing momentum in early primary and caucus states is the major factor in who gets the nominations. This has resulted in campaigns started far in advance of the party conventions. It also means those with the most money for ads and those who are media favorites have a decided advantage.

Eliminate Party Designation

Another change I believe would have a salutary effect on our political process would be to make elections at all levels non-partisan – meaning a candidate's party would not appear on the ballot. Each election would have a primary where the top two candidates would move on to the general election – regardless of party. This does not mean there wouldn't be parties. Some have supported the elimination of political parties, but people with common political beliefs will always join together to get those who share their views elected. People should have that right. In fact, if we were to try to outlaw parties, they would likely just be driven underground.

However, if elections were held without candidates needing official party designations, it would be likely many more political parties would be formed. Thus, the stranglehold the Republicans and Democrats have on elections would be broken. It is likely some candidates might get the endorsement of more than one party. Also endorsement by non-party interest groups may well carry more weight. This would not be a parliamentary system, such as many countries like the United Kingdom and Canada have, where the parties select a Prime Minister. We would still have a separate election of a president.

I do hope all Americans would return to a belief in those ideas that made the United States a great nation and which we have largely abandoned. I believe a large majority of both Christians and non-believers need to adopt such views if we are to turn the country around.

I have a major concern about the future of America. I think it is possible that young people in the future will turn to the right and become quite serious about removing the shackles of government. However, there is also a trend among the young of accepting homosexuality as normal and favoring "gay" marriage. This will make it difficult for conservatives and Christians to coalesce with them behind freedom candidates that are needed to restore our nation. I don't have a good answer on how to address that problem. I do believe Christians need to continue to stand up for what is right.

Christians need to take the threat we face seriously. I fear too many think the battle is just about electing people who will keep taxes low so we can take home a few more dollars in our paychecks. I believe we are in a struggle, the outcome of which will determine whether civilization survives. If a Christian is just concerned about improving their financial situation, I would question whether there is any reason to put any time or effort into politics.

A Most Important Action

While my main objective in this book is influencing Christians and others to adopt what I believe are the proper political views, my primary objective in life is to do what I can to get more people to accept Jesus Christ as their Savior. This should be the most important goal for all Christians. One stumbling block to some, if not many, in the path of considering such a decision is their perception of Christian involvement in politics. I would hope a non-believer reading this book might lose some of their misconceptions about such involvement and be more open to Christianity as a result.

Beyond the restoration of our nation, I have an even greater hope for those who are not believers in Jesus Christ: that they would acknowledge their need for a Savior and ask Jesus to forgive their sins and come and be the Lord of their lives. That is, at the bottom line, what is most important for all people.

Bibliography

Prologue.

Dobbs, Zygmund. *Keynes at Harvard.* New York, NY: Probe Research, 1969.

The Veritas Foundation. *The Great Deceit: Social Pseudo-Sciences.* West Sayville, NY: The Veritas Foundation, 1964.

Chapter 1. God's Purposes for Life on Earth

Bowen, Catherine Drinker. *Miracle at Philadelphia.* Boston, MA, New York, NY, London, UK: Back Bay Books, 1986.
(The story of America's constitutional convention.)

Eidsmoe, John. *Christianity and the Constitution.* Grand Rapids, MI: Baker Books House, 1987.
(The faith of the founding fathers.)

Marshall, Peter and Manuel, David. *The Light and the Glory.* Grand Rapids, MI: Fleming H. Revell, 1977.
(How God's hand was on the development of our nation from the time of Columbus to the Revolutionary War.)

Marshall, Peter and Manuel, David. *From Sea to Shining Sea.* Grand Rapids, MI: Fleming H. Revell, 1986.
(A sequel to *The Light and the Glory* – continuing the story up to the Civil War.)

Chapter 2. Christians Involvement in Affairs on Earth

Eidsmoe, John. *Historical and Theological Foundation of Law* (Volumes I-III). Powder Springs, GA: Tolle Lege Press, 2012.

Schaeffer, Francis. *How Should We Then Live?* Westchester, IL: Crossway Books, 2005.
(Influences of Christianity on Western Civilization including those that have impacted politics.)

Chapter 3. Thinking Politically as a Christian

Noebel, David. *Understanding the Times* Manitou Springs, CO: Summit Press, 2006.
(Evaluates the views of different worldviews in various academic disciplines.)

Sowell, Thomas. *The Vision of the Anointed.* New York, NY: Basic Books, 1995.
(How liberals insist on imposing their will on society.)

Whitehead, John. *The Separation Illusion.* Milford, MI: Mott Media, 1977.
(Refutes the idea that the First Amendment calls for a complete separation of anything spiritual and the government.)

Chapter 4. Christians on the Political Spectrum

Eidsmoe, John. *God and Caesar.* Eugene, OR: Harvest House, 1984.
(Discussion of the role of government from a Christian standpoint.)

Goldberg, Jonah. *Liberal Fascism.* New York, NY: Doubleday, 2007.

McManus, John. *Overview of America* (DVD). Appleton, WI: The John Birch Society, 2013
(A comparison of different governmental and economic systems.)

Paul, Ron. *Liberty Defined.* New York, NY, Houston, TX: Grand Central, 2011.

Taylor, John. *New Views of the Constitution of the United States.* Washington DC: Regnery Press, 2000.
(Early Virginia senator's analysis of the constitution.)

Woods, Thomas and Gutzman, Kevin. *Who Killed the Constitution?* New York, NY: Crown Forum, 2008

Chapter 5. Morality, Government, and the Christian

Bastiat, Frederic. *The Law.* Auburn, AL: Ludwig von Mises Institute, 2007.
(Deals with economics from a moral standpoint – rather than just the practical aspects of what works.)

Chapter 6. Life and Health Issues

Kurisko, Lee, MD. *Health Reform: The End of the American Revolution?.* St. Paul, MN: Alethus Press, 2009.
(A Canadian doctor's experiences with their government healthcare system.)

Chapter 7. School and Work Issues

Blumenfeld, Samuel. *Is Public Education Necessary?* Old Greenwich, CT: Devin-Adair, 1981.
(Includes the history of public education in America.)

Blumenfeld, Samuel. *NEA: Trojan Horse in American Education.* Boise, ID: The Paradigm Company, 1984.
(Political influence of the National Education Association.)

Kjos, Berit. *Brave New Schools.* Eugene, OR: Harvest House, 1995.
(Describes left-wing and anti-Christian curriculum in the public schools.)

Marsden, George. *The Soul of the American University.* New York, NY, Oxford, UK: Oxford University Press, 1995.
(Secularization of American Christian Universities.)

Chapter 8. Financial Issues

Carney, Timothy. *Obamanomics.* Washington, DC: Regnery Press, 2009.
(Details how Barack Obama helps big business with corporate welfare.)

Greaves, Percy. *Understanding the Dollar Crisis.* Auburn, AL: Ludwig von Mises Institute, 2008.

Griffin, G. Edward. *The Creature from Jekyll Island.* Westlake Village, CA: American Media, 2002.
(The story of central banking in the U.S. and the founding of the Federal Reserve System.)

Hazlitt, Henry. *Economics in One Lesson.* New York, NY: Three Rivers Press, 1988.

The John Birch Society. *Dollars and Sense (DVD).* Appleton, WI: The John Birch Society, 2007.
(Discussion of money.)

Richards, Jay. *Money, Greed, and God.* New York: HarperOne, 2009.

von Mises, Ludwig. *The Free and Prosperous Commonwealth.* Princeton, NJ: D. Van Nostrand, 1962.

Woods, Thomas. *Meltdown.* Washington DC: Regnery Press, 2009
(Includes discussion of the 2008-2009 bailouts.)

Chapter 9. Foreign Policy

Buchanan, Pat. *A Republic, Not An Empire.* Washington D.C: Regnery Press, 1999.
(How the U.S. went from non-interventionist foreign policy to policing the world.)

Chambers, Whittaker. *Witness.* Washington, DC: Gateway Editions, 2011.
(The autobiographical story by Chambers of his days as a Soviet spy.)

Golitsyn, Anatoliy. *New Lies for Old.* New York, NY: Dodd, Mead and Company, 1984.
(How the USSR used deception - by a high-level defector.)

Sutton, Anthony. *Wall Street and the Rise of Hitler.* Forest Row, UK: Clairview Books, 2011.

Welch, Robert. *The Politician.* Belmont, MA: Belmont, 1964.
(The political career of Dwight Eisenhower by the founder of the John Birch Society.)

Chapter 10. Civil Liberties

Lance, Peter. *Triple Cross.* New York, NY: Harper, 2009.
(The failures of U.S. intelligence in detecting Mideastern terrorists.)

Chapter 11. What about Faith-Based Initiatives?

Olasky, Marvin. *The Tragedy of American Compassion.* Washington DC: Regnery Press, 1995.
(The story of the many private organizations that ministered to the needy in America's past.)

Chapter 12. Is Globalism Good?

Griffin, G. Edward. *The Fearful Master.* Boston, MA, Los Angeles, CA: Western Islands, 1964.
(An exposure of the United Nations, focusing on its founding.)

Jasper, William. *Global Tyranny...Step by Step.* Appleton, WI: Western Islands, 1992.
(A more current look at the activities of the United Nations.)

Sutton, Anthony. *Trilateralists Over Washington* (Volume I). Scottsdale, AZ: The August Corporation, 1978

Sutton, Anthony. *Trilateralists Over Washington* (Volume II). Scottsdale, AZ: The August Corporation, 1981
(The two volumes talk about the influence the Trilateral Commission has asserted over U.S. politics.)

Wormser, Rene. *Foundations –Their Power and Influence.* Sevierville, TN: Covenent Books, 1993.
(How tax-exempt foundations fund the left.)

Chapter 13. Are There Conspiracies?

Perloff, James. *Shadows of Power.* Appleton, WI: Western Islands, 1988.
(The story of the Council on Foreign Relations.)

Quigley, Carroll. *Tragedy and Hope.* New York, NY: The Macmillan Company, 1966.
(Insider admission of a secret global elite impacting historical events.)

Skousen, W. Cleon. *The Naked Capitalist.* Catchogue, NY: Buccaneer Books, 1998.
(A review of *Tragedy and Hope* above.)

Smoot, Dan. *The Invisible Government* Boston, MA, Los Angeles, CA: Western Islands, 1977.
(An earlier look at the Council on Foreign Relations.)

Sutton, Anthony. *America's Secret Establishment.* Walterville, OR: Trine Day, 2004.
(About the Skull and Bones organization at Yale University.)

Sutton, Anthony. *Wall Street and the Bolshevik Revolution.* Catchogue, NY: Buccaneer Books, 1993.

Chapter 14. What Should the Role of the Courts Be?

Thomas, Clarence. *My Grandfather's Son.* New York, NY: Harper, 2007.
(Thomas' autobiography.)

Woods, Thomas. *Nullification.* Washington DC: Regnery Press, 2010
(How states have and still can nullify unconstitutional laws and actions by the federal government.)

Chapter 15. How Should Christians Relate to the Environment?

Coffman, Michael. *Saviors of the Earth.* Chicago, IL: Northfield Publishing, 1994.
(The politics and religion of the environmental movement.)

Michaels, Patrick. *Meltdown.* Washington, DC: Cato Institute, 2004.
(Discussion of global warming.)

Ray, Dixie Lee. *Environmental Overkill.* Washington, DC: Regnery Publishing, 1993.

Singer, Fred. *Hot Talk Cold Science.* Oakland, CA: The Independent Institute, 1999.
(A refutation of global warming.)

Chapter 16. The Religious Left

Sowell, Thomas. *Quest for Cosmic Justice.* New York, NY: The Free Press, 1999.
(About the liberals' efforts to try to create a perfect world where everyone experiences their notion of justice.)

Chapter 17. The Christian Right

McManus, John. *William F. Buckley: Pied Piper for the Establishment.* Appleton, WI: The John Birch Society, 2002
(Also provides information about the neoconservative movement.)

Nash, George. *The Conservative Intellectual Movement in America.* (Wilmington, DE: Intercollegiate Studies Institute, 1996.)

Schlossberg, Herbert. *Idols for Destruction.* Nashville, TN: Thomas Nelson, 1983.
(A Christian critique of the culture and political beliefs of contemporary America.)

Chapter 18. Where Do We Go From Here?

"The New American" (magazine). Appleton, WI: American Opinion Publishing,
(A must-read to keep on top of current political issues and events.)

About the Author

Keith Johnson is a lifelong student of history, politics, economics, and Christian apologetics, having read hundreds of books and thousands of articles on those topics. While he believes Christians should be informed on these topics, he also spurs believers on to make a difference in the political realm. Equipped with a Christian worldview and an understanding that we are "endowed" by our Creator with specific rights, his understanding of these topics has motivated him to take an active role in political education and advocacy organizations, as well as being involved in partisan politics – including running for the U.S. Congress and the Minnesota State Legislature.

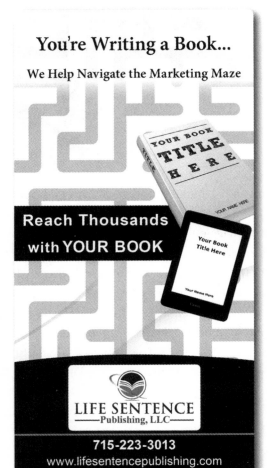